PROBLEMS IN FOCUS SERIES

Each volume in the 'Problems in Focus' series is designed to make available to students important new work on key historical problems and periods that they encounter in their courses. Each volume is devoted to a central topic or theme, and the most important aspects of this are dealt with by specially commissioned essays from scholars in the relevant field. The editorial Introduction reviews the problem or period as a whole, and each essay provides an assessment of the particular aspect, pointing out the areas of development and controversy, and indicating where conclusions can be drawn or where further work is necessary. An annotated bibliography serves as a guide for further reading.

TITLES IN PRINT

European Warfare 1815–2000
    edited by Jeremy Black
European Warfare 1450–1815
    edited by Jeremy Black
The Wars of the Roses
    edited by A. J. Pollard
The Reign of Henry VIII
    edited by Diarmaid MacCulloch
The British Problem, c. 1534–1707
    edited by Brendan Bradshaw and John Morrill
Culture and Politics in Early Stuart England
    edited by Kevin Sharpe and Peter Lake
The Origins of the English Civil War
    edited by Conrad Russell
Reactions to the English Civil War 1642–1649
    edited by John Morrill
The Reigns of Charles II and James VII & II
    edited by Lionel K. J. Glassey
Enlightened Absolutism
    edited by H. M. Scott
Popular Movements, c. 1830–1850
    edited by J. T. Ward

Problems in Focus
Series Standing Order
ISBN 0-333-71704-X hardcover
ISBN 0-333-69348-5 paperback
(outside North America only)

You can receive future titles in this series as they are published. To place a standing order please contact your bookseller or, in the case of difficulty, write to us at the address below with your name and address, the title of the series and the ISBN quoted above.
Customer Services Department, Macmillan Distribution Ltd
Houndmills, Basingstoke, Hampshire RG21 6XS, England

European Warfare 1453–1815

Edited by

JEREMY BLACK
Professor of History, University of Exeter

palgrave
macmillan

First published 1999

Published by
PALGRAVE MACMILLAN
Houndmills, Basingstoke, Hampshire RG21 6XS and
175 Fifth Avenue, New York, N.Y. 10010
Companies and representatives throughout the world

PALGRAVE MACMILLAN is the global academic imprint of the Palgrave Macmillan division of St. Martin's Press, LLC and of Palgrave Macmillan Ltd. Macmillan® is a registered trademark in the United States, United Kingdom and other countries. Palgrave is a registered trademark in the European Union and other countries.

ISBN-13: 978-0-333-69223-3 hardcover

ISBN-13: 978-0-312-22118-8 paperback

This book is printed on paper suitable for recycling and made from fully managed and sustained forest sources.

A catalogue record for this book is available from the British Library.

First published in the United States of America by
ST. MARTIN'S PRESS, LLC.,
Scholarly and Reference Division,
175 Fifth Avenue, New York, N.Y. 10010

Transferred to digital printing 2008

For
Alyson and Stephen Barter

Contents

Introduction

JEREMY BLACK

Modern images of early modern European warfare centre on battles, the pikemen/musketeer chequerboard squares of the sixteenth and seventeenth centuries, and the linear formations of musketeers on the eighteenth-century battlefield. These images have been animated by modern film and television treatments, such as *Barry Lyndon*. At sea, ships of the line beat the waves. Such images make the warfare seem readily understandable, but they slight questions of the wider significance of military attitudes, forces and action. Furthermore, there is the issue of how far the images mislead even as accounts of the operational side of war. This introduction will consider attitudes, forces and action, and will also seek to focus on what was distinctive about European warfare. This offers one way of approaching the question of whether there was a military revolution in early modern Europe without becoming overly concerned with the historiography of the subject.

I

Attitudes are important because they create the context within which war is instrumental and functions. There are no necessary ways in which armies and navies function, no obvious reasons why conflict should arise in particular circumstances but not in others. Instead, these issues reflect wider cultural assumptions and practices. So also do attitudes towards loss and suffering, towards inflicting and risking pain and death, towards hierarchy, obedience and discipline, and towards the readiness to serve, in both war and peace, all of which are crucial to military capability.

These issues do not commonly rise to the fore when scholars debate military history. Thus, early modern European military history is generally considered in terms of the so-called 'Military Revolution',[1] whether located in 1560–1660 or earlier, and, more

1

generally, of the weaponry and tactics of the period. This is misleading because the latter were functional, designed both to serve purposes that were not immutable, and to do so in ways that reflected social and cultural structures and notions. Furthermore, it is difficult to show that attitudes to war changed in accordance with the means and methods of conducting it, or that there was a revolution in these attitudes.

If attention is focused on cultural assumptions and practices, as with Tom Arnold's argument that the Renaissance had a military dimension, then war becomes an aspect of the general history of the period, not a separate subject ringfenced as military history. This is appropriate, because war, indeed, was both central to the general history and a product of it. Thus, the military reflected the nature of society and its actions exemplified current attitudes towards both human life and the environment. Killing was not seen as unnatural, but was, instead, generally accepted as necessary, both for civil society, against crime, heresy and disorder, and in international relations. A willingness to accept pain and privation was part of ordinary labour, and military service was another aspect of it. Although there were dissatisfaction and mutinies,[2] the soldiery were not consulted about their conditions or instructions. It was assumed that they would serve, and at the behest and under the control of their social superiors.

War was seen as a source of glory for rulers and the officer class, much of which was made up of the nobility. The latter justified their special status by drawing attention to such service, but command was more than a matter of ideology. It was seen as fun as well as duty, the major activity and recreation for the landed orders of Europe. This became more the case in the second half of the period, as military entrepreneurs were replaced by clear command structures in royal armies and these structures were dominated by the nobility. The hierarchy and collective discipline of officership 'worked' and was made effective in large part because it rested on a definition of aristocratic honour and function in terms of military service. Aristocratic leisure activities responded to changing military needs. Tournaments changed with the phasing-out of the joust, the invention of new forms using handguns, and the introduction of combat on foot.[3]

War itself seemed natural. In modern terms it was the necessary product of an international system that lacked a hegemonic power. However, to contemporaries, it was natural as the best means by which to defend interests and achieve goals. The idea that such objectives might be better achieved through diplomacy enjoyed limited purchase in a society that took conflict for granted. Warfulness encouraged war, and the frequency of conflict ensured that a fresh turn to force seemed natural.[4]

This situation ensured that an effective military was necessary, and that was further encouraged by the general absence of police forces at other than the limited local level. A reliance on force to deal with internal opposition, especially if from below the level of the elite, was also crucial to the context of military needs, action and change, although this internal policing function is commonly slighted in the literature.

Did the cultural context change greatly in the period? There is scant evidence of such change as far as attitudes to death were concerned. However, the impact, first, of state-building and, secondly, of the ideological tensions, first, of the 'Wars of Religion' stemming from the Protestant Reformation and, secondly, of the French Revolution, is less clear. In particular, it is uncertain how far these changes accentuated a propensity to fight, both at the level of decision-makers and at that of ordinary soldiers. Ideological tensions may well have made compromise less easy and contributed to the repeated conflicts of 1585–1609, 1618–48 and 1792–1815. Such tensions also encouraged intervention in the internal affairs of other states, as from the mid-1580s, when Philip II of Spain played a direct role in the French Wars of Religion and Elizabeth I of England sent forces to aid the Dutch Revolt against Philip. These tensions may also have made it easier to overcome domestic limitations to the mobilisation of resources for war. Furthermore, a more heightened atmosphere acted to break down the monopolisation of war by the military. This was seen clearly in popular resistance to Napoleonic forces in Calabria and Spain, but there were many other examples, such as the Genoese rising against Austrian occupation in 1746 and the subsequent successful resistance of the city to Austrian attempts to recapture it.[5]

Popular participation cut across the general impact of state-building on the military. This was a matter crudely of the state taking over control of formal military activity, seeking to limit unofficial activity, and also employing military power in order to enhance its power and prestige. That, however, is too schematic an account of what was a more complex process and one, furthermore, that could not be abstracted from the social system. Far from being outside society, 'states' reflected social structures, practices and attitudes, and the process of growing governmental control was, generally, one achieved through co-operation with social elites, and was greatly dependent on it. This co-operation reached its apogee with Peter the Great's attempt to classify society through state service with his Table of Ranks (1722), and with Napoleon's creation of a new imperial aristocracy in which military service played a major role. Aristocratic officership was also important in less prominent armies: nearly 90 per cent of Spanish officers after 1776 were from the nobility. Such officership affected aristocratic conduct, encouraging a greater interest in the military arts in their upbringing. The Jesuit College founded by the Duke of Parma in 1601 included in its curriculum training in weaponry, horsemanship and movement in formation.

Precisely because an expansion of governmental military strength was a matter largely of co-opting elites, rather than coercing them, it proved difficult to limit unofficial military activity. Military entrepreneurship could be redirected through more regular military channels, especially thanks to a system of the aristocratic proprietorship of regiments,[6] but it proved far harder to suppress feuds, brigandage and duels enjoying elite support.

The extension of state control was far easier at sea, because navies required substantial fixed, and recurrent, expenditure, and operated from a limited number of ports. Furthermore, much of Europe's coastline, especially the Atlantic coastline, was under the control of a small number of powers that did not wish to encourage naval forces that were not under control. The situation in the Mediterranean was different, but, even so, there also the net result was a concentration of naval power, and a degree of governmental direction, that was not matched on land. Thus, in the British Isles, the Jacobite risings on land were not matched by comparable activity at sea.

There were private naval forces, but states strove to license them by means of privateering. Piracy within non-Mediterranean

European waters was less of a problem for warships than for merchantmen, and much of the piracy was from outside areas under the authority of the major states.[7] Indeed, the major pirate forces were those of the Barbary States of North Africa.

In the case of navies, it is possible to present a model of military change driven by military technology and operational considerations. In this model, the prime reason for change would be the rise in the sixteenth century of the large specialised warship, the ship of the line built and maintained just for war, rather than also acting as a peacetime trader. These ships, able to take part in sustained artillery duels at close range, were expensive to build and maintain, and could only be deployed by major states, and, even then, only with considerable difficulty, as the French discovered in the mid-1690s. As a consequence, the number of potential maritime powers was restricted, and the naval state was no longer coterminous with the commercial territory or port.[8] Such an account, however, has its flaws, not least because it neglects the question of why particular states chose to develop their naval power, and to invest substantial sums accordingly. Issues of identification and image played a major role, and political cultures that placed an emphasis on commercial interests were possibly best suited for this development, although such an approach has to be treated with care, because strength, not commerce, was the prime rationale for naval power.

Any emphasis on attitudes does not serve simply as a critique of the technological account of war. It also directs attention to reasons for variation in military strength and activity. In place of a diffusionist model, based essentially on technology and training, and the rate and reasons for their spread, it is possible to direct attention to a more varied military topography in which differences arose from complex, and often obscure, causes. This is important, not only in explaining why European practices differed from those elsewhere, but, also, in revealing how and why the European way of war itself was far from a monolith.

The contributors to this volume, however, face the same problem as other scholars on military history, namely how best to provide descriptive and explanatory form to the variety of the period. Any schematic model would be misleading, but so also is a mere listing of different military events and situations. The challenge is greater if one moves from a short period, say a

century, where a single descriptive account might, however
misleadingly, seem appropriate, and, instead, seek to comprehend a longer timespan, such as that of this volume. Then the
problem of discussing change through time becomes more pressing. It is also a more important question, for it was through time
that changes occurred in the comparative advantage of particular
military methods and systems, both within Europe and globally.
Any discussion of these changes requires an understanding of
what constituted comparative advantage.

II

Military organisation has to be located socially and politically.
The most essential point tends to be forgotten. For most of
history, military organisation has been essentially a matter of
male activity, although women have had to bear many of the
resulting costs. This situation is currently changing, in part because the premium on human strength is now far less, but also,
largely, due to ideological, rather than functional, considerations. No such change occurred in the early modern period, and
this affected both the military resources available to states and the
image of war.

The social and political character and contexts of naval organisation were different to those of land warfare. In his valuable
study of English naval development, Nicholas Rodger has suggested that land-based military systems require and encourage
an authoritarianism, in organisation and political context, that
is inappropriate and, indeed, ineffective in the case of naval
power. Instead, he argues that for the United Provinces (Dutch,
modern Netherlands) and England, later Britain, it was the
creation of consensual practices and institutions that was crucial
in producing the readiness to sustain naval power.[9]

Rodger's approach, however, can be queried in both general
and detail. It excludes all non-European naval powers. Even
within Europe, Rodger's account is necessarily limited in its
examples. Russia, for example, built up an effective navy in
the eighteenth century, and Scandinavian rulers not associated
with consensus, such as Gustavus III of Sweden, also invested
heavily in naval power. Furthermore, Rodger fails to consider

adequately the counter-factuals that might be advanced in the case of English naval developments. His emphasis on consensualism offers a Whiggish teleology that is seductive, yet also open to empirical and methodological debate.

If military organisation is, in part, understood as an exercise in the control, deployment and sustaining of force, then the situation at sea was obviously different to that on land. The force–number ratio was very different, increasingly so as the force-projection (and cost) of each warship increased from the sixteenth century with successive advances in gunpowder-weapons technology. In the eighteenth century individual warships had greater artillery power than entire field armies. The chronology of naval organisational development is different to that for armies in the West recently outlined by John Lynn,[10] because professionalisation, specialisation, machinisation and state control all became more evident in Western navies in the sixteenth and seventeenth centuries, and the situation has not in essence changed since.

Thus, the technical specialisation seen by Lynn as crucial to the situation in the modern Western army began earlier at sea. Recruitment entailed systems of forcible enlistment that mirrored the situation on land, but these ended earlier at sea, and there was a greater role for volunteer service, a consequence, in part, of the greater professionalism of sea service. Cohesion and state control of the officer class were greater at sea than on land, in large part because military entrepreneurship played a smaller role at sea, while greater professionalism was expected there, and was, indeed, necessary. This was true of sailing skills, fire control, logistics and the maintenance of fighting quality and unit cohesion.

Any emphasis on differences between land and sea invites questions about the timing and appropriateness of particular descriptive and analytical models, such as that of an early modern 'military revolution'. In the case of 'modern', i.e. specialised navies, the appropriate model is state-driven and centred, to a degree that was only later true for armies, but it is still reasonable to ask how far the general patterns of social behaviour affected military organisation and force structures and practices. At the basic level, there was no role for operational consent on the part of sailors in state forces, no more than there was for soldiers. An element of contractualism might pertain for service conditions, especially in terms of payment and the provision of food, but this was lessened in Europe from the mid-seventeenth century, as governmental control over the military increased and the provision of services improved. Furthermore, in state forces, contractualism on the part of soldiers and sailors did not extend to operations.

This was very different to the situation in a range of independent or autonomous forces within the European system, such as mercenaries, irregular troops, privateers and pirates, and was also very different to many, but by no means all, non-European forces.[11] One shift in European military organisation was the demise of contractualism, as the nature and power of the state were defined and developed from the decline of feudal practices. This process was given added force and pace in the late eighteenth century as the autonomy of corporate institutions came under attack, first from the 'Enlightened Despots' and then, more brutally, from the French Revolution and the subsequent expansion of French power. Although their power has been exaggerated, the 'Enlightened Despots', such as Frederick II, 'the Great', of Prussia (1740–86), wielded more control over their armies, both soldiers and officers, than their sixteenth- or seventeenth-century predecessors had done.

The demise of contractualism, on land and sea, was an aspect of the more general problem of control posed by the military. The issue is difficult to integrate into a typology and chronology of military organisation, because, in response to particular domestic political developments, circumstances varied so greatly between particular countries. Any theory of military organisation has to take note of problems of internal and external control.

Lynn's model places due weight on organisation. He proposes a developmental pattern that, for the early modern period, sees a shift from 'aggregate-contract' to 'state-commission' and then 'popular-conscript', as the 'core army style matrix'. The first was exemplified in the sixteenth century by France and then Spain, the second, in the late seventeenth and early eighteenth centuries by France, and from mid-century by Prussia, while the last was created by Revolutionary France. Like earlier scholars, for example Michael Howard,[12] Lynn essentially offers a paradigmatic model, and one that centres on conflict *between* European states, especially in the France–Germany region. His is an account of the pressures of symmetrical warfare, conflict between essentially similar forces, a point emphasised by his opening example, drawn from the battle of Rossbach in 1757 between France and Prussia.

Yet such a paradigm is unhelpful as an account both of Europe's military position in the wider world and, indeed, of European warfare itself. It also presupposes a paradigmatic approach that *may* be appropriate for certain periods, but that is generally unhelpful. Any taxonomy and analysis of military style has to be able to comprehend asymmetrical as well as symmetrical warfare. This is true of Europe's military history. Over the last two millennia, and, indeed, earlier, there have been repeated attacks on European states by peoples from 'outside' Europe, the latter understood in terms of what was to be the Romano-Christian nexus. Thomas Arnold's essay is a valuable reminder of the importance of the challenge posed by the Ottoman Turks.

The challenge was not simply that of the quantity of force brought to bear against Europe, but also of different military methods that were effective and remained so until the eighteenth century. Indeed there was no significant disparity between Turkish and European abilities to mobilize and finance major campaigns until the mid-seventeenth century, and maybe even later. The Turks were effective in feeding and supplying their troops and their logistics were important to their operational capability. Thus, an emphasis on asymmetry is appropriate. Any paradigm, organisational or otherwise, based solely on inter-European military competition is questionable.

This analysis can be taken further by suggesting that such conflicts – on the geographical 'periphery' in Lynn's terms – had a greater impact on the European 'core' than a model that privileges developments within the latter might claim. In short, methods and organisations devised to deal with threats and challenges from outside, in this period the Turks, might well have affected not only 'peripheral' states, a term that in the seventeenth century included Venice, Austria, Poland and Russia, all of which bordered the Turkish empire, but, also, those further removed from the direct confrontation with 'non-European' states. Austria and Poland acted as crucial intermediaries in the seventeenth century, not least in maintaining a role for light cavalry within European warfare. In part, this issue of military core-periphery within Europe is an aspect of the primitivisation of the East in Western analysis, a primitivisation that greatly affected and affects perceptions of Eastern Europe in a misleading fashion. In the eighteenth century the flow of military influence was indeed rather West to East, as in the use of weaponry, experts and commanders, at land and sea, in Russia and, to a far lesser extent, Turkey. However, it is necessary to be cautious before deriving from that flow any hierarchy of military capability. Furthermore, it has been argued that infantry columns originated in fighting against the Turks.

The essay by Brian Davies is a valuable reminder of the vitality of Russian military developments, and this point can be taken further by drawing attention to the structure of the book. Four chronological chapters provide the major thematic approach, namely that of change through time, but they are complemented by five other chapters that focus on particular spheres over the entire period. Aside from the naval chapter, the other four chapters are designed to direct attention to Turkey, Russia, Scandinavia and Gaelic Britain – regions that do not generally receive sufficient attention in accounts of European military history. This list could be expanded to include, for example, England and Poland,[13] and it serves as a reminder of the danger of assuming a paradigmatic/diffusionist model. In his chapter on Gaelic warfare, Michael Hill argues the case for a distinctiveness of the military arts in Scotland and Ireland based on infantry shock tactics combined with tactical flexibility.

The book could have been organised differently by, for example, military arm – cavalry, infantry,[14] artillery,[15] etc. – or aspects of war – recruitment, logistics, etc. – or types of engagement – battles, sieges,[16] etc. However, such thematic approaches tend to minimise the attention devoted to variations in time and place. Such variations are an important corrective to an overly static interpretation.

III

Armies and navies are organisations with objectives, and, in assessing their capability and effectiveness, it is necessary to consider how these objectives changed, and how far such changes created pressures for adaptation. In short, a demand-led account has to be set alongside any supply-side assessment that might present improvements in weaponry or increases in numbers without considering the wider context.

Territorial aggrandisement was an important theme throughout the period, but so, also, was a related interest in preventing threatening developments in international relations. The latter might be presented in various terms, not least that of preserving the balance of power, but it ensured a continual sense of the need for vigilance. This sense was heightened when uncertainty about international relations was combined with concern about the domestic situation. This was especially true of the period of the so-called 'Wars of Religion', 1560–1648, and, again, of that of the French Revolution. Foreign encouragement of domestic disaffection was not restricted to those periods, but it was especially strong then, both because restraints on intervention greatly lessened and because ideological factors subverted senses of dynastic or national loyalty.

This subversion increased the difficulties of controlling armed forces. They could be compromised by disaffection, as with the naval mutinies in Britain in 1797. There could also be questions about the reliability of troops when called upon to act against compatriots. This encouraged reliance on men hired from other areas. Thus, in suppressing Jacobitism in the British Isles in 1689–1746, William III of Orange and the Hanoverians used Danish, Dutch and Hessian units as well as British troops.[17] Such a transfer of military resources was not solely motivated by the need to deal with rebellion, but could also reflect the particular characteristics – in terms of motivation, training and weaponry – of troops from different areas. In the sixteenth and seventeenth centuries, the Spanish military system had, in large part, rested on the ability to move units within the empire in order to serve in distant parts, for example by transferring troops from Italy to fight in the Low Countries.[18]

Religion might focus and accentuate domestic disaffection, which was an issue that rulers had to consider, when recruiting and employing troops, throughout the period. The possibility of disaffection affected attitudes to the development of armed forces and to force structure. An emphasis on fortified positions away from external frontiers was one major consequence of concern about disaffection. Thus, Louis XIV built a citadel at Marseille. After its rebellion was suppressed in 1678, Carlos II of Spain imposed a substantial garrison in a new citadel at Messina.

In simplistic terms, the period of the Wars of Religion challenged reliance on national levies where there were important heterodox religious movements, as in the (Austrian) Habsburg hereditary lands, and, instead, encouraged a use of units, sometimes mercenaries and/or foreign units, in which reliability was a key factor. This became less of an issue in the seventeenth century, particularly after Protestant autonomy was suppressed in France and the (Austrian) Habsburg hereditary lands in the 1620s, and then after the so-called mid-seventeenth-century crisis of internal control in much of Europe in the 1640s and 1650s.

The altered situation ensured that domestic stability was less important for military action and organisation than hitherto, although it was still a factor, as shown by the use of troops to suppress risings in Brittany (1675), Bohemia (1680) and the South-West of England (1685). The absence of police forces meant that troops were frequently used for policing purposes; but the limited nature of royal control in many, especially frontier, regions was such that the army was the appropriate solution anyway. Thus, in 1681 Victor Amadeus II of Savoy–Piedmont used 3000 men to suppress resistance in Mondovi to duties on salt. After the Ukrainian leader Mazepa defected in October 1708, Peter the Great stationed ten Russian dragoon regiments permanently in the Ukraine.[19] This accompanied the destruction of the Zaporozhian Sich and the subordination of the Hetmanate's Cossack regiments to Russian commanders.

The reduced fear of insurrection after the mid-seventeenth century encouraged a reliance on indigenous troops, whether raised by limited conscription or as volunteers, although this was far less the case where governmental control was limited, as in Hungary and Highland Scotland. Reliance on indigenous forces was further enhanced by the demographic downturn or stagnation in much of Europe from the early seventeenth century until the mid-1740s. The military market was less buoyant than in the sixteenth century, a period of population growth, and it was correspondingly more important to control and employ domestic military manpower. This tendency also owed much to a stronger emphasis on 'standing' (permanent) armies that reflected both 'military' factors – the need for training in order to make best use of gunpowder weaponry – and the 'political' context – the greater extent of international competition, stemming, in particular, from the aggressive tendencies of Louis XIV and the expansionist plans of the Russian Romanovs and the Austrian Habsburgs. Whereas, for example, France and the Austrian Habsburgs in the second half of the sixteenth century had not been, or been perceived as, growing and threatening powers, this was not the case in the later seventeenth century and from the mid-1680s to the late 1720s respectively. Within Germany, the prolonged conflicts against Louis XIV and the Turks from the 1660s encouraged medium and small territories to militarise.[20]

Systems of conscription were less effective than in the twentieth century, not least because of the limited amount of information at the disposal of the state and the weakness of its policing power. Nevertheless, the spread of conscription greatly altered the social politics of military service and war. It was crucial to the process by which rulers asserted more direct control over their armies. In 1693 each Prussian province was ordered to provide a certain number of recruits. This was achieved by conscription, largely of peasants. The same year, French militia units were sent to fight in war zones; from 1688 they had been raised by conscription among unmarried peasants Conscription was imposed in Denmark in 1701, Spain in 1704 and in Russia the following year, and in Austria and Bohemia in 1771. These systems were extended during the eighteenth century, and then again during the Napoleonic Wars. In Prussia, a cantonal system was established between 1727 and 1735. Every regiment was assigned a permanent catchment area around its peacetime garrison town, from where it drew its draftees for lifelong service. Such systems increased control over the peasantry, who were less able than mercenaries to adopt a contractual approach towards military service.[21]

These recruitment practices were as important an aspect of rising state military power as the number of troops which is sometimes employed in a somewhat crude fashion as the sole indicator of such power. This is one reason why the period 1660–1760 was an important one of military change. New recruitment systems were mediated by aristocratic officers, but they reflected an enhanced control on the part of government, and the impact of this can, in part, be seen by contrasting the politics of army control in the French Revolutionary and Napoleonic Wars (1792–1815) with that earlier in the 'Wars of Religion'. In 1792–1815 there was no figure equivalent to Wallenstein, the independent entrepreneur who raised armies for the Austrians in the 1620s and the 1630s, no system of military entrepreneurship to sap governmental control, both politically and operationally.[22] The latter was crucial to the ability to think and act in strategic terms. Napoleon was able to direct his marshals without any sense that they owned their armies.

The ability to think strategically was scarcely novel, but the increase in discipline, planning, and organisational regularity and predictability that characterised European armies and navies in this period made it less difficult to implement strategic conceptions. The greater effectiveness of the military forces of the period were demonstrated most obviously by Russia under Peter the Great, and by Prussia from 1740, but there were other examples. The Spanish army had been very weak in the 1670s, but in 1717 the island of Sardinia was successfully invaded and in 1734 the Spaniards overran Naples and Sicily. The old organisation of *tercios* was replaced in 1702–04 by a new structure of regiments, battalions and companies, and only the king had the right to assign officers to units. The Spanish navy was also revitalised in the 1710s.

It would, of course, be misleading to exaggerate the nature of the changes of 1660–1760. Firearms were difficult to aim accurately. At sea, 'no tactical system could resolve the fundamental problem related to the fact that sailing men-of-war moved and fought along axes that lay at right angles to each other'.[23] On both land and sea, operations were still greatly affected by the constraints, circumstances and accidents of climate and weather. Thanks in large part to the combination of the wind and the poor manoeuvrability of warships, naval battles frequently did not develop as suggested by fighting instructions and admirals had only limited control once battles had begun. Operations on land were also greatly affected by the weather. The surprise attack on Belgrade mounted by the Austrians on 2–3 December 1787 failed because most of their force lost their way in fog. Rain turned roads into quagmires, hindering, for example, the Neapolitan invasion of the French-occupied Papal States in November 1798.

Logistical – supply – difficulties were exacerbated by the rise in the size of armies, and failures to maintain adequate supplies of food both sapped the strength of soldiers and affected their morale.[24] Logistical demands pressed on societies that could not readily increase their production of food or munitions. Indeed, the low level of agrarian productivity ensured that the accumulation of reserves was difficult. As a consequence, the ability of states during a period of sustained conflict to retain their military effectiveness was affected by factors over which there was limited control, principally the weather. Logistical difficulties encouraged an emphasis on the strategic offensive, because it then became possible to tap the economies of occupied areas, either by pillage or by 'contributions' – taxes enforced under the threat of devastation. However, advancing armies could run short of food, especially in areas without much arable agriculture, such as the Khanate of the Crimea, a problem that helped to thwart the Russian advances in 1687 and 1689.

The system of transferred costs both enhanced the destructiveness of war and made it more important not to lose control of territory. The burden of war rose if armies were forced to fight on the defensive on their own territory. This affected the French in the War of the Spanish Succession as they were driven from Germany (1704), Italy (1706) and the Low Countries (1706). Transferred costs also contributed to the situation in which the bulk of the burdens of war were borne by the peasantry of combatant powers. This was a major part of the social politics of war, although, as rural devastation inhibited the ability to pay rents, tithes and taxes, the costs were widely spread.

These costs can be minimised by referring to the regenerative capability of an unmechanised agrarian economy and to the extent to which these were societies accustomed to pain and sudden death. However, neither point lessens the human and social cost of military service, casualties and devastation. Soldiers' diaries and correspondence testified to their fear of injury.[25] The crippled, limping, gun-laden ex-soldier, dependent on begging, depicted by the Florentine Giovanni Ferretti in *Harlequin Returning from the Wars* was an all-too-present image of an everyday scene. Recent work on early modern social attitudes has, for example, emphasised that high childhood mortality rates did not encourage callousness or lessen a sense of loss. Thus war powerfully contributed to a mental world dominated by chance and a frequently malign fate. It encouraged a providentialism in which the world appeared outside human control. War was presented as one of the curses or plagues of life.

This aspect of the impact of conflict forms an ironic counterpoint to the usual emphasis on a growing bureaucratisation and planning of war in early modern Europe. Such a gap between intention and impact is common to war, but it is worth considering how far the bureaucratisation has been exaggerated. It is more appropriate to stress governmental capability and planning in the case of naval warfare, but, even so, under the strain of conflict, navies found it difficult to fulfil their potential. At the outset of wars, even Britain, the leading naval power in the eighteenth century, found it difficult to ensure victory, as was shown in indecisive clashes with the French off Minorca (1756) and Ushant (1778). The individual ships' companies were newly recruited or pressed, their captains were still working up the sailing capacities of their ships and crews, and the admiral was still working up and determining the capacities of his captains, who were equally unsure of their commander. In both 1756 and 1778, the component parts of the British fleet displayed a serious lack of cohesion. The chances of holdness going wrong were therefore far higher than, for example, in 1759 when Boscawen and Hawke won the battles of Lagos and Quiberon Bay with well-tried and experienced ships and captains on whose capacities they could rely.

On land, the situation, especially in wartime, was far more confused than might be suggested by much of the teleological language of governmental development and military revolution(s). Indeed, far from war being won by planned action, it was frequently the side that was less handicapped by deficiencies that was successful: coping with problems was the major skill of command. This was true both on campaign and on the battlefield. In the latter case, the retention and use of reserves amidst the uncertainty of battle was often crucial. Such a situation did not, however, preclude a degree of change.

Command issues were affected by the rise in the number of troops and by developments in weaponry. Having argued that these factors should not be placed first, either in description or analysis, it would, however, be misleading to neglect their role. This is particularly the case because so much of the discussion of change has been in terms of weaponry, army size and type of fortification. These have been linked, as in Geoffrey Parker's claim that the impact of cannon on siegecraft – for both the besiegers and the besieged – was such that a new system of fortification – the *trace italienne* – developed, and that this led to requirements for more extended siege lines and thus more troops.[26]

Such claims have been central to the debate over the existence, character and impact of a military revolution or revolutions in this period, a debate discussed by a number of the contributors. An emphasis on weaponry and fortification has also been crucial to the claim that the balance of military advantage between Europe and the outer world shifted dramatically in this period.[27] Furthermore, the notion of a military revolution, driven or at least permitted by technological developments, appears both to make sense of the expansion of European power and to locate the impact of gunpowder in the history of Europe.

However, timing is again an issue, and this is linked to the need to consider which aspect of gunpowder weaponry was most important. In both Africa and India the flintlock musket was more important than earlier hand-held firearms, or indeed than cannon. As a consequence, it is more appropriate in those cases when focusing on the role of gunpowder weaponry to emphasise the late seventeenth and eighteenth centuries. It is unclear how far it is reasonable to downplay the introduction and spread of the flintlock in European firearms conflict, as is generally the case in work on military change on the continent.

A crude technological determinism is clearly inappropriate in military history. It neglects the more complex character of military capability and achievement, and misunderstands technology by treating it as an independent variable, and one that was readily understood and easily adaptable. In addition, the multi-faceted nature of the European military environment was such that what might be appropriate or considered appropriate, in weaponry and tactical terms, in one setting, was not necessarily so in others. This was especially true on land, but was, also, the case at sea, although there was a far greater degree of standardisation there. Nevertheless, the deep-draught warships characteristic of the Atlantic powers were of only limited use in shallow inshore waters, such as those of the Gulf of Finland where Russia and Sweden competed in the eighteenth century. Galleys and frigates played a greater role than in the Atlantic.

On land, there was a tension between firepower and shock tactics, for infantry, cavalry and siegecraft, and the different choices made reflected not only the views of particular generals (such as Gustav Adolf, Charles XII, Saxe, Frederick the Great, Rumiantsev and Suvorov), but also wider assumptions in military society. Choices were not dictated by technology. Such cultures have received insufficient attention, but it is worthy of note that an emphasis on the attack can be frequently seen in the case of Gaelic, Swedish, Russian, Polish and Turkish forces. Mention of Saxe, the leading French general of the 1740s, and of Frederick the Great make it clear, however, that the strategic and tactical offensive in Western Europe was not banished by the enhancement of firepower from the 1690s thanks to the widespread addition then of socket bayonets to flintlock muskets. Shock won over firepower in the case of cavalry tactics. Shock also played a major role in victories over non-Europeans, as in the defeats of the Turks, by the Austrians at Vienna (1683), Zenta (1697) and Belgrade (1717), and by the Russians in 1770 and 1774.

Any emphasis on shock does not necessarily lessen the role of firepower, not least because this could be used to prepare for the assault. However, it suggests that an account that approaches tactical success in terms of the technological (weaponry) and organisational (tactics, drill, discipline) factors that maximised firepower is limited. The real point of drill and discipline was defensive – to prepare a unit to remain whole in the face of death, regardless of casualties. The issue of shock versus firepower – of offensive efficacy or effectiveness in causing casualties – was not as important as a unit remaining able to act and tractable to its commander while receiving casualties.

This criticism of the primacy of firepower can be extended from the battlefield to the siege by drawing attention, first, to the large number of positions, often major ones (for example Prague in 1741) that fell to assault and, second, to the numerous positions that were not strengthened in accordance with the latest fortification techniques. The latter were too expensive to be comprehensively adopted. Furthermore, the effectiveness of fortified positions as a control over territory and their importance in military operations varied in different parts of Europe.

The journal *War in History* recently carried two important and thoughtful reviews that neatly exemplified the problems of arriving at a synthesis of early modern European military developments. Robert Frost emphasised the

> sheer pace of innovation, as Europeans rapidly expanded the possibilities of the military art in an utterly unparalleled manner . . . . The trajectory and chronology of change varied according to local political and geographical circumstances, but all societies, sooner or later, had to face up to the challenge; that some proved temporarily or permanently inadequate does not undermine the idea of the Military Revolution.[28]

In the preceding review, however, David Parrott warned:

> It is easy to fall into the Whiggish trap of assuming that military theorists and commanders in the field consistently recognized and appreciated the salient points in the western tradition, that 'progressive' European rulers modernized their states and reshaped their societies to facilitate war fought on these recognized western principles. What is played down in much of this account is the extent to which western war has been as much about fashion, prejudice and vanity as about the progressive evolution of superior military systems.[29]

Parrott's comment is a valuable guide to the need to think carefully about the processes by which military change occurred. It is all too easy to employ a model of a competitive states system driving military development and to forget the recurrent element of choice and the role of the individuals, groups and institutions that made and implemented these choices, and also of training in particular techniques. This factor is enhanced if attention is devoted to European ways of war, for the reminder that there were choices of weapons, weapon systems, tactics and strategy serves again to underline the role of choice. Commentators in the early sixteenth century could debate the value of mercenaries or militia, pikemen or swordsmen, musketeers or

heavy cavalry, and how best to use and to combine them.
A quarter-millennium later, in the late eighteenth century, commentators could consider column versus line.[30]

The role of debate and choice can be seen in more than one
light. They might complicate modern analysis, but they are re-
minders of a dynamic aspect of European culture, its *relative
freedom of debate*. This was, of course, limited and constrained
– by gender, social, economic and political factors – but it nevertheless appears to have been far greater than anywhere else in
the world. The culture of print was of limited value to the illiter-
ate or poor, but of considerable importance for military development. This was readily apparent in direct terms. Printed manuals
on gunnery, tactics, drill, fortification and siegecraft spread
techniques far more rapidly than word of mouth or manuscript. *Uchenie i Khitrost' ratnogo stroeniya pekhotnykh lyudei*, the first
Russian printed book on military matters, was published in 1647.
An infantry manual, it emphasised training and included a large
number of sketches and plans to teach drill. Aside from specifics,
the manual emphasised the very value of military education, and
associated military skill with knowledge. Manuals also permitted
and made possible a degree of standardisation that both helped
to increase military effectiveness and was important for the
utilisation of military resources.

Literacy and printing had other values. They fostered discussion of military organisation and methods, and encouraged a
sense of system. Literacy and printing were important to command and control, and to military administration. It became less
difficult to survey the quantity and state of military resources.
Military statistics became more accessible. The official report of
the Russian Ordnance, *Kniga Pushkarskogo prikaza, za skrepoyu
d'yaka Volkova* (1680), *Book of the Gunners' Chancellery, with the
certification of secretary Volkov*, listed all arms and ammunition as
well as current production. The number of cannon located in
towns was revealed to be 3575 pieces. Another 400–500 field
guns were probably available for the field army. Literacy and
printing also aided the positive interaction of resources and requirements, of different military branches, in particular localities,
and of forces that were in different locations. This was true even
of armies that were not at the forefront of military development:
'on the eve of the demise of Habsburg rule [1700] the Spanish

Monarchy remained a relatively powerful, functioning military structure or "system", a surprisingly integrated and coherent war machine'.[31]

It would be misleading to adopt a teleological approach and to suggest that discussion in print necessarily enhanced military effectiveness. Much of it was platitudinous and some novel suggestions, for example Saxe's interest in the eighteenth century in the revival of the pike, were unhelpful. Work on the history of science warns against any simple assumption of linear progress. Even if new ideas were useful, there were still major questions of diffusion and implementation.

This accepted, it is clear that the culture of print helped foster a dynamic relationship between applied science and military practice. This was true of fortification and ballistics, with works such as Tartaglia's geometrical models of artillery trajectories in the 1530s and Galileo's kinematics of ballistic motion in a vacuum. In the 1530s there was already great interest in the possibilities of measuring cannon fire. The century 1660–1760 was especially important, because it witnessed the linkage of Newtonian science to military engineering, artillery and military thought. Ballistics were revolutionised between 1742 and 1753 by Benjamin Robins and Leonhard Euler. Robins invented new instruments enabling him to discover and quantify the air resistance to high-speed projectiles. He also furthered understanding of the impact of rifling. The author of *Neue Gründsatze der Artillerie* (1745), Euler also solved the equations of subsonic ballistic motion in 1753 and summarised some of the results in published tables.

These theoretical and empirical advances greatly increased the predictive power of ballistics, and helped turn gunnery from a craft into a science that could and should be taught. These advances affected the use of artillery and influenced military education.[32] An artillery school was opened in Naples in 1744, and an engineering academy ten years later, and in 1769 they were amalgamated into the *Reale Accademia Militare*. It taught ballistics, tactics, experimental physics and chemistry to officer cadets, all of whom were supposed to attend classes.[33]

Scientific advance was not always immediately helpful. Under Louis XIV the French government sought to establish naval shipbuilding on a theoretical basis, but 'mathematical description of the theoretical principles of *la manoeuvre*, the disposition of sails and the positioning of rudders, made not the slightest contribution to the improvement of warships. The actual construction of warships continued to be carried out after age-old practices by shipwrights who received their training by apprenticeship.' The Jesuit Paul Hoste, author of *Art des Armées Navales* (1697), complained, 'It is by luck that a good ship is built, for those who still make them are no better than those who build without knowing how to read or write.' Ironically, Hoste's explanation of why ships do not capsize was itself wrong. In the eighteenth century progress was not achieved by the investigation of mechanical principles, for 'the content of science moved ever farther away from the descriptive, ambiguous world of the shipbuilder, filled with limitation and constraints, toward a more extensive use of abstract concepts' defined by mathematics. Instead, it was the development of the profession of naval engineering that was decisive. It combined a general mathematical culture and the study of the old rules for building ships to find the best practice.[34] Furthermore, the superiority of French ships was outweighed by superior British shiphandling.

As already suggested, the concept of a military revolution is problematic, and the chronological delimitation of the peak period of scientific application in order to establish when such a revolution occurred may be of limited value. As with other aspects of military change, early developments may have been more significant than a greater rate of change later, but it is also possible to argue the opposite. Nevertheless, it is worth noting just such an acceleration in scientific innovation and application from the later seventeenth century. Before turning to the specialist chapters, it is important to emphasise the centrality of war to the international and domestic politics of the period, to its culture and its confessional development, and to the experience of society and the people of the period. Causal relationships can be obscure, ambiguous and controversial, but there is no doubt of the importance of military preparedness and conflict.

1. War in Sixteenth-Century Europe: Revolution and Renaissance

THOMAS F. ARNOLD

A REVOLUTIONARY CENTURY OF WAR?

For over forty years – ever since Michael Roberts's 1956 article 'The Military Revolution, 1560–1660' first introduced and defined the idea of an early modern military revolution – historians have been debating the question of whether the sixteenth century can be identified as a – or perhaps even *the* – revolutionary period in the history of warfare in the Western world.[1] In the last decade, particularly in the wake of Geoffrey Parker's *The Military Revolution* (1st edition 1988; 2nd edition 1996), attention to the issue has only intensified. At this date no survey of war in sixteenth-century Europe, not even the present limited chapter, can honestly avoid taking a position on this dominating historiographical problem. So, then: was there an early modern military revolution, and did it principally take place in the sixteenth century?

Any answer to that question necessarily involves a review of the debate so far. In a nutshell, Michael Roberts's original thesis identified four revolutionary tendencies in the warfare of the late sixteenth and early seventeenth centuries: first, the superiority of disciplined infantry – musketeers rather than pikemen – armed and drilled to prosecute a field battle by the ordered application of firepower, not the hurly-burly of man-to-man combat; second, the manifestly greater size of these new-style, mostly musketeer armies; third, the emergence of bolder, more dramatic strategies designed to seek a decisive battle at the culmination of a sharp campaign; and fourth, a need for larger and more reliable and intrusive commissariats and military bureacracies to supply and support these larger armies. Not surprisingly, given that he was

23

a historian of the Swedish imperial experience in the seventeenth century, Roberts saw the complete expression of these revolutionary trends – tactical, strategical and administrative – in the armies and the campaigns of Gustavus Adolphus, particularly in that monarch's celebrated whirlwind invasion of Germany in 1630–32. Though important elements of this military revolution (such as the so-called 'linear tactics' of massed musket fire) could be traced to prominent late sixteenth-century reformers – in the case of infantry tactics, to Maurice of Nassau, reformer of the Dutch Protestant army fighting Philip of Spain in the 1590s – for Roberts the critical date in his essay's title was 1660, not 1560. Thus he concluded, in the last paragraph of his essay, that:

> The armies of [the Austrian Habsburg Emperor] Maximilian II [died 1576], in tactics, strategy, constitution, and spirit, belong to a world of ideas which would have seemed quite foreign to Benedek and Radetzky. The armies of the [Prussian] Great Elector [died 1688] are linked infrangibly with those of Moltke and Schlieffen, By 1660 the modern art of war had come to birth.[2]

Therefore, in Roberts's original formulation, the military revolution really a problem of seventeenth-century history (and an achievement of northern and Protestant Europeans). But above all, in terms of chronology, Roberts emphasised the long-term importance of this military transformation within the broadest scheme of modern European history, To quote the final words of Roberts's essay, as the result of this military revolution 'the road lay open, broad and straight, to the abyss of the twentieth century'.[3]

Roberts's concept of an early modern military revolution has been borrowed and transformed by Geoffrey Parker, first in a 1976 essay, and subsequently and much more thoroughly through the two editions of his book *The Military Revolution*.[4] In his 1976 essay, Parker accepted the broad categories of Roberts's thesis, but Parker challenged Roberts's identification of northern, Protestant armies as the first to be fully or significantly transformed. Noting the continued success of Catholic and Habsburg armies throughout the 1560–1660 period (most tellingly by referring to the crushing Catholic Habsburg victory over a Swedish army at Nördlingen in 1634) Parker brought the threshold of the military revolution back to the massive – if not fully successful – Spanish effort to contain and roll back the Dutch revolt in the Netherlands from the 1570s. And Parker even more directly critiqued Roberts's chronology, asserting that Roberts's 'choice of the year 1560 as the starting point of the military revolution was unfortunate' and that 'many of the developments described by Roberts also characterized warfare in Renaissance Italy'.[5] While Roberts's military revolution was an achievement of the seventeenth century with antecedents in the sixteenth, Parker made the military revolution a firmly sixteenth-century phenomenon with antecedents in the fifteenth.

Parker followed up on his 1976 essay with the first book-length treatment of the question, his *The Military Revolution* of 1988. (The second, 1996 edition of this work is unchanged except for an 'Afterword' responding to criticism.) In terms of chronology, Parker's fully developed military revolution thesis – the thesis that now forms the base line for debate on the topic – is firmly grounded in the sixteenth century (though one important chapter, on supply and logistics, does privilege developments of the seventeenth). Besides an elaborated discussion of infantry musket drill and tactics from the later sixteenth century, a feature of the military revolution argument since Roberts's original essay, Parker identified other, equally fundamental – or revolutionary – technical and tactical changes in the management of gunpowder weapons; changes that dated to even earlier in the sixteenth century. Most importantly, Parker strongly emphasised the importance of siege warfare throughout the period (by any historian's count, there were many more large-scale sieges than major field battles) and the particular importance of a new, modern style of military architecture, one based on low, thick bastions and ramparts rather than the tall, thin towers and curtain walls of medieval castles and towns. As Parker made clear, from the early decades of the century, first in Italy and then throughout Europe, the true bastion, a truncated artillery platform ingeniously angled so as to depend for its defence on the flanking fire of neighbouring bastions, completely remade both the theory and the practice of fortification. The physical changes that resulted were interesting and notable enough: in plan, European cities and citadels conformed to a star or snowflake design as bastions literally became the ruling form, or shape, of military architecture. This formal, architectural transformation of European cities has been well studied outside the military revolution debate. But Parker argued that the demands of a materially intensive new-style siege warfare based on defending and taking bastions helped drive larger, structural trends in warfare: basically, the need to man and provision extensive siege lines (while on the offensive) and garrison numerous friendly towns and citadels (while on the defensive) steadily drove up the total number of soldiers required to prosecute any sustained war, leading to the growth-of-army phenomenon considered, since Roberts, as a salient feature of any early-modern military revolution, Besides emphasising the consequences of bastion fortifications, Parker also identified the broadside sailing warship, with its cannon (often as many as in a good-sized fort) mounted in tiers along either side of the hull, as a critical technical innovation of the sixteenth century. Together with bastion fortresses and the other important new martial techniques of the century (again, especially infantry fire drill), these broadside warships critically contributed towards what Parker now identified as the single most important consequence of his reconfigured military revolution: a new-found European dominance on the battlefields of the world. Now Europeans could sail the seven seas with impunity, coasting distant continents in their far-cruising and powerfully armed carracks and galleons, pausing to literally stake out (with a fortress trace) and so claim any good harbour or desirable stretch of coast that appealed. Economic advantage came immediately in the wake of these naval and military advantages, while territorial expansion inland (in the near or the very long term) could follow as opportunity knocked. It was thus that tiny – in world terms – but militarily sophisticated European states such as Portugal, Spain, the United Provinces and England came to tap, and eventually command, the ocean-going trade of the globe. For Roberts, the early-modern military revolution amounted to the birth of modern war within Europe; for Parker, the early-modern military revolution allowed the birth of the modern world order. The difference in scope is notable, Parker insisted that the military revolution was not just a European revolution of modern over medieval, but a revolution of European over non-European. Roberts, in the final paragraph of his 1956 essay (quoted above), indicated that the fundamental changes of early-modern warfare led directly to 1870 and August 1914; Parker's thesis hinted that the same – or rather, a revised and amplified and firmly sixteenth-century military revolution – led to colonialism new and old, and perhaps even to the politics of force that shore up our present global order today, at the very close of the twentieth century. (Witness the 1991 Gulf War, the latest and most decisive triumph yet of a Western over a non-Western military or, in Iraq's case, what is best called a pseudo-Western military.) As Parker has reconstructed the idea of an early-modern military revolution, this is an historical process that ranks with the Industrial Revolution in terms of shaping the modern world.

Parker's thesis, though generally well received, has not escaped criticism. However, very little attention has been paid to critiquing Parker's real conclusion: that Europeans first demonstrated their future military dominance over non-Europeans in the sixteenth century. Instead, criticism has tended to focus on the particulars of his argument, such as the connection between bastioned fortifications and the growth-in-army-size phenomenon – and on his *chronology* of significant or revolutionary change. Indeed, the timing of a military revolution has become the overriding question in the debate, as historians – generally championing the area of their greatest personal knowledge – have plumped for one century or string of decades or another. Even before the first edition of Parker's *The Military Revolution* appeared, Günther E. Rothenberg, in the first two sentences of a 1985 essay on warfare in the seventeenth century, noted that 'the concept of a "military revolution" in Europe during the early-modern era has come to be generally accepted. There is, however, disagreement about the exact time frame of this development.'[6] As already explained, for Parker the revolution begins in the sixteenth century, with bastioned artillery fortresses, disciplined battlefield firepower, and far-sailing broadside sailing ships. His critics – or better, his amenders – have focused on other eras. Jeremy Black, reviewing the arguments of both Roberts and Parker, has rejected the relative importance of the sixteenth century entirely, instead arguing that 'innovation and development were concentrated in the late fifteenth and then again in the late seventeenth century'.[7] Black is particularly keen to emphasise the half-century after 1660, when 'the introduction of the bayonet and the phasing-out of the pike were of considerable importance' and the emergence of a small number of dominating great-power states ('France, Austria, Russia, Prussia and Britain') established the geopolitical framework of modern European conflict.[8] Medievalists have also entered the fray to argue for the decisive innovations of their own, earlier centuries. Clifford Rogers, taking the biologists' theory of 'punctuated equilibrium evolution' as his model, has presented a carefully crafted chronology for a series of military revolutions reaching back to the dawn of the fourteenth century.[9] Rogers identifies several distinct peaks of fundamental change within an overall landscape of steady-state gradual improvement or stasis: first, an 'infantry revolution' based on the achievements of English longbowmen and dismounted knights and Flemish, Scots and Swiss pikemen in the early fourteenth century (c.1302–15 for the pikemen; his chronology for the English is less specific); second, an 'artillery revolution' flowing from the newly powerful and more numerous cannon that first appeared, in various parts of Europe, between the 1420s and 1440s; and third, an 'artillery fortress revolution' of the early sixteenth century ('after 1520') that finally countered the earlier 'artillery revolution' of c.1420–c.1440 with the familiar ditches, ramparts and bastions of early modern military architecture.[10] With Black pulling the chronology of revolution forward to the very end of the seventeenth century, and Rogers pushing it back to the dawn of the fourteenth century, the sixteenth century looks less and less like a watershed era in the history of warfare. Also, the very idea of a historiographically useful military revolution has been stretched to breaking point, as contradictory examples of technical innovation are offered up to support various chronologies of change. To give one flagrant example of conflicting claims, it is hardly possible for both the *introduction* of the pike in the early fourteenth century (Rogers) and the *suppression* of the pike in the late seventeenth century (Black) to be truly revolutionary breaks with the past. Given such conflicts, the possibility of constructing a grand unified theory of early-modern military revolution that embraces all the chronologies on offer seems impossible. Better, then, to put the old war-horse out to pasture – or send it to the knacker's yard. Bert Hall, in a very recent and comprehensive survey of tactical and technological developments across the breadth of late-medieval and early-modern Europe, has concluded, in furtherance of Rogers's evolutionary model, that 'It is necessary to move beyond the concept of a single "military revolution" occupying a singular moment in historical time. A series of military transformations took place over a much longer period of time, ranging from the fourteenth through the early seventeenth century.'[11] Such a conclusion, besides politely advising that the military revolution is indeed a dead horse we can now all stop beating, also suggests that the sixteenth century is just one of three or four contiguous centuries during which Europeans gradually honed, sharpened, changed and modernised their technical military knowledge and ability.

THE REAL REVOLUTION: WEST VS EAST

But this conclusion neatly avoids the real heart of the matter. The unambiguously revolutionary nature of sixteenth-century European warfare is sharply confirmed once one focuses, as did Parker in his *The Military Revolution*, on the larger issue of Europeans vs non-Europeans. Here the operational experience – the campaigns and battles – of the sixteenth century contrasts strongly with the preceding, medieval centuries, and begins a long-term pattern that still obtains. Parker concentrated on the new-found military success of Europeans on the high seas (broadside sailing ships) and on distant shores (bastioned fortress bases), but an examination of the all-important Mediterranean and Balkan military frontier between the Christian West and the Muslim East even more dramatically highlights the critical, revolutionary importance of the sixteenth century. Between the fall of Acre in 1291 (the last toehold of the once-impressive Crusader presence in Palestine) and the fall of Constantinople in 1453 (the practical death of the long-expiring Byzantine empire) the relative balance of power between the European and non-European world relentlessly slipped to the advantage of the latter, and after 1453 a rapidly rising Turkish tide lapped at the edges of Western, Catholic Europe. The grave seriousness of that Turkish threat needs to be underlined – the essentially continuous war between cross and crescent was no mere background game of raid and reprisal, but a clash of two civilisations, a clash of two ways of war.

For Western Europe, the serious tests came from the last decades of the fifteenth century. In 1480 a Turkish armada seized the Italian town of Otranto in Apulia, a perfectly positioned beach-head on the very heel of the Italian boot, directly across the narrow straits of Brindisi from Ottoman-occupied Albania. A mixed army of Italian allies led by the king of Naples successfully contained this Turkish lodgement with earthworks, and then retook Otranto in 1481, but this specific experience of an actual, if limited invasion of Italy dramatically reinforced the general Turkish threat. Luckily for Europe, the coincident death of Mehmed II 'the Conqueror' in 1481 saved Italy from an immediately renewed assault. Nonetheless, among Italians at least there was a real sense of looming Turkish power, and a real fear that fuelled periodic panics. Once the rumour was that the Pope himself had been seized by Muslim corsairs while out riding near a seaside villa; another time rumours of an invading Turkish army so alarmed the poor people of the Friuli region, in the north-east of Italy, that they fled *en masse*, imagining themselves to be just ahead of Turkish outriders who had come with mastiffs to tear them apart. Though fanciful, such an invasion was by no means unimaginable; after all, Ottoman raiders had reached the Piave in 1463 and 1469. There were also real disasters. In 1499 a Turkish fleet smashed the Venetians at Zonchio (today Navarino, on the Greek side of the crucial Brindisi straits linking the Adriatic and the western Mediterranean). Despite these turn-of-the-century alarms and defeats, a sustained Turkish invasion of Europe did not come until well into the sixteenth century, when the Ottoman state was once again in the hands of a westward-looking sultan, Suleiman 'the Magnificent'. But once that assault came, its pace was relentless. In 1521 Suleiman took Belgrade; in 1522 he evicted the Knights of St John from their island-fortress at Rhodes (they had outlasted an earlier ferocious siege in 1480); in 1526 he smashed the army and kingdom of King Louis II of Hungary at Mohács; and in 1529 he lay siege to Vienna, nearly taking the city. Europe seemed on the brink of inundation.

But within a generation of 1529 the Turkish tide had crested, and in the 1560s and very early 1570s a series of epic encounters

demonstrated the mounting effectiveness, even the relative superiority, of European skill at arms. For one thing, there was now a
large European state with the resources to match the sultan:
Habsburg Spain. Even as Ottoman power had expanded westward, Spanish power had stretched eastward, beginning with the
fall of the last Muslim state in Iberia, Granada, in 1492. From
1496 Spain was master as well of the Kingdom of Naples, and in
a series of well-coordinated amphibious operations, Spanish galley fleets and armies seized several of the most important port-
cities along the coast of North Africa: Melilla in 1497, Oran in
1509, Bougie and Tripoli in 1510, Bizerta and Tunis in 1535.
Not all was success. In 1541 a massive Spanish army besieged, but
failed to take, the city of Algiers, and there was never much real
Spanish penetration into the Maghreb; beyond the coastal bases
and local clients there were only raiding parties. Service in these
hot, alternately boring and dangerous, ill-supplied African
fortress-enclaves (a foretaste of centuries of European colonial
service to come) was seldom popular; morale was often perilous,
and communication with Sicily, Naples and Spain unsure. Not
surprisingly, most of these Spanish bases in North Africa were
eventually lost (though Melilla and Ceuta along the Moroccan
coast remain Spanish to this day).

More important than this scattering of limited Spanish offensive victories along the Barbary cast was a growing general European defensive prowess. Here the key was the new European
military architecture based on mutually supporting bastions, low
and relatively invulnerable to artillery attack, yet bristling with
well-hidden cannon able to sweep all assault routes with a withering, enfilading fire. Against such a scientific system – and the
word scientific is exactly correct – the Turks had no similarly
systematic response, only a brute reliance on human-wave
assaults and massive but imprecisely directed cannon battery.
Even the enormous resources of a now fully-expanded Ottoman
Empire – an empire comprising Anatolia, Egypt, the Levant,
Syria, Iraq and the Balkans – could not overpower this European
advantage in fortifications science, an advantage at once tactical
and strategic, given that defensive strong-points could now be
depended on to block Turkish advance. The most famous demonstration of this European advantage came at the siege of Malta
in 1565, where a few thousand Knights of St John and crusade-

minded volunteers, manning sophisticated new-style defences, outlasted a furious, nearly four-month-long Ottoman siege until a Spanish relief army landed and forced a Turkish evacuation. The importance of modern, bastioned fortifications had already been proven by the failure of the Turkish siege of Venetian Corfu in the summer of 1537: had that siege been successful, the several thousand Turkish horse landed in Apulia earlier that year (shades of 1480!) would certainly have been followed by a genuine army of invasion. What worked at Malta and Corfu could be depended on to work elsewhere. Listening to their architect-engineers those states most menaced by the Turkish threat poured their resources into the construction of elaborate fortress systems: Austria fortified the Danube basin; Venice her long chain of islands and mainland bases from the head of the Adriatic to Crete and Cyprus; Spain her coasts and ports throughout the western Mediterranean. The result was an effective military frontier marking the high-water mark of Turkish penetration into Europe. Modern fortresses, however, were not invincible bulwarks. Their limitation was proved by the too-easy loss of the Venetian fortress-city of Nicosia on the island of Cyprus, the very first European town (from 1565) to be completely surrounded by a geometrically perfect perimeter of textbook bastions, in this case eleven in number. Despite its model walls, Nicosia fell to the Turks in 1570: besides being indifferently defended, the city was too close to the heartland of Ottoman power, and too far from Venice – fortifications alone could not completely control the strategic situation. But even when European fortifications failed, their strategic purpose could be served. An example is the Turkish siege of Szigeth in Hungary in 1566, an operational victory for the Turks that was morally and strategically hardly more satisfactory than their failure at Malta in the previous year. At Szigeth a tiny Hungarian garrison defending a modern citadel held out for just over a month, withstanding a sustained bombardment and three mass janissary assaults while the sultan Suleiman, at seventy-two still directing operations in the field, lay dying in his tent. By the time Szigeth fell on 8 September (the first anniversary of the Turkish evacuation from Malta in the previous year) the Turkish army was badly bloodied, the sultan dead, and the campaign year exhausted. All things considered – averaging the histories of Malta, Corfu, Nicosia, Szigeth and a host of other sites – the bottom line is that from the last third of the sixteenth century a cordon of rampart- and bastion-defended fortifications effectively blocked Ottoman expansion westward. And that, at the time, was a revolution indeed.

Fortifications were Europe's trump card in the sixteenth-century confrontation with the Turk, but European technical advantages emerged in other areas as well. In naval warfare, the great and famous victory of a combined and allied – even if warily allied – Spanish, Venetian and Papal galley fleet at Lepanto in 1571 erased the consequences and memories of earlier Turkish victories in the same waters in 1538 (the battle of Prevesa) and 1499 (Zonchio). Lepanto also avenged the destruction of a Spanish fleet at Djerba off Tunisia in 1560. Between the 1530s and the 1560s Turkish war fleets – not just Muslim pirates – had operated at will in the western Mediterranean. No coastline had been safe. In 1543 the Turks sacked Nice – with the assistance of their desperately anti-Habsburg French allies – and temporarily held it as a base of operations from which to systematically attack Spanish and Spanish allied (Genoese, Tuscan) shipping. In the same year they sacked Reggio in Calabria. In the summer of 1555 a Turkish flotilla landed troops on the coast of Tuscany and the island of Elba (in support of Franco-Sienese resistance to the Hispano-Florentine occupation of Siena), where they were defeated by the local forces of duke Cosimo de' Medici. The Turkish fleet appeared again off the Tuscan coast in the summer of 1558. In the far western Mediterranean, Ottoman fleets several times operated off the coasts of Spain and the Balearics, including in 1529, 1535 and 1540. When the Muslim Moriscos in Granada rebelled against Spanish Catholic rule on Christmas Day 1568, the real fear at the court of Philip II – and in Rome – was of massive Turkish naval intervention. Christian fears were by no means groundless: there was steady small-scale support for the revolt, in men and muskets, from Algiers and Constantinople, and the uprising was only suppressed in 1570 after a bitterly cruel guerrilla war and the heartless – but necessary – mass deportation of Morisco families sympathetic to the rebels. Large-scale Turkish intervention in Granada in 1569 might well have reversed the Spanish conquest of 1492. Before Lepanto, then, Turkish naval power was fully as impressive as the sultan's land forces. After Lepanto, the Ottoman navy never recovered its

earlier near-mastery of the Mediterranean: the successful operation that took Tunis in 1574 proved its swan-song. Even before
1571, some Europeans suspected that they now held the upper
hand, technically, in war at sea. In a 1567 treatise published in
Venice, one Matteo Cicogna remarked that the Turks 'sail in
badly made ships [*brutti vasselli*] poorly equipped with artillery'
but that they individually 'fight with desperation'.[12] Courage
and numbers were well enough, but European ships and shiphandling now more than made up the difference. Lepanto,
where a smaller but better-armed Christian fleet won spectacu-
larly, proved that the tide had turned at sea as well as on land.
The long-term future was one of further Turkish naval disasters
at Western hands, including Navarino in 1827 – fought in the
same waters as Lepanto – and Sinope in 1853.

   Though no great field encounter matched the Christian victories at Malta and Lepanto, new European battlefield tactics
suggest that here, too, technical superiority was passing to the
West. European battlefield successes tended to come in small-
scale encounters – such as the defeat of a Turkish landing party
in Tuscany in 1555, mentioned above – in circumstances where
Ottoman numerical advantages could not tell. Even without a
great and signal victory, European confidence, at least, was
restored by the end of the century. In a work published in 1587,
the French Huguenot captain François La Noue, referencing an
actual Spanish exploit in North Africa, explained how two small
squares of well-ordered infantry, a balanced force of 2500 pike
and 1500 arquebusiers, could safely march a great distance –
'three French leagues' – across open ground in the face of a
strong force of hostile cavalry.[13] Before the sixteenth-century
development of systems for marching and fighting in order, and
managing firepower, any such operation would most likely have
been a disaster, the European infantry shot to pieces by a feint-
ing, swirling mass of light horsemen, especially horse archers.
(This had often been the fate of European armies confronting
the Turks in the later medieval centuries, the most complete
disaster coming at Nikopolis in 1396.) In a real way, La Noue's
tactical model – in which well-ordered European infantry use
defensive discipline and offensive firepower to hold at bay any
number of impetuous 'native' warriors – prefigured the standard
operating procedure of colonial conflict. At the battle of the

Pyramids in 1798, squares of French infantry (with artillery at the angles) slaughtered their superbly mounted and caparisoned Mameluke attackers, the French losing only some 300 men. Exactly a century later, at Omdurman in the Sudan, British and British-trained Egyptians shot and machine-gunned over 10 000 Dervishes with a negligible loss – only 48 killed. These and other overwhelmingly one-sided European victories of the colonial era depended on tactical doctrines and attitudes, particularly an emphasis on regular formations and the management of fire-power, that originated in the sixteenth century. (Even as late as the Sudan campaign, European-style infantry still 'formed square' to fight a more numerous and encircling 'native' foe.) While no major sixteenth-century field battle reflected the grow-ing superiority of European tactics – and Christian armies were comprehensibly defeated by Islamic foes at Alcazarquivir in Morocco in 1578 and Mezokeresztes in Hungary in 1596 – the future belonged to the drill, discipline and tactical doctrine of the West. The truly revolutionary importance of this sixteenth-century shift has not gone unnoticed. In 1924, decades before Michael Roberts proposed his formula for an early-modern mili-tary revolution, Charles Oman, the pioneering English historian of medieval warfare, wrote in passing of 'the military revolution of the sixteenth century' by which European infantry of the new discipline, musket- and pike-armed, finally learned to hold their own against the Ottoman hordes.[14]

THE MILITARY RENAISSANCE

How to explain this very real sixteenth-century military revolu-tion, the West's new and expanding superiority in the areas of fortifications and siegecraft, naval warfare and infantry tactics? The source of Europe's emerging technical advantage was not primarily technological, as might be suspected: it was not simply a question of muskets and cannon. The Ottoman sultans had embraced the destructive possibilities of gunpowder weapons as early as any European prince; it was cannon that had finally laid low the walls of Constantinople in 1453, one of the first great demonstrations of the power of artillery anywhere. Cannon and arquebus-armed janissaries materially contributed to the sultan

Suleiman's victory over the Hungarians at Mohács in 1526 – at that great battle, it was the Christians who were outgunned. And in the course of the sixteenth century, Muslim armies, just like European, used a brute advantage in gunpowder weapons to vanquish less technologically sophisticated peoples: the Persians defeated the Uzbeks in 1528; from 1526 (the battle of Panipat) the Mughals carved out an Indian empire; and the Moroccans conquered sub-Saharan Songhai (based on Timbuktu) in the 1590s. It is true that the workshops of the Muslim east never developed the tinkering ingenuity that characterised Western centres of gunfounding and gunsmithery, but it is hard to demonstrate how Europe's frankly more inventive gun-culture provided anything more than a marginal edge in this period: the basic weapons – matchlocks and muzzle-loading artillery – were essentially the same, in both East and West, from the early sixteenth to the eighteenth centuries. In terms of sheer numbers of firearms and cannon, the armouries of the East were almost certainly as well stocked as those of the West. Only in naval warfare (always sensitive to purely technological factors) was there a marked ship-to-ship European advantage in the number of cannon and total weight of shot. Also, raw technological knowledge tended to flow quite easily from West to East; there were always Christian renegades willing to sell their expertise in casting or aiming cannon, making maps, or any other militarily useful craft. After all, the princes of the East – the Ottoman sultan above all – could afford tantalisingly handsome stipends for their hired Western experts. No less a savant than Leonardo da Vinci, the consummate Western technologist, offered his services to the Turk: he proposed a bridge across the Bosporus.

If Europe's advantage was not purely technological, it was still technical; it sprang from the distinctive way Europeans thought about and used their gunpowder weapons. The difference between East and West lay in the doctrines, the tactics, that Europeans created to harness the revolutionary potential of gunpowder weapons. Unlike the people of any other world civilisation (with the possible and temporary exception of late sixteenth-century Japan), Europeans were not content to simply retrofit gunpowder weapons to their existing military culture. Even in Europe, this was the tendency through the fifteenth century: hand-gunners stood with crossbowmen, and the cannon that replaced the old trebuchets were still used like super-catapults. Outside Europe, in the Ottoman armies – or the Safavid Persian, or the Mughal, or the Ming Chinese – warriors took up gunpowder weapons quickly enough, and appreciated them for their power, but this adoption sparked no basic rethinking of warfare. That happened only in Europe (again, with the possible exception of Japan), and within Europe the period of real transformation, the real revolutionary moment, was the early sixteenth century.

What made early sixteenth-century Europe a crucible for military experiment and change was the conjunction of three circumstances: first, the awkward presence in warfare of a powerful, aesthetically exciting (stinking, smoking, noisy, expensive) but culturally still half-alien military technology, the technology of gunpowder weapons; second, a grave military crisis, not only the Ottoman threat but a connected series of wars that embroiled every major European state; and third, a current within the larger culture of Europe's social elite, namely the Renaissance, that allowed and encouraged – even demanded – the wholesale reconceptionalisation of every custom and art, including the art of war. The first of these three trends, the presence of powerful gunpowder weapons, requires more explanation than might be expected: what was critical was not just the physical presence of firearms and cannon, but their mental presence in the minds of Europe's ruling class. In the course of a long, gradual and now rather clearly understood process of technological improvement, by the second half of the fifteenth century gunpowder weapons were no longer supplementary novelties, but necessary tools of war. However, even into the sixteenth century there was some lingering distrust – or disgust – regarding gunpowder in the minds of some members of Europe's ancestral military elite. The French knight Bayard, the gallant embodiment of a self-conscious, centuries-old chivalric military culture of horses, swords and single combat, despised firearms as unseemly – just as he despised the low trick of aiming a lance to kill a horse rather than its rider. (It is worth noting that an arquebus ball felled Bayard himself in a skirmish in 1524.) But in Bayard's own time he was already something of a relic; most members of Europe's hereditary military class were, by the sixteenth century, passionate gun lovers. Many princes (the emperor Maximilian I, duke Ercole d'Este of Ferrara) doted on their extensive artillery parks of individually named pieces; they cared for their big guns in much the same way they cared for their horses and hunting dogs. In peacetime as well as in war, cannon salutes – from forts, from ships at sea, from armies in review – added a sonorous, deeply impressive flourish and flash to arrivals and departures, births and weddings, and other great moments in the lives of the powerful. Europe's nobles liked little guns, too. The emperor Charles V made a hobby of messing with the mechanisms of clocks and pistols (at this time fired by a clock-like mechanism, the wheel-lock), even though some aristocratic critics continued to think the short and handy pistol fit only for assassins. It would take time before a true 'officer and gentleman' could use a firearm in battle against a social equal without having to explain himself; the gentrification of the pistol, its transmogrification into the officer's sidearm and the gentleman's duelling companion, took generations – and the long firearm, the musket or rifle, never did become genteel. And into the twentieth century the social hierarchy of European armies placed cavalry above infantry, and infantry above the tradeschoolish gunners and engineers. Nonetheless, despite a real and deep cultural reluctance to fully accept firearms (a reluctance very similar to the prejudices of the Japanese samurai), by the sixteenth century Europe's military and political ruling class were prepared, even enthusiastically prepared to make muskets and cannon the central instruments of war. Before 1500 that conspicuously modern attitude was not yet widespread enough to allow a revolution in warfare.

The political conditions of the early sixteenth century also propelled significant military changes – and the creation of an international, truly European art of war. The specific circumstances were the Italian Wars, a series of campaigns that began in 1494 with a French march down the Italian peninsula in pursuit of a claim to the kingdom of Naples. In itself this event was nothing new, but the French occupation of Naples upset the military balance between the major and minor Italian states – a diplomatic and political *modus vivendi* formed in the 1450s, not least because of a perceived Turkish threat following the fall of Constantinople – and attracted the intervention of almost every outside European power, including the king of Spain and the

Holy Roman Emperor. A lasting peace came only in 1559. Meanwhile, though the wars were not continuous (significant activity peaked in the 1520s), for two or three generations Italy was, in the phrase of the day, the 'school of war' for all Europe. The 'lessons learned' – to use modern military jargon – encouraged the emergence of homogenous military doctrines. In fact, the wars became an open, brutal competition between various existing national or ethnic styles of warfare; in terms of military culture, Italy was a melting pot.

At first, the camps were a colourful miscellany: Italian crossbowmen and handgunners; Swiss and German *landsknechts* armed with pikes, halberds and great double-handed swords; Venetian stradiots from Greece and Albania, tough light horsemen armed with lances; Spanish light cavalry skilled with javelins; even mounted bodyguards armed with shot crossbows. But the experience of war identified some techniques of war as superior to others. One victor was the Italian system of fortification. Experiments with bastion-like towers had begun before the Italian Wars; now, all Europe could see the advantage of the newfangled military architecture. First, from about 1530 on, all the Italian states enthusiastically rebuilt, at least in part, their most important defences. Subsequently, almost every other European nation hired Italian engineers, and the new military architecture spread to the rest of Europe, by mid-century to Spain, Austria and France; later to other areas – England, northern Germany – further from involvement in the Italian campaigns.

As important as the emergence of an international military architecture was the emergence of an international infantry discipline. The Italian Wars quickly identified the style of the Swiss and their first imitators, the German *landsknechts*, as superior; their hallmark was a deep formation of disciplined pikemen supplemented by smaller companies of expert handgunners. Observers – like the Venetian official Alessandro Benedetti, who reviewed a corps of Germans parading before the walls of Novara in the Milanese in 1495 – marvelled at their cohesion, their ability to hold together in ranks and files, perform various movements, and shift formations. Emulation of what Benedetti called the 'new military order' (*nova pugnatium instituto*) quickly followed admiration.[15] At about the same time that Benedetti praised the new-style discipline in the north, in southern Italy, after a minor defeat by Swiss pike in French service, the practical Spanish general Gonsalvo de Cordoba retrained his Spanish infantry in the Swiss style (with his own variation: 'sword-and-buckler men' intended to slip between the long and unwieldy pikes of an enemy formation and cut it to pieces from within; this idiosyncratic variation essentially died out after the battle of Ravenna in 1512). As Spain cemented her position in Italy by taking control of Naples and then Milan, Italian recruits – there must always have been some – drilled in the same fashion as Spanish regulars from Spain. (Long-term cohabitation in Italy of course led to cross-cultural contact: in Naples the many children of Spanish servicemen and Italian women were jocularly known as 'janissaries' – once they reached their teens these boys would have made natural recruits for the Most Catholic King.) The new infantry discipline, based on the Swiss example but no longer connected to or dependent on the peculiar martial culture of the Swiss mountain valleys, spread in other ways than official mimesis. Individual mercenaries – particularly sergeants and other old veterans – who moved from one service to another brought their knowledge with them. The Venetian diarist Marin Sanuto wrote of the era's 'Noah's Ark armies', containing two of every kind: though a unit might officially be labelled German or Italian, individual soldiers might be from anywhere in Europe – say, Irishmen in Spanish service, or Scandinavians in the Dutch (both examples were common in the later sixteenth century, and helped spread the new discipline to the fringes of Europe not politically connected to the wars of its heartland).[16] Such soldiers were walking synthesists of drill and discipline.

Finally, and most importantly, the printing revolution encouraged the diffusion and the homogenisation of infantry doctrine like no other force. The very first printed drill book – a practical little manual known simply as 'Vallo's' – appeared in Italian in Naples in 1521. Printed drills proliferated from mid-century, and by its end an Englishman could complain, in print, of his countrymen who only knew war from a page, and who attempted to drill their charges book-in-hand. Though subtle variations existed, in the main all these books insisted on the same main point: that modern infantry was a business of pike and shot, disciplined and ordered, prepared to fight more by firepower than by press of pike. Europe – not just various regions of Europe – now had its own way of war.

But why did anyone – particularly the decision-making elite – care to so radically restructure Europe's military institutions? World history is full of examples of headstrong military cultures that preferred defeat and death to changing the heroic customs of the ancestors (such a scenario unfolded almost everywhere in Africa and North and South America). To explain why Europe acted so uncharacteristically (when compared to human beings the world over) it is necessary to remember the larger intellectual culture of Europe in the early sixteenth century. Frankly, Europe's military elite – in the main, the descendants of medieval knights – no longer thought like medieval knights. For Europeans, the military customs of the ancestors were still revered, but they were no longer sacrosanct (except for the chevalier Bayard and his fellow Don Quixotes). What captured the mind of the sixteenth-century noble military man was the Roman way of war. There was, both in print and in practice, a real military renaissance afoot; Europe's military men were culturally awash in what the French historian Frédérique Verrier calls 'l'humanisme militaire'.[17] This humanist spirit was still novel at the turn of the sixteenth century; and was only yet seriously influential in Italy – exactly where the coming great military confrontation and competition would take place. By 1500, the educated Italian prince – the social model – would have been educationally exposed to the classics of ancient military history; if not in detail, at least in spirit and outline.

We have clues as to the coming of this new mentality. At the palace of the Gonzaga – a family of important mercenary commanders, not effete idlers – in Mantua in Lombardy, fifteenth-century Arthurian frescoes depicting a tournament of the knights of the round table, a very medieval topic, were covered over before they could be completed; a late fifteenth-century Gonzaga chose to redecorate his palace with a series of paintings depicting the triumphs of Caesar – and his artist (Andrea Mantegna, no hack, but a fashion-maker) depicted the equipment and costume of the Roman soldiers he painted with a scrupulous, even archaeological regard for their correct appearance. What we think of as a Roman soldier is still based on a concern that originated in Renaissance Italy. Another clue:

around 1460 a miniaturist painted the great mercenary commander Francesco Sforza (he ended his career as duke of Milan) as a Roman general wearing an ancient-style muscled cuirass and holding conversation with a committee of famous ancient generals, including Hannibal, Julius Caesar and Epaminondas: what did he expect to learn from their advice? By the early sixteenth century a military man didn't have to be a reader – or even well exposed to the Latin classics – to think of the Roman example as apropos. There was a fashion for modern armour – parade stuff, but real steel made by real armourers – made *alla antica*: Charles V had a suit. In Italy, some prominent military men of the sixteenth century were named for ancient martial heroes, including Ercole ('Hercules') d'Este and Alessandro ('Alexander') Farnese. And then there was the turn-of-the-century fashion for ultra-short Roman-style hair. Men who dressed and groomed themselves like Romans – who were named after Greek heroes – could see nothing particularly anachronistic about acting like an ancient professionally. (Particularly since the ancient example dictated the style of so much else in their cultural world, from church façades to coin faces.) And so they did ape Roman and Greek warfare. There were operational examples: it is possible that Prospero Colonna's successful campaign to take Milan in 1522 was based on his understanding of Julius Caesar's siege of Alesia in the Gallic War. Certainly contemporaries saw an ancient connection: the humanist historian Francesco Guicciardini laurelled the careful and cautious Colonna with the title 'Cunctator' after the great Roman commander Fabius 'the de-layer'. But what gave this classical revival its lasting importance was that many early sixteenth-century witnesses of the battles and drillfields of the Italian Wars compared what they saw or experienced with what they knew from their beloved ancient texts. Therefore, when Machiavelli observed Swiss-style infantry tactics, the ancient Greek pike phalanx immediately came to mind: in fact, he seems to have erred in thinking that the Swiss valleys had somehow preserved intact the tactical virtues of ancient days. Machiavelli could not have been alone in making this connection: Alessandro Benedetti, the man so struck by the drill of German pikemen and handgunners in 1495, described what he saw in Latin – using the vocabulary of ancient warfare. Melding modern and ancient was an obvious exercise: which is exactly what Machiavelli proposed in his *Art of War*, published in 1521, the first printed theoretical drill ever. It appeared in exactly the same year as Vallo's entirely practical treatise: theoreticians and practitioners were thinking along parallel lines. These converged between 1534 and 1536, when king Francis I of France – desperate for military glory, still smarting from his complete defeat and humiliating capture by Spanish forces at Pavia in 1525 – invested what must have been huge sums in a truly grand experiment: refounding the legions of ancient Rome. The actual discipline of these new French legions owed as much to the Swiss example as it did to what intellectuals could glean from ancient sources like Livy, Polybius and Aelian, and in time the legions seem to have both decayed and evolved into normal regiments. But Francis's grand experiment was a shining example of a full-force military renaissance, a total willingness on the part of Europe's military and political elite to remake their martial institutions and customs. This humanistic tendency, the desire to rebuild *in toto* and *ab ovo* on the basis of ancient texts, was not limited to a few cranks and wayward monarchs. In 1529 the gerontocrats of Venice – noted for their gravity and fiscal shrewdness – invested a serious amount of money in a reconstruction of a Roman quinquereme (the sea trials of the massive craft proved unsatisfactory). Most famously, in the 1590s Maurice of Nassau, inspired by a reading of Aelian, reformed the fire discipline of the Dutch army on an explicitly ancient model. And his Roman-inspired reforms worked. Historians have tended to see Maurice's experiment as the dawn of a new era, but in fact he was part of a community of military intellectuals who had been exploring the same possibility for at least seventy years.

To bring the arguments of this chapter full circle, there were direct connections between the Turkish threat and the military renaissance: together they made for the real military revolution of the sixteenth century. Obviously, the threat of Turkish seapower spurred Venetian interest in the possibility of reconstructing ancient Roman galleys. And some military intellectuals of the day explicitly connected their work with the ever-looming Turkish threat. Tartaglia, the first great theorist of ballistics, had reason to hate war: as a boy in 1512 he was so badly beaten by French troops sacking his home town of Brescia that he acquired a permanent speech impediment and his nickname, *tartaglia*, meaning 'the stutterer'. But he published his 1537 treatise on ballistics anyway, in the hope that it might improve Christian gunnery in a future crusade against the Turk (and in his dedication Tartaglia encouraged king Henry VIII of England to take up that crusade). A 1595 treatise by Francesco Patrizi, the *Paralleli Militari* – published even as Maurice of Nassau was drawing his own parallels in the Netherlands – explicitly connected the essence of the new-style infantry discipline with its virtues in war against the Turk: the book revealed, according to its title page, 'the various customs and the regulations of the Ancients accommodated to our firearms; by the power of this true art of war a few men can defeat the great multitudes of the Turks'.[18] Though preoccupied with the affairs of Europe, Western statesmen and intellectuals could never completely forget the horsehair standards, the crescent flags and the brazen cymbals of the sultan's vast and infidel hosts. It was to fight those hordes that the military revolution was in part proposed; it was in matching those hordes on the field of battle that the military revolution was proved.

2. Warfare in the Age of the Thirty Years War 1598–1648

RONALD G. ASCH

POLITICS AND ARMED CONFLICT:
THE ORIGINS OF WAR

The years 1598–1648 were for many parts of Europe a period of almost permanent warfare. After 1618 central Europe was engulfed by the Thirty Years War, which involved not only the Emperor and the principalities of the Holy Roman Empire, but also the Netherlands, Spain, and at later stages of the conflict Denmark, England, Sweden and France. Nor had the years before 1618 been particularly peaceful, although the first decade of the seventeenth century saw a number of prolonged armed conflicts come to an end. The Spanish attempt to intervene in France during the French Wars of Religion had been abandoned in 1598 with the Peace of Vervins. The war between England and Spain – which went back to 1585 – had been ended in 1604, a year after the end of the Nine Years War in Ireland (1594–1603), which had been closely connected with the Anglo-Spanish contest. Even the conflict between Spain and her 'rebellious' provinces in the Low Countries had been interrupted in 1609 by a twelve-year truce, and the long war between the Emperor and the Sultan which had begun in 1593 was ended in 1606 by the treaty of Zsitvatorok. Peace between Turkey and the Austrian Habsburgs remained somewhat uneasy, small-scale warfare continued, and the Prince of Transylvania was to intervene in the Thirty Years War more than once with Turkish support, but a somewhat uneasy cessation of hostilities on any large scale was, nevertheless, achieved in 1606.[1]

But smaller conflicts continued to jeopardise the uneasy peace gradually achieved in Europe between 1598 and 1609. As early as

45

1600 France had occupied by force of arms the provinces ruled by the Duke of Savoy north of the Alps on the western bank of the river Rhône (Bresse, Bugey, Gex), a conquest which Savoy had accepted in the following year. Savoy was involved between 1612 and 1617 in another armed dispute over the inheritance of Duke Francesco Gonzaga of Mantua, who had died without direct male heirs. Charles Emmanuel of Savoy claimed the Montferrat, a part of the Gonzaga inheritance which formed an enclave in Savoy territory. He only abandoned this claim in 1617 under Spanish pressure, when he realised that he could not expect much support from France.

The war over the Gonzaga inheritance was a conflict of limited dimensions, but everything that happened in northern Italy immediately threatened to provoke a major European war, as France had never entirely abandoned her claim, going back to the end of the fifteenth century, to exert some influence in Italy, which had been dominated in the second half of the sixteenth century by Spain. Essentially it was only because France was too weak to embark upon a major war after the death of Henry IV in 1610 that the confrontation in northern Italy did not escalate into a more serious European conflict.[2]

If Italy was a trouble spot between 1600 and 1618, so was the Lower Rhine, where the death of the last Duke of Cleves in 1609 nearly provoked a major European war. The inheritance was claimed by various German princes who tried to gain the support of either Spain or the Dutch Republic and France. In fact, Henry IV had been about to intervene in the dispute at the head of his army in 1610 when he was murdered by a Catholic fanatic.[3] Finally, the Baltic was another area where the tensions between the various powers repeatedly led to war before 1618. In a brief confrontation with Sweden, Denmark had asserted her superiority in 1611–13 for the last time. Poland and Sweden had intermittently been at war from 1600 onwards. Though hostilities died down after 1605 and were in fact settled temporarily by occasional truces, they resumed in earnest in 1617. After another truce, they flared up again in 1620–22, and did not end until 1629. During the same period Russia and Sweden were at war between 1614 and 1617.[4]

Thus the beginning of the Thirty Years War had been preceded by quite a number of minor or not so minor regional conflicts (only some of the more important ones have mentioned here). Why was peace so difficult to achieve and often so unstable once it had been achieved, as in 1609 in the form of a truce between Spain and the Dutch Republic, or in 1598 between Spain and France? One obvious answer could be that the increased ability of the major European powers to wage war – growing financial resources, and a greater number of soldiers serving in the armed forces, for example – inevitably led to armed conflict, given the absence of any institution capable of settling disputes between rulers with conflicting legal claims, at least outside the Holy Roman Empire. Here, in Germany, the highest law courts did provide a mechanism for this purpose before the constitution of the Empire gradually broke down between the 1590s and 1618. However, for a number of conflicts the opposite answer is far more plausible, that is, that it was not the growing strength but the weakness of existing states and political systems which caused wars, or at least was responsible for the escalation and prolongation of hostilities once war had broken out. This point has recently been made by the German historian Johannes Burckhardt, who interprets warfare essentially as part of a long-term state-building process.[5]

Many of the larger European states were, in fact, composite monarchies, that is, they consisted of a number of individual kingdoms and principalities owing allegiance to the same dynasty but otherwise governed according to their own particular constitutional traditions.[6] The Spanish empire in Europe and the dominions of the Austrian Habsburgs are the best known examples of such composite monarchies, but in fact the Stuart monarchy, comprising England, Scotland and Ireland, and the Danish monarchy (Denmark, Norway, Schleswig and Holstein), can also be considered composite states. The problem with such political structures was that any attempt to make them more coherent could easily have the opposite effect. The attitude of the individual provinces towards the dynastic centre was often far too ambivalent to guarantee their loyalty if it was put to the test by raising taxes or enforcing religious conformity. Spain had been confronted with the problem in the Netherlands as early as the 1560s. Later, in the first two decades of the seventeenth century, the Emperors Rudolf, Mathias and Ferdinand II were successively to encounter similar forms of provincial resistance against centralising policies in their dominions. It was the revolt in

Bohemia in 1618 which provoked the outbreak of the Thirty Years War. Ferdinand II had too few resources and troops to put the rebellion down himself and had to appeal for outside help from Spain and Bavaria, a decision which immediately transformed the Bohemian war into a struggle in which the entire Holy Roman Empire and – directly or indirectly – the great European powers were involved.[7] Later still, at the end of the 1630s and in the early 1640s, Charles I faced rebellions first in Scotland and then in Ireland, which in their turn triggered off a civil war in England in 1642.[8]

The Holy Roman Empire can hardly be described as a composite monarchy. Rather, it was a political system *sui generis*, certainly more than a mere federation of states, but clearly less than a state in the sense in which France or England were states during this period, with nationwide administrative and fiscal structures providing an institutionalised link between central and local government. Nevertheless, the relationship between the political centre, the imperial court, and the periphery, the principalities and imperial cities outside the Emperor's immediate control, was a major cause for political friction in Germany as much as in other monarchies. Ultimately, in combination with the Bohemian rebellion, it was the cause of the greatest military conflict of the early seventeenth century, the Thirty Years War. The crucial questions in this respect were, to what extent the Emperor, with or without support from the Imperial Diet, should be entitled to limit the options available to individual princes in matters of confessional policy, and to what extent his interpretation of the Empire's fundamental laws should be binding.[9]

The internal tensions afflicting the Holy Roman Empire and composite monarchies such as the dominions of the Spanish and the Austrian Habsburgs caused wars which are difficult to categorise. Were they civil wars or conflicts between states? In fact civil wars and 'international' war merged into each other during this period – one of the reasons why peace proved so elusive. Whereas the wars of the eighteenth century could in some ways be described as moves in a well-established game in which the European states fought for power and status, the wars of the early seventeenth century were still conflicts in which the very rules of the game themselves were at stake. Could German princes who were the Emperor's liegemen legitimately enter into an alliance with France or Sweden, or even wage war against the Emperor without committing the crimes of high treason and felony, for example? Questions such as these were to bedevil the peace negotiations in Osnabrück and Münster at the end of our period. The Peace of Westphalia did make a contribution to a clearer definition of the *ius ad bellum*, the right to wage war, although it never quite managed to clarify the status of the German princes once and for all: they gained some of the attributes of sovereignty such as the right to pursue their own foreign policy, without becoming fully sovereign, because they still owed allegiance to the Empire and its ruler.[10]

In the years before 1648 it had been quite normal for princes and Estates who were subject to an overlord to appear as independent agents on the stage of European politics. The Estates of Bohemia deposed their King in 1619 (not to mention the older example of the Dutch provinces which had seceded from the empire of the Spanish Habsburgs in 1581), and the French Huguenots tried to defend their privileges by force of arms against Louis XIII in the 1620s, supported in 1627–28 by England. The Estates of Catalonia rose against Philip IV of Spain and received help from France in the 1640s. French noble magnates, including for a long time the Duke of Orléans, Louis XIII's heir-presumptive until 1638, co-operated intermittently with Spain during the 1630s and 1640s, and in particular during and after the *Frondes* of 1648–53, while France was at war with the Habsburgs.[11]

The inherent instability of many European states and monarchies was an important cause of military conflicts or their escalation, but confessional antagonism certainly also loomed large as a factor exacerbating existing tensions within and between states. In fact it provided a decisive link between domestic conflicts and European politics. Without the conflict between Protestants (in particular Calvinists) and Catholics in the Holy Roman Empire, the Thirty Years War would have been inconceivable. It was the all-pervasive atmosphere of mistrust and hatred between the religious opponents which made a political solution to the constitutional problems of the Empire so difficult. There was certainly no area before 1618, or during the first half of the war, in which the authority of the Emperor – or indeed the imperial Diet in so far as it took majority decisions – was more hotly contested than in confessional matters.

Nevertheless, it should not be forgotten that outside Germany and even within the Empire, conflicts between princes who subscribed to the same confession were by no means exceptional. France and Spain were, with the possible exception of the years 1610–24, almost always on the brink of war, if not actually at war. Relations between Denmark and Sweden, both Lutheran countries, were hardly much better. Even the Duke (later Elector) of Bavaria and the Austrian Habsburgs, who co-operated very closely during the Thirty Years War, did not really see eye-to-eye on many issues. Maximilian of Bavaria certainly did not want the Emperor to become an absolute ruler in Germany, nor was he prepared to give more than token support to Spanish policy in Central Europe.[12] Within the Protestant camp the Elector of Saxony followed a pro-Habsburg policy. Admittedly, in this case the implacable hatred felt by the leading Saxon theologians (all orthodox Lutherans) for Calvinism in any form did play a role in influencing policy – the Elector Palatine, leader of the radical Protestants in the early 1620s, was a Calvinist.[13]

However, with the possible exception of the period between the Edict of Restitution and the Peace of Prague (1629–35), the war in Germany was never a straightforward religious conflict. Too many Protestant princes remained neutral, or co-operated with the Emperor most of the time. Outside Germany the influence of religion on foreign policy and war was often even less obvious. Although Swedish intervention in Germany in 1630 was interpreted by pro-Swedish pamphlets published in Germany as a crusade for the liberty of true religion, and did in fact assume some of the characteristics of such a crusade, Swedish fears of Habsburg–Polish military and naval co-operation, and the desire to secure Swedish control of all trade in the Baltic, originally loomed at least as large as enthusiasm for the Protestant cause in Gustavus Adolphus's decision to intervene.[14]

Another example is the war between Spain and the Dutch Republic. Although the Republic and Spain still appealed in all sincerity to religious ideals to legitimate their policy, economic interests (for example Spain's wish to reopen Antwerp as a port, which was impossible as long as the Dutch blockaded the entrance to the river Scheldt), commercial and colonial conflicts outside Europe and questions of prestige and status were, probably in the last resort, more important for refuelling the conflict between Spain and the Dutch, with the result that the truce was not prolonged in 1621.[15] However, in many countries, religious loyalties were the only reliable basis for any sort of popular or even elite support for foreign policy – difficult to dispense with if war had to be financed by taxes granted by parliaments or assemblies of Estates, as in England. It could pose a serious problem if the objectives actually pursued by a government were impossible to justify in confessional terms, as in the case of Richelieu's anti-Spanish policy.

The Franco-Spanish conflict was in many ways a special case. On the one hand its roots lay in a classic dynastic dispute which went back to the sixteenth, if not the late fifteenth, century. The Valois – the predecessors of the Bourbons as Kings of France before 1589 – and the Habsburg dynasties had already confronted each other in the dispute over the Burgundian inheritance after the death of the last independent Duke of Burgundy in 1477, and from the 1490s onwards in Northern Italy. On the other hand, the long-term elements in the confrontation between France and Spain should not be overemphasised. Cardinal Richelieu, who was in charge of French policy between 1624 and 1642, was anxious to avoid a full-scale war with Spain. He felt that France could not match the resources of the Spanish empire and that an open alliance with Protestant powers such as Sweden (as opposed to the mere payment of subsidies), which would be difficult to avoid in an all-out war against the house of Habsburg, would create all sorts of problems for a Catholic country like France, both at home and abroad. He nevertheless went to war with Spain over Mantua in 1629. The last Gonzaga Duke had died and the potential heir with comparatively the best claims was a French nobleman, the Duke of Nevers. The Spanish tried to prevent Nevers from taking possession of the Gonzaga dominions, Mantua and Montferrat. For Richelieu this was an opportunity too good to be missed, given that Spain could be attacked in Italy without appealing to the help of Protestant states, and that it seemed possible to confine hostilities to Italy. The dispute over the Gonzaga inheritance was indeed settled largely in Nevers's and, therefore, France's favour in 1630–31 because the Emperor, allied with his Spanish cousin, had deserted Madrid at a crucial moment, when confronted with growing opposition among his allies in Germany and facing the threat of Swedish intervention in the Empire.[16]

Nevertheless, the war had also demonstrated that the fighting capacity of the French army was very limited. It was therefore by no means a foregone conclusion that Spain and France would go to war again in 1635, and this time openly and on all fronts. Essentially both Richelieu, and the Conde-Duque Olivares acting for Spain, took this decision more because they felt vulnerable – inspired by a sort of worst-case scenario – than out of a feeling of strength. France had pursued a covert war against the Habsburgs in Lorraine and the neighbouring German territories in the early 1630s. Olivares felt that only by converting this undeclared small-scale war at a favourable moment into an all-out military confrontation could he gain the full support of the Emperor who had already demonstrated in 1630–31 that he was an unreliable ally. By attacking French troops on the Moselle in March 1635 and thereby provoking an escalation of the conflict, Olivares hoped to create a situation in which a war between France on the one hand and the Emperor with all the German princes on the other hand became inevitable.

Richelieu for his part could not ignore the Spanish provocation, reluctant though he still was to commit himself to a war *à l'outrance* because he had staked his entire political fortune on a belligerent anti-Spanish foreign policy since autumn 1628. He had made many enemies in France in the process: devout advocates of a confessional foreign policy, protagonists of financial and administrative reform, and all those who opposed high taxation in the name of the 'soulagement du peuple', relief for the hard-pressed populace. If his policy now turned out to be a failure, Richelieu's opponents would win the day, as the Cardinal could never be entirely sure of Louis XIII's wholehearted support.[17]

Domestic issues and problems of foreign policy therefore remained inextricably linked in the early seventeenth century, not just in the French case, and the military conflicts of this period were as much or more a result of the inherent instability and weakness of most European monarchies and states as of their strength.

THE STRUCTURE OF WARFARE:
TACTICS, STRATEGY AND NUMBERS

The early seventeenth century is often considered to be a period in which warfare underwent important changes, in fact, a crucial phase in the 'military revolution' of the early modern age.[18] Many years ago Michael Roberts, the biographer of Gustavus Adolphus of Sweden, argued that this military revolution culminated in the reforms undertaken by the King of Sweden, who managed to perfect the improvements accomplished in the Dutch army during the war against Spain before 1609. The Swedish infantry, the argument runs, was better trained and better disciplined than that of other armies, achieved a higher firing power and was more flexible in battle, because in combat it was deployed in comparatively small units only about six lines deep.[19] The best infantry of the day, the Spanish, originally had a tradition of fighting in massive *tercios*, square formations of up to thirty lines deep, although this pattern of deployment had already been substantially modified by the beginning of the Thirty Years War.[20] Furthermore – and Roberts strongly emphasised this point – Gustavus Adolphus revived the cavalry's offensive role on the battlefield. Whereas it had become customary for horsemen to attack infantry units or even hostile cavalry formations by trotting up to them, discharging their pistols, and, more often than not, retreating, Gustavus allegedly had them attack at full gallop with drawn sabre or sword, perhaps after an initial volley of shots.[21] In ordering this change of tactics he was apparently inspired by the Polish horse regiments which he had encountered on the battlefields of Eastern Europe.

More recent research, however, has shown that the Swedish horse never entirely abandoned the *caracole*, the attack with firearms at a comparatively slow trot; in fact, attack at full gallop with the *arme blanche* as the principal or only weapon did not become customary in the Swedish cavalry until the 1680s. Gustavus Adolphus did, however, at times have only the first line of an attacking squadron fire one of their pistols (not both). The second and any further lines used only their swords to attack, although the pistols – still loaded – could be useful in the ensuing mêlée with the enemy.[22]

On the other hand, the tactical approach of Tilly, Gustavus Adolphus's opponent at Breitenfeld in 1631, was not as outdated as has sometimes been maintained, although he had been trained in the Spanish army. He relied far less on massive, unwieldy infantry squares than the *cliché* of the determined and courageous but old-fashioned and unimaginative Catholic general would suggest.[23] What did give the Swedish army a certain advantage was the combined operation of infantry with artillery, and of cavalry with both musketeers and mobile artillery, but of course even this innovation was soon imitated by others, such as Wallenstein's Imperialists at Lützen in 1632. The superiority of Swedish armies in Germany, demonstrated in battles such as Breitenfeld or Jankov in 1645 but also in a number of minor victories, was probably primarily due to the fact that the entire Swedish state was organised much more consistently for the purposes of warfare than other states of the time. A system of conscription existed which provided the Swedish army with a core of comparatively cheap but reliable regiments, whose soldiers were motivated by religion and national sentiment.[24] Admittedly, for most of the time Swedish soldiers were only a small minority of the troops fighting for the northern kingdom; mercenaries, mostly Germans, formed the bulk of the army (in most battles as much as 90 per cent). But at critical moments, such as in 1630–31 at the beginning of the intervention in Germany, and again in the later 1630s after the defeat of Nördlingen in 1634, the Swedish conscripts provided an elite striking force which was not easily demoralised by temporary setbacks, unlike mercenaries, who always had a tendency to desert in such moments. This reserve of highly motivated soldiers allowed Sweden to overcome defeats which would have spelt doom for other powers, such as Denmark, which had to withdraw from the war in 1629, three years after Christian IV's army suffered a crushing defeat at Lutter at the hands of the Catholic League.[25]

The tactical innovations, on the other hand, first introduced in the Dutch army in the 1590s and later perfected in Sweden, had only a limited impact on the outcome of battles in the Thirty Years War and hardly amounted to a full-scale military revolution. In fact, one could argue, as Geoffrey Parker has done, that ultimately changes in fortification techniques achieved during the sixteenth century were more important than changes in battlefield tactics as such. According to Parker, the development of a new style of fortress with an elaborate system of bastions and moats initiated in Italy in the first half of the sixteenth century revolutionised warfare much more effectively. Known outside Italy as the *trace Italienne*, this style of fortress was gradually imitated in other parts of Europe, although it did not reach some peripheral regions, for example Ireland, until the second half of the seventeenth century. Such fortresses, whose walls could resist even heavy artillery bombardment, could be taken only after long sieges which, so the argument runs, required a far greater number of professionally trained troops than in the past.[26] The impact of battles was very limited, because no number of victories won in battle would overcome the resistance of the enemy's garrison troops in the almost impregnable fortified towns. Thus warfare was largely dominated by long sieges and a strategy of attrition.[27] This description certainly fits the war in the Netherlands well enough. In particular, during the second half of the 80-year contest, after the 12 years' truce had expired in 1621, hardly a major battle was fought between the Spanish and Dutch armies. Sieges, positional warfare and other measures calculated to wear down the opponent, including trade embargoes, blockades of rivers and ports, and attacks on trade at sea by privateers prevailed.[28] But this was certainly not the sort of war waged in Germany between 1618 and 1648. On the contrary, pitched battles and the rapid movement of armies over long distances, sometimes hundred of miles, remained quite common in the Thirty Years War. Certainly, there were a number of fortresses of strategic importance. The capture of Breisach, for example, by the French in 1638, after a prolonged siege of five months, was crucial for the later success of French operations in southern Germany. Nevertheless, the great battles such as Lutter, Breitenfeld, Lützen, Nördlingen and Jankov on the one hand, and small-scale warfare at the local level, in which villages and small towns were burned down or plundered or forced to pay contributions, or enemy supplies seized by cavalry squadrons on the other, characterised warfare in Germany.

　　The dense network of fortresses and fortified towns – its effectiveness strengthened by natural obstacles which advancing armies encountered (the sea and the many waterways) – which provided the framework for warfare in the Netherlands, just did not exist in Germany. Many urban fortifications were out of date and therefore comparatively easy to take by assault or after a short bombardment. And whatever the strategic role of fortified towns, their political and economic weight was certainly much smaller than in the much more urbanised Dutch Republic. Here at least in the most important province, Holland, urban trade and industry produced much more wealth than agriculture, unlike the situation in most other countries. The limited economic and social significance of the towns was another reason why sieges did not dominate warfare in Germany between 1618 and 1648.[29]

Moreover, in Germany, a victory in battle promised considerable political benefits beyond the destruction of the enemy's field armies. Many princes and free cities in Germany were either neutral during long phases of the war or less than fully committed to one of the two sides. This holds good for Brandenburg and Saxony, both important electorates. Princes such as the Electors of Brandenburg and Saxony quickly changed sides after a seemingly decisive victory. Thus a victory in battle had a considerable psychological impact which went far beyond the immediate military effects. The near-total collapse of Sweden's military position in Germany after the defeat at Nördlingen in 1634 must ultimately be explained in psychological terms, for nearly all of Sweden's pre-1634 allies now joined Saxony in seeking peace with the Emperor. To fight pitched battles therefore remained worthwhile, in spite of the high risk and the heavy casualties. Admittedly, after about 1635, the impact of battles clearly diminished for logistical reasons. Operations now had to concentrate on securing control over regions which were not yet totally devastated so that contributions could be raised there. Under such circumstances it became difficult to follow up a victory in battle with further attacks designed to defeat the enemy once and for all.[30]

In fact, during the last phase of the war, after 1635, the capacity of almost all armies to mount major offensive operations with enough troops to besiege and take major fortified places – even if their fortifications were not up to date – and to conquer large stretches of enemy territory permanently, diminished considerably.[31] The number of troops deployed in any battle tended to become markedly smaller. At Breitenfeld, for example, admittedly the largest battle on German soil during the entire war, about 41 000 Swedish and Saxon soldiers had fought 31 000 Imperialists. After 1635, however, the Swedes as well as the Emperor were rarely able to send more than 15 000 and were hardly ever capable of sending more than 20 000 men into battle at any given time. Outside Germany the number of troops participating in individual battles remained greater. At Rocroi (1643), for example, 27 000 Spanish troops fought 23 000 French soldiers, but there the devastation caused by warfare was generally not as extensive as in many regions of Germany, so that supplies could more easily be organised.[32]

The small size of the armies actually fighting in any given battle was due to the fact that an increasing number of troops was tied down in garrisons which secured the routes of supply and the areas which provided the armies with money and provisions. In the long drawn-out war of attrition which the military and political contest in Germany had become after 1635, the cavalry became the dominant arm of service outside the garrisons. Mounted units, though needing more supplies, in particular, fodder for the animals, were able to requisition food over a wider area and could move more quickly to regions which were not yet totally devastated. In Germany many armies now had as many horsemen as footsoldiers or even more, whereas in the earlier years of the war the cavalry had normally made up between 15 and 25, or at most 35 per cent of the fighting forces.[33]

The overall size of armies during the first half of the seventeenth century is not easy to ascertain. Many soldiers, and sometimes entire companies or regiments existed only on paper. The colonels commanding regiments and the captains in charge of companies had a vested interest in creating the impression that their units had their full complement of men. Only then could they expect to receive the maximum amount of provisions, munitions and wages for their soldiers, and if these soldiers were non-existent they could pocket the surplus themselves. In the French army, where admittedly absenteeism and desertion may have been particularly widespread, the theoretical strength of infantry companies had originally been 120 men. Even in official documents this had to be reduced to as little as 50 in the 1630s and 1640s, and in the period 1645–46 to 40 men. But the real strength was smaller still, and sometimes not more than 15 or 20. Thus the French infantry, which on paper had a strength of more than 200 000, and in the late 1640s of as many as 270 000 men, could in reality send no more than 170 000 soldiers at most into battle, and when things were going badly, as between 1640 and 1643, fewer than 100 000. Including the cavalry, the French armies in Germany, in northern France, in the South-East and in Catalonia may have reached an overall strength of about 200 000 men in 1639–40 and again in 1645–46, according to André Corvisier. John A. Lynn's more sceptical estimates, however, give the maximum strength for the late 1630s as 125 000 or, at most, 152 000. This was a considerable size, given the fact that at the beginning of the century the peacetime strength of the army was not much more than about 10 000 men. But it could not yet be maintained over a longer period of time.[34] Desertion, death and disease reduced the numbers rapidly once a campaign had started, especially if it did not bring any immediate success and the logistical problems could not be solved, as was so often the case.[35]

The number of around 150 000 (or at most 200 000) soldiers also seems to have been a maximum for the combined Spanish armies in Europe in the 1620s and 1630s.[36] Wallenstein apparently had between 100 000 and 150 000 men under his command in the second half of the 1620s.[37] The Dutch Republic, which probably managed to finance its troops more efficiently than most other European powers, with the result that official figures are possibly more reliable than in other countries, had a standing army of 55 000 men at its disposal when warfare against Spain was resumed in 1621 (this was about the same size as that of the Dutch army during the last years of war before the truce of 1609). In the 1620s and 1630s this standing army, which excluded the at times very considerable number of mercenaries hired just for one campaign or recruited by military entrepreneurs for the Republic, grew to a maximum of 75 000 men. If mercenaries are included, the fighting strength of the army was 128 700 men in 1629.[38] When Gustavus Adolphus intervened in Germany in 1630 he had an army of about 70 000 men at his disposal (though not all of them were in Germany at this time). After the victory of Breitenfeld more mercenaries could be recruited, and the King envisaged an army of 200 000 men, including the troops of his allies. In fact the Swedish army in Germany had a strength of about 120 000 men in March 1632 (of which only 10 per cent were native Swedish or Finnish soldiers). This army was supported by the Elector of Saxony's troops, comprising another 20 000 men.[39]

During the second half of the Thirty Years War such enormous armies became increasingly difficult to maintain in Germany. The different imperial armies, for example, numbered only about 70 000 men in 1644, including the troops under Bavarian command and the other allies of the Emperor (but excluding the Elector of Saxony's troops and imperial garrisons in Hungary). They maintained approximately this strength until the end of the war, and the Swedish army was hardly larger at this stage.[40]

FINANCE, WARFARE AND THE TRANSFORMATION OF THE STATE

Whatever the number of troops, warfare was continually hampered by the shortage of funds and provisions. During the first half of the seventeenth century warfare was nearly always underfinanced, probably on an even greater extent than in other periods of history. It is traditionally assumed that the expansion of the state in the early modern period was largely an answer to the challenges of warfare. For our period this is only partly true, for states clearly had ways and means of avoiding major changes in their administrative and fiscal system and waging war on a considerable scale all the same.[41] The easiest solution was to entrust the task of warfare to military entrepreneurs. These were men who recruited and equipped soldiers for a campaign or a series of campaigns. The regiments or companies, which they recruited at their own cost, were in many ways their property. They could expect to be reimbursed for their expenses in some way or other. If it proved impossible to provide them with wages and supplies for their soldiers (including those who only existed on paper, so that they could make a profit), the simplest method was to let them raise contributions and requisition provisions in an area allocated to their regiment or company. Raising contributions often implied looting or holding to ransom towns and villages occupied during the war. Rewards in the form of confiscated estates which the rulers of the time gave their officers to compensate them for unpaid debts were also a possible source of financial profit.[42]

This system worked well enough as long as an army operated in enemy territory. In this case the military entrepreneurs, normally noblemen of some wealth, provided the prince who had hired them with funds and credit facilities which he lacked himself. In the end, however, it was the population of occupied provinces which had to foot the bill. On the other hand, if an army recruited by military entrepreneurs should be defeated and destroyed, it was unlikely that the colonels and captains of such an army would be able to insist on the payment of debts owed to them. Matters, however, became more complicated when the army was forced to retreat into friendly provinces or never managed to leave them. In this case, the fiscal costs which the state had avoided in the first place by having the soldiers recruited and equipped by the military entrepreneurs were quickly transformed into social costs in one form or another. Provisions levied in kind, contributions and various services required of the local population were only one of the forms these social costs could take. Another was the legal, political and economic privileges granted to the military entrepreneurs in lieu of cash payments. Rewards of this kind were particularly widespread in Spain, where military administration and warfare itself were gradually privatised during the first half of the seventeenth century. Because the ever increasing financial crisis made it impossible to pay the contractors who supplied the troops with provisions, arms and ammunition and the great noblemen who recruited them, in any other way they received extensive economic monopolies or rights of jurisdiction over formerly royal towns and districts (cf. below pp. 66–7).

Among the military entrepreneurs of the early seventeenth century the commanders who recruited not just individual regiments but entire armies were a special case. Some of the best known examples in Germany were Albrecht von Wallenstein (1583–1634), Count Ernst von Mansfeld (1580–1626) and Bernhard von Weimar (1604–39). Wallenstein had more than a hundred thousand men and perhaps as many as 150 000 under his command at the height of his power in the late 1620s. By systematically and ruthlessly exploiting the areas his troops controlled, he managed to pay this enormous number of soldiers comparatively effectively, although taxes raised in Bohemia, Moravia and Silesia also served to finance Wallenstein's army. However, Wallenstein's system could only work if his troops were kept on the move – to keep such large numbers of troops permanently in one place or one region, even if they were to some extent dispersed, was impossible; a purely defensive strategy was therefore difficult to pursue. This was one of the reasons for Wallenstein's dismissal in 1630, when the Emperor's political priorities had changed. Reappointed commander-in-chief of the imperial armies in December 1631, he failed to fulfil the Emperor's expectations of him and showed a dangerous tendency to pursue his own political objectives. In the end the Emperor had him killed because it seemed too dangerous to dismiss him once more, not least because it would have been extremely difficult to pay off the debts the imperial treasury owed him.[43] Bernhard von Weimar, who served France with an army of 18000 men after 1634, was spared such a fate, but his death from natural causes in June 1639 was certainly not inconvenient for the French crown as he could lay claim to the Landgraviate of Alsace as a reward for his services.[44]

After Wallenstein's and Bernhard von Weimar's death the role of military entrepreneurs was reduced once more, although it survived to a greater or lesser extent at the regimental level. Moreover, the system of contributions on which Wallenstein had relied so largely was also modified. For those parts of the Holy Roman Empire under imperial control or allied with the Emperor, a new legal basis for contributions was devised by the Peace of Prague in 1635. The Council of Electors and the Regensburg Diet of 1640–41 officially granted taxes to finance the Empire's armies, and the assemblies of the various Circles of the Empire, or at least of those Circles which still maintained some coherence and which were willing to co-operate with the Emperor, did the same.[45] Apparently this system worked quite well until the mid-1640s. Recent research has demonstrated that the Elector of Bavaria was able to finance his army successfully out of the contributions raised in the imperial Circles of Swabia and Bavaria (the Bavarian Circle was considerably larger than the electorate itself), in accordance with the official assessments by the Diet and the assemblies of the Circles. In fact Maximilian of Bavaria, like other commanders, expected his army to live off the land. Only when his troops were concentrated in order to fight a battle or besiege a town did he spend money out of his own treasury on the troops, because such offensive operations were impossible to undertake without extra funding. His own dominions thus contributed only a limited amount to the upkeep of his army.[46]

Sweden had also tried to put the financial system which formed the basis of her campaign in Germany on to a firmer legal footing by establishing the Heilbronn League, which was joined by most of her German allies in April 1633. However, with the collapse of the League after the battle of Nördlingen, the Swedish commanders had to return to a more primitive system of exploiting the areas occupied by their troops. The results were often less than satisfactory, as demonstrated by the series of mutinies in the Swedish army after 1634 – a reaction to the non-payment of wages. Nevertheless, Sweden managed to pursue the war in Germany until 1648, while investing hardly any revenues raised by domestic taxation at all. During the last years of the war only 4 per cent of the Swedish crown's ordinary budget was spent on the war in Germany.[47] Admittedly, further funds were provided by French subsidies and by loans from Swedish or foreign financiers, not to mention the fact that the Swedish crown owed huge sums to the army officers and soldiers at the end of the war (unpaid wages, etc.), as well as to the contractors and merchants who had provisioned the army. This fact made the indemnity to be paid by the Empire such an important issue for Sweden during the negotiations in Osnabrück.[48] Nevertheless, the Swedish example shows that by relying on the principle 'the war feeds itself', a comparatively poor country could finance a major war for nearly 20 years without unduly burdening the taxpayer at home.

However, military entrepreneurship and contributions raised in occupied or allied provinces and principalities were not the only way to finance warfare. Some countries did rely on taxation and credit raised at home. This holds good, for example, for the Dutch Republic. The Netherlands were the only major power successfully to draw on domestic taxation as the principal source of war finance without provoking major internal revolts, or facing the repeated, or indeed permanent, threat of financial collapse. The central provinces, in particular Holland, were particularly urbanised and commercialised; it was one of the economically most advanced areas of Europe. Moreover, the biggest town in Holland, Amsterdam, was not only a focus of international trade, but also the dominant centre of the European money market north of the Alps. The bankers of Amsterdam provided half of Europe with credit, and the Dutch state therefore found it easy to raise loans at fairly low rates of interest. The merchants, rentiers and financiers of Amsterdam were often only too glad to provide the Dutch republic with funds. After all, the finances of the Republic were sound, and domestic creditors had the great advantage of being able to control the budget and policies of their debtor themselves through the Estates of Holland and the Dutch Estates General.[49]

France also tried to finance warfare through taxation, but with less success. Because the crown mistrusted the French nobility which was prone to join provincial revolts led by aristocratic magnates, it avoided a full-blown system of military entrepreneurship, at least after 1635. Although aristocratic patronage was rampant in the army and commands had as a rule to be purchased, the king remained legally in control and regiments did not really become the full property of their colonels. Officers were expected to finance their companies or regiments to a large extent out of their own pocket, without a chance – at least officially – to recoup their losses by raising contributions, and without any guarantee that regiments which they had recruited would not be dissolved or merged with other troops ('reformed') at the first opportunity. The result was that the morale of French officers was not particularly high, absenteeism and corruption were widespread and the fighting capacity of the French army, theoretically under closer royal control than the mercenary armies of other powers, was for a long time inferior to that of its opponents.[50]

Nor was the attempt to finance troops out of taxation entirely successful. Undoubtedly royal income form taxation did rise very considerably. During the 1620s, when royal revenues were already increasing, the central treasury in Paris received about 43 million *livres tournois* each year from revenues of all sorts; in the decade 1630 to 1639 this figure went up to 92 million, and in the decade 1640 to 1649 to 115 million *livres*.[51] Even if we take into account the fact that the silver content and the purchasing power of the *livre tournois* was falling, the increase was striking. Counted in grain equivalents, in order to assess the real value of these revenues, French taxes, direct and indirect, had brought in about 4.9 million hectolitres in 1620 and 9.2 million hectolitres in 1640. According to one estimate, a French peasant who had to work about 10 to 15 days per annum to pay his taxes before Richelieu became the King's first minister in 1624, had to work about 35 days in 1641 shortly before the Cardinal's death.[52]

All these figures show that the years of Richelieu's government and the subsequent years of the Thirty Years War until 1648, when the Peace of Westphalia was signed and the outbreak of the *Fronde* put paid to all attempts to increase the level of taxation even further, were a revolutionary period for French crown finances. Within two decades, the income of the French crown doubled in real terms. In terms of monetary units the increase was even steeper. Of all European states participating in the Thirty Years War, France was probably the most deeply transformed by the impact of the war as far as the burden of taxation was concerned.

The French example shows what it meant to finance warfare for long periods of time primarily out of domestic taxation, without the benefit of a vast income from overseas colonies or the ability to transfer most of the costs of warfare to occupied enemy or neutral territories. For France the only way to raise credit seemed to be to sell royal offices and regalian rights, such as the right to retain a certain percentage or even all of the proceeds of newly introduced taxes.[53] During the war against the Huguenots, the Mantuan war, and the covert warfare against Spain in 1631 to 1635, the French crown had, in fact, largely relied on this system to finance its policy. Income from the sale of offices and related regalian rights reached an all-time high, amounting to as much as 55 per cent of regular royal income, considerably more than the income from direct taxation. This is not to say that direct taxation did not increase from the late 1620s onwards, but a very considerable share, probably the greater part of the new taxes, went to officeholders and owners of alienated surtaxes, *droits aliénés*.[54]

In 1634, with open war against Spain imminent, however, the crown changed its policy: the surtaxes granted to private parties were now largely resumed. Those who had bought these rights were compensated, but inadequately; that is, in effect the crown declared a partial bankruptcy in 1634. Thus the level of taxation and, more importantly, the actual crown income from taxation could be raised even further. But the new financial policy put considerable pressure on the peasant population, who had to pay the bulk of the taxes, and at the same time antagonised important vested interests, the (former) owners of the *droits aliénés* and hereditary officeholders in general. The result was stiff resistance to the increased taxation, often encouraged by the officeholders and regional elites. The later 1630s also saw a series of provincial rebellions which threatened the foundations of the French monarchy and, of course, reduced the amount of taxes actually collected. One of the most serious of these provincial risings was the revolt of the *Nu-Pieds* in Normandy in 1639, which required 10 000 regular soldiers to put it down.[55] After 1640, any attempts to increase taxation further foundered on the resistance of the peasantry and the local elites.[56] Thus French finances were by no means in a healthy state in the 1640s. The expansion of taxation in the preceding years had only been achieved at a high price, that of abandoning most projects for administrative reform. The basic structures of the highly illogical and inefficient French taxation system, with its many exemptions for certain provinces and privileged social groups, had remained largely unchanged.

Essentially, France, like Spain, was just muddling through in the 1640s as far as meeting the ever-increasing financial demands of warfare was concerned. Nevertheless, whereas in France, in spite of all setbacks, the power of the state and its capacity to extract taxes grew during the war, the opposite was true of Spain. Here, in particular in Castile, the heartland of the Spanish monarchy, a deep economic and demographic crisis undermined the crown's ability to raise higher revenues from taxes. The economic crisis was all the more serious as it hit the towns which bore the main burden of taxation in Spain in the form of indirect taxes particularly hard.[57] Moreover, royal income from silver imports from South America also declined, although the extent of the decline remains controversial.[58] The stagnation or decline (in real terms) of the crown's revenues also reduced Spain's ability to raise credit; in the past Spain had never encountered any real problems in finding bankers eager to lend money, in spite of the long series of state bankruptcies from the mid-sixteenth century onwards, because it was widely expected that royal income would increase each year (at least nominally), so that future revenues could be anticipated in the form of loans.[59]

With credit facilities and income from taxation in Castile drying up in the late 1630s, the Spanish crown was forced to fall back on expedients which other participants in the Thirty Years War had already employed earlier. When fighting started along the border between Spain and France after 1635, the frontier provinces were asked to contribute in cash and kind to the upkeep of the troops stationed in these areas. If they refused, the troops would be used to enforce compliance or let loose to plunder villages and towns. Such measures helped to provoke the Catalan revolt of 1640.[60] Nevertheless, with warfare concentrated on Spanish soil much more after 1640 than before – in addition to the war in Catalonia, Spanish troops were fighting against the Portuguese after 1640 – the system of raising contributions locally in or near the areas where troops were actually operating was maintained. It ensured that Spain could go on fighting (in the case of the war against Portugal, until 1668), despite the collapse of her finances and her credit system. During the course of the war, Spain underwent a gradual regression from a fairly sophisticated system of taxation and raising credit to comparatively more primitive forms of financing warfare – a regression exacerbated by the increasingly widespread devolution of formerly public rights and services, such as the recruiting of soldiers or the provisioning of troops, to noble magnates and private contractors respectively.[61] They were rewarded with extensive legal and economic privileges. Spain, or rather, Castile, could go on fighting only by 'liquidating' the crown's sole remaining capital, its own authority, and by transforming the fiscal costs of war (in the form of taxation) into social costs in the form of the burdens the population had to bear (contributions in kind and in cash, labour services, etc.) and the form of privileges for noble magnates and military contractors, as I. A. A. Thompson has pointed out.[62]

According to Thompson, this form of warfare was only possible because Spain, on the Iberian peninsula at least, was mostly fighting a defensive war after 1635, so that the war effort could be organised and financed locally.[63] However, this explanation is only partially convincing; in many ways the system of military entrepreneurship prevailing in central Europe tended to privatise war as much as the methods employed in Spain, although the social costs of warfare had to be borne primarily by the population of occupied foreign provinces. What seems at least as significant in explaining the difference between France and Spain is the fact that France had seen almost 40 years of civil war before 1598 and that a relapse seemed quite possible until the late 1650s.[64] An aristocracy raising private armies or any other form of full-blown military entrepreneurship recalled the trauma of the Wars of Religion, and was therefore unacceptable in France, whereas in Castile, which had seen no serious domestic warfare since the Communeros Revolt of the 1520s, the great aristocratic families had risen as a service nobility, and therefore seemed to pose a much small threat to the coherence of the state.[65]

Sweden, the Dutch Republic, France and Spain present contrasting examples of the interaction between warfare and the development of state and society. Further variants are provided by the German principalities, where the wartime emergency measures and the considerable amount of contributions levied by friendly and hostile armies alike defined the preconditions for political developments after 1648 – a higher level of taxation and a reduced role for the provincial Estates in high politics, though not necessarily in local administration,[66] and by England, torn apart by a civil war in the 1640s. In England, 'The tax state was rooted, chronologically, in the 1640s: structurally its roots lay in the localities, in the activities of local officeholders.'[67] Here it was, in a manner of speaking, their revolt against the crown's centralising policies which forced local elites to rethink their attitude towards taxation and reorganise the traditional system of raising revenues. Otherwise their fight against the King would have collapsed for lack of resources. Thus it was a revolt against higher taxes imposed from above which laid the foundation for a taxation system which became one of the most efficient in Europe by the end of the seventeenth and the beginning of the eighteenth century. In this respect, the English case is perhaps best comparable to developments in the Dutch republic but rather unusual in a wider European context.

Ronald G. Asch

The effects of warfare on state formation in the early seventeenth century remained ambivalent. In some cases protracted war led to the contracting out or 'privatisation' of formerly public functions and tasks as in Spain, and to a decentralisation of political authority. In other cases it did not affect the constitutional structures and the fiscal system very deeply at all, because the cost of warfare was partly or totally transferred to conquered or occupied provinces. France was perhaps the only country where warfare led directly to political centralisation and some sort of 'absolutism', although even here this process was qualified by the survival or indeed growth of a venal bureaucracy and of innumerable fiscal and legal privileges. These phenomena were as much a result of the financial crisis which the war had brought about as an obstacle to a truly efficient system of financing the war effort, which only one European country managed to create in this period on any considerable scale: the Dutch Republic, seemingly one of the least warlike of the European powers.

3. Warfare in the Old Regime 1648–1789

PETER WILSON

THE CHARACTERISTICS OF OLD-REGIME WARFARE

At about 11 a.m. on 11 May 1745 a large column of British and Hanoverian infantry approached a line of French troops near the village of Fontenoy, close to the modern Franco-Belgian border. When the opposing forces were only 30 metres apart, an English officer allegedly stepped forward and cordially invited the French to fire first. This story, though almost certainly apocryphal, nonetheless seems to epitomise warfare in old-regime Europe.

Conflicts in this period are almost universally thought of as more sedate, narrow and limited in comparison with earlier and later wars.[1] Those of the sixteenth and early seventeenth centuries are regarded as particularly ferocious, but also as a source of military innovation, when new tactics and weaponry were developed and standing armies came into being. Similarly, the Revolutionary and Napoleonic Wars (1792–1815) seem the dawn of a new era of mass-citizen armies, grand strategy and military decisiveness. War in both periods involved fundamental issues stirring the passions of the participants; religion and domestic political power in the former era, nationalism and revolutionary ideology in the latter.

These military factors are related to wider social, political and economic aspects characterising these periods generally as distinct phases in European history. Thus, the religious and civil strife of the so-called Confessional Age (1517–1648) was replaced by relative tranquillity under the rule of largely absolutist monarchies. These monopolised violence, depriving their inhabitants of the means to oppose them militarily, and directed their efforts outwards into limited external war fought in their personal dynastic interest. Armies, it is widely believed, became divorced from the societies they were paid to protect, recruiting themselves from the politically and economically disenfranchised, while remaining under the command of a privileged, aristocratic elite. The changes associated with the French Revolution disturbed these structures, just as they undermined the rest of the old regime, heralding a new era for military, as well as political and social history.

This is not the place to debate the validity of this standard periodisation of European history, nor to re-examine its implicit relationship between military and wider historical change. One important point does, however, need to be made. Like many other accepted generalisations about European development, the concept of old-regime warfare as limited is based primarily on French and German historiography. Given both the German tradition of regarding political structures as largely militarily determined, and the historical pre-eminence of Louis XIV's France as Europe's premier absolutist monarchy and great power, the link between absolutism and permanent, professional armies has been assumed as a defining characteristic for the continent as a whole. The subsequent rise of Prussia and the influence of its army as a general European model only serves to reinforce this point.[2]

Similarly, there has been a tendency to regard the campaigns waged in north-western and central Europe as paradigmatic of all old-regime warfare. Not only are the exploits of great German and French generals, like Prince Eugene and Maurice de Saxe, exceptionally well documented, but this geographical area also saw most of Britain's limited involvement in continental land warfare prior to the Peninsular War. The understandable interest in the Duke of Marlborough, as well as the forces under later, generally less successful, British generals, has helped concentrate Anglophone research on the same areas, even to the relative neglect of British military involvement in Spain in the early eighteenth century. This has been valuable for highlighting aspects that were indeed important features of the period as a whole. However, inevitably, there has been a tendency to measure other developments against these, especially French models, as well as a neglect of change over both time and space.

The standard scheme looks far less logical when viewed from the perspective of eastern Europe, or the continent's northern and southern fringes. The political events used to define and delineate the time-span derive from French and German history and make only partial sense when applied elsewhere. The Peace of Westphalia (1648), which ended the Thirty Years War in central Europe and confirmed the independence of the Dutch Republic from Spanish rule, did not end other major conflicts. Franco-Spanish hostilities continued until 1659, and even the terms of the Westphalian Settlement relating to the Baltic were not fully implemented until 1653. Disputes over maritime access to this area, as well as the lucrative river tolls and customs duties levied along its shoreline, flared up again only two years later, representing not a new departure, but the continuation of a regional power struggle dating from the early sixteenth century. These conflicts were related to similarly protracted hostilities between Poland and Russia for the control of an area between the Baltic and the Black Sea larger than the total extent of France. Though increasingly open to western influences, neither Poland nor Russia ever became a carbon copy of French or German models, filtering instead new ideas through indigenous traditions, themselves still capable of producing innovations, and pursuing distinct military paths; for the Poles an ultimately disastrous one. Both the Baltic and eastern conflicts continued until the complex peace settlements of 1718–21 confirmed Sweden's relative decline and Russia's emergence as a world power.[3]

Equally, the epochal character of the French Revolution must be questioned when seen from a pan-European perspective. True, the revolutionaries abolished the French monarchy and eventually marched across most of Europe, redrawing a large part of its political map in the process. All the major powers were compelled to adapt, either by adopting French methods wholesale, or by accelerating existing reform processes. However, neither France nor its revolution was the sole source of change. Both Russia and especially the Austrian Habsburg monarchy drew on long experience of warfare against the Ottoman Turks which influenced their military traditions in ways often overlooked. In particular, Austria's geographical location gave its military establishment a Janus face, incorporating the experience derived from conflicts with conventional western opponents like France, as well as lessons learnt under very different conditions against

Hungarian rebels and the Ottoman hordes. In this sense, the Habsburg army acted as a conduit for eastern and western influence to spread in both directions. For example, its light infantry (*Grenzer*) and cavalry (hussars), initially raised to oppose the Turks, were employed in the West, where they were widely emulated. Similarly, confrontation with Austrian disciplined tactics and mass firepower compelled the Turks to modify their own forces with French and renegade German expertise.[4]

The protracted struggles between the Habsburgs and the Sultan also provide evidence that the era of religious wars did not end with the Westphalian compromise between Catholics and Protestants. The relief of Vienna, besieged during the great Turkish attack of 1683, was a pan-European enterprise, celebrated as an achievement equal to the great Christian naval victory of Lepanto (1571). Later wars still displayed the spirit of a baroque crusade long after the Habsburg court gave up its initial hopes of recovering Jerusalem. Both sides fought with great determination and brutality, massacring the civilian population of captured cities even in the last Turkish War of the eighteenth century in 1787–92.[5]

Even Britain cannot be slotted easily into the usual generalisations, not least because it was never an absolute monarchy and yet became one of Europe's most powerful states. Indeed, the British experience, along with that of the Dutch Republic, stands as an important corrective to the standard linkage of absolutism and military power. The Dutch defeated the monarchical pretensions of their own House of Orange, as well as their former Spanish overlords, while even after the Restoration of 1660, England remained very different from absolutist France. Yet both states were already significant powers by 1648, particularly at sea, and developed fiscal–military infrastructures of great potential. Unlike France, where the crown used the reworked ideology of absolutist kingship to legitimise taxation and sustain creditworthiness, both Britain and the Dutch Republic created formal mechanisms to foster a relatively broad consensus across the landed and commercial elite. In the British variant, as it became established after the 1688 political settlement, this enabled the state to tap an expanding economy without provoking the sort of elite protest which had undermined many sixteenth- and early seventeenth-century European states. Britain's island location enabled such fiscal power to be translated into military power without the need for a large domestic military establishment. Cash subsidies, along with political influence and naval support, won Britain the continental allies needed to match France's superior human and material resources.[6]

Nonetheless, the concept of British exceptionalism should not be pushed too far. Its standing army was still relatively numerous and expanded greatly in wartime. It was also deployed as a guardian of civil order in a manner not dissimilar to continental forces, and was likewise used to crush political opposition to English rule in the subject kingdoms of Ireland and Scotland. Similarly, absolutism was not without its own mechanisms to foster legitimacy and consensus, even where it sought to curb and remove traditional representative institutions. Centred on court patronage and the public representational display of royal rule, these could be comparatively successful, as indicated by the resilience of the Austrian monarchy despite the continued pressure of major wars. However, these structures were cumbersome and relatively inflexible, making it difficult for reforming monarchs, like Joseph II (1780–90), to tap other sources of wealth. Critically, where they broke down completely, absolutism had little to put in their place, as the experience of late eighteenth-century France graphically illustrates.

Finally, the orthodox interpretation of limited warfare looks less certain when its implicit comparisons over time are reconsidered. Given the obvious importance of weapons technology, writing on war is prone to chronicling a 'progress of destruction'; a false teleology based on the real, but misleading, premise that modern weapons clearly have a far greater destructive potential than their predecessors. Technology cannot be wrenched from its wider context, and to write the history of warfare around the development of weaponry produces a distortion. For example, modern weapons systems are extremely expensive, yet most states, including the superpowers, spend proportionally less of their total central budgets on defence than those of eighteenth-century Europe.[7] Moreover, when set against the general level of technological development and manufacturing ability, old-regime weaponry was clearly at the contemporary cutting edge, or as one recent writer has put it, in the 'category of a space shuttle rather than an aircraft carrier'.[8]

WAR AND SOCIETY

The themes raised in the previous section can be continued in an examination of the wider impact of war and its relation to society; areas which have been opened up by new research. For military–civil relations to exist at all, soldiers first have to emerge as a distinct social group. This process began in the late fifteenth century with the growing employment of professional mercenaries whose clothing, attitudes and behaviour already set them apart from the rest of society. The economics of early modern warfare widened the divide by compelling most soldiers to become migrants, travelling from one source of insecure employment to the next, in contrast to the bulk of the rural population which remained tied emotionally, economically and often legally to a fixed locality. Attempts by the state to regulate and control soldiers' behaviour, along with the requirements imposed by weaponry and military necessity, also helped set soldiers apart. Already under separate jurisdiction in the early sixteenth century, soldiers were subject to a growing body of disciplinary codes, joined from the 1580s by different forms of drill prescribing precise physical movements and intended to instil a new sense of obedience and subordination.

Improvements in the state's ability to maintain soldiers over longer periods of time failed to diminish its desire to impose its authority upon them. On the contrary, the system of regulation hardened as the military population became more sedentary with permanent employment in standing armies. The earlier emphasis on drill and discipline gave way after 1648 to a host of regulations fixing recruitment, conditions of service, clothing, billeting and discharge. Simultaneously, uniforms became standardised and extended even to the officers by the early eighteenth century. By the 1720s the period of innovation and experimentation was essentially over and the issue of regulatory codes declined in both frequency and volume, as most armies had their essential administrative systems already in place. While these were still subject to repetition and modification, the basic shape remained unchanged until the next century.

While this certainly marked soldiers out as a distinct group, it would be wrong to see them as isolated or detached from the rest of early modern society. First, they were simply one group among many in an already highly stratified social system. All sections of the population, including the nobility, were subject to codes of behaviour and marked by varying degrees of privilege and burdens. These rules were enforced not only by church and state, but by the groups themselves, which often enjoyed their own semi-autonomous jurisdiction, as with the internal management of universities, monasteries and urban guilds. Thus, the internal structure of an army, with its own hierarchy of ranks, customs, jurisdiction and forms of punishment, was indeed uniquely military, but not entirely dissimilar to the basic structure of other social groups.

Furthermore, though conscious of its own distinctiveness, no army was entirely cut off from other sections of society. Despite the permanence of armies as organisations, the composition of their actual personnel continued to fluctuate. Most armies had a core of long-serving soldiers whom they sought to retain, but filled the rest of the ranks with men for whom military service was often one source of employment among many over their lifetime. Even states using limited forms of conscription, such as Sweden, Prussia and later, Denmark and Austria, tended to release soldiers back into the civilian economy for large parts of the year to economise on their maintenance. The remaining professionals often only did duty on two or three days a week, supplementing their meagre pay by working on the remainder as servants, building workers, hawkers and, usually illegally, tradesmen.

In addition, many soldiers were married or had long-term unofficial relationships, something which became more feasible with the greater permanence of military formations. Around half or more of Prussian privates were married in the late eighteenth century, a proportion often exceeded in other armies, despite official restrictions. Further daily contact with civilians came from the practice of billeting soldiers in towns and villages. France began accommodating its army in barracks comparatively early on, partly thanks to the vigorous fortress-building programme which turned many frontier towns into military installations. Over 300 towns had barracks by 1742 and by 1775 total capacity reached 200 000 men, equivalent to its peacetime establishment.[9] This, however, was exceptional, and most soldiers were lodged in inns, as in Britain, or in sheds and shacks scattered throughout a town or clustered along its fortifications, or as was more often the case, simply quartered directly in the poorer burghers' houses and peasant farms. The phenomenon of the garrison town remained, until the barrack construction programmes of the 1790s, characterised by the intermingling of soldiers and civilians rather than by a distinct military presence.[10]

These points of contact could also operate in the opposite direction. Most continental states used militias as a reserve to supplement or augment the field army in times of crisis. Militiamen were either drafted temporarily into the regular forces or embodied as field formations, as in Bavaria and many other German territories, or mobilised as second-line troops for garrison duty and home defence as in France, Spain and the Italian states. Either way, the training and service of militiamen, along with the discharge of professional soldiers temporarily or permanently back into civil society, transmitted a general familiarity with weapons handling and military service that is surprising in an age otherwise characterised by the state's attempts to monopolise violence and demilitarise society.

This raises the question whether, as some have argued, eighteenth-century society was militarised. Certainly, there is considerable evidence that, after 1648, most Europeans came to accept the permanence of armies and the validity of war as a means of resolving international disputes. However grudgingly, they also bore the heavy fiscal and manpower demands without resorting to the sort of violent protest that had characterised the early seventeenth century. That they should do so was clearly in the interests of the state, which made great efforts to encourage compliance, using exaggerated images of the disorderly soldiery and the horrors of the Thirty Years War to magnify the virtues of its new, disciplined forces.

Military ways of thinking were probably most pronounced within the social elite, particularly the old aristocracy, which reasserted its control of command positions in the later seventeenth and early eighteenth centuries in most countries, displacing officers of non-noble origin who had formed a significant proportion of the earlier mercenary captains. The aristocracy's near-monopoly of officer posts proved vital in the defence of noble privilege and allowed it, particularly in central and eastern Europe, to accommodate itself with absolutism by partially reinventing itself in the concept of state service.[11]

It has been argued[12] that this was particularly pronounced in Prussia, a factor of general historical importance given that state's later domination of Germany. The nobles' hold on command and administration, along with their stake in the process of recruitment, fused military attitudes with political authoritarianism so that the means of maintaining national defence became those sustaining the rule of a narrow, socially conservative elite. In short, society was militarised in the interests of those in power. The case for 'social militarisation' has, undoubtedly, been exaggerated, certainly for the period before 1789, and there is the danger, not always avoided, of generalising from the Prussian example. Even here, recent research reveals that there was no direct link between the famous Prussian Canton system of limited conscription, and the Junkers' defence of their socioeconomic position and political influence.[13]

Re-examination of military–civil relations before 1789 also casts doubts on the standard explanation of the old regime's failure to withstand the French revolutionary armies. By championing the concept of the citizen-in-arms, itself hardly a novelty, the revolutionaries supposedly bridged the gap that separated army from society, uniting both through the common ideology of nationalism, universal rights and the defence of the homeland. Much of this stems from an uncritical acceptance of what the revolutionaries and later European liberals *said* they wanted, especially their rhetoric of national sovereignty mediated by a liberal, representative assembly, rather than direct monarchical rule. As the alleged henchmen of the discredited monarchies, old-regime armies were naturally portrayed in a poor light to legitimise the Revolution's own claims.

While much did change after 1789, this should not blind us to important elements of continuity. The recruitment base of most old-regime armies, including the British, was not as narrow as is commonly supposed. Given the fluctuation in personnel, the total proportion of the population with direct experience of military life may have reached 3 per cent, while even in peacetime established strengths of major powers stood at half this or more, a figure roughly comparable with levels in the next century. The fact that the majority of soldiers came from the poor or propertyless classes, while the officers were drawn from a narrow privileged elite, might well be reprehensible in liberal terms, but nonetheless reflected the social distribution of power under the old regime.

It was the 'middle class' of propertied, non-nobles that was under-represented and it was precisely this group that was pushing for control over war-making. The Revolution and post-revolutionary political settlements did grant this group greater influence, but left the broader social composition of armies relatively unchanged. French conscription was far from universal in the 1790s as, in practice, there were still exemptions and ways to dodge the draft. Such exemptions were confirmed in most early nineteenth-century systems, and though the bourgeoisie did gain greater access to officer posts, this too was partly reversed in most countries after 1815. Conversely, some important links between soldier and civilian were eroded after 1789, particularly by the construction of barracks, which accelerated in the nineteenth century as governments feared that the political reliability of their armies might be compromised by contact with subversive social elements.

THE GROWTH OF EUROPEAN ARMIES

The evolution of the standing army was a long and complex process, dating back to the mercenary companies paid to guard palaces and castles by many sixteenth-century rulers. However, it was only after 1648 that these were consolidated in their final form. The leading military power and model for most of late seventeenth-century Europe was unquestionably France, which reorganised the administration and structure of its forces in the 1660s to create the largest single permanent force in the continent. Directed by the war ministers Le Tellier and Louvois, these reforms were a direct response to the problems encountered when fighting Habsburg Austria and Spain in 1635–59, when the existing fiscal–administrative structure proved incapable of meeting the mounting demands. Centralised and subordinated to direct royal authority, the new structure reduced the abuses and wastage which had undermined earlier French military efforts and enabled Louis XIV to field forces which were qualitatively as well as quantitatively superior to those of his predecessors. However, this process was never completed before the collapse of the Bourbon monarchy, and its scope and effectiveness were constantly constrained by the very nature of French absolutism, which relied on the management and appeasement of privileged interest groups to sustain its political authority.

Though numerically superior, the French were not alone in maintaining permanent forces by 1648 (see Table 3.1). The Austrians already had substantial numbers and continued to field the largest German army throughout the old regime. Old powers like Spain, as well as new or emerging ones like Sweden, Denmark, England and the Dutch Republic, also had considerable forces. Unlike France, however, none reformed or modernised the structures developed during the early seventeenth-century wars, retaining instead existing systems of funding, recruitment and organisation, with only limited or piecemeal efforts to assert greater uniformity and state control.

Significant change came only when these armies encountered the 'new-model' French forces after 1667. The latter's rapid defeat of Spain in the War of Devolution (1667–68) was followed by further successes in the more serious test of Dutch War (1672–79), when Louis XIV made the largest territorial gains of the last 250 years of the French monarchy. Not only did established powers like Spain and Austria suffer reverses, but the Dutch found serious deficiencies in their more recently developed system of defence. Similarly, Sweden, whose successes in the Thirty Years War had discouraged reform, was defeated by comparatively insignificant Brandenburg–Prussia in 1675, with the subsequent temporary loss of its German possessions.

The shock of defeat, along with the sheer extent of French power – by 1648 Louis XIV had the largest army seen in Europe since the Roman Empire – forced these states to reform and expand their own forces after 1679. The next decade saw an explosion of activity lasting till the 1720s which gave shape to most of Europe's standing armies. Often this was associated with a political shift to more absolutist rule. For example, Swedish military reforms after 1680 involved the recovery of alienated crown lands to provide a more secure financial base for military expansion. Denmark witnessed a similar process and both monarchies sought to increase their executive authority. James II's reorganisation and expansion of English and Scottish armies was also related to his efforts to reduce Parliament's fiscal control.

Table 3.1 *Effective Strengths of Major European Armies 1650–1790*

Year	France	Spain	Austria	Prussia	Other German states	Denmark–Norway	Sweden–Finland	Poland–Lithuania	Savoy–Piedmont	Dutch Republic	Britain
1650	125 000	100 000	33 000	800	15 000	–	50 000	10 400	18 000	30 000	70 000
1660	50 000	77 000	30 000	12 000	20 000	25 000	70 000	40 000	5 400	–	16 000
1667	85 000	30 000	60 000	14 000	58 000	25 000	–	–	–	70 000	15 000
1670/72	76 000	–	60 000	25 700	60 000	39 600	63 000	66 000	26 200	37 000	10 000
1675/78	253 000	70 000	60 000	45 300	120 000	44 000	–	18 000	6 000	70 000	15 000
1682/83	130 000	–	60 000	25 000	87 000	54 000	–	–	7 500	50 000	6 000
1688/90	273 000	30 000	70 000	29 000	87 000	32 000	65 000	38 000	8 670	50 000	43 000
1695/97	340 000	51 000	95 000	31 000	150 000	36 000	90 000	38 000	23 000	63 000	68 700
1702/05	220 500	20 000	100 000	40 600	170 000	32 000	110 000	35 000	26 550	74 500	71 400
1710	255 000	50 000	120 000	43 800	170 000	74 000	38 800	12 000	22 400	76 800	75 000
1714	150 000	–	130 000	46 000	120 000	74 000	50 000	20 000	22 500	–	16 400
1730	205 000	–	130 000	66 900	85 000	56 000	–	20 000	24 000	–	23 800
1735	309 400	–	200 000	76 000	150 000	56 000	–	20 000	43 000	–	34 400
1740	201 000	67 000	108 000	77 000	115 000	56 000	15 000	20 000	28 300	30 000	40 800
1745	345 000	–	200 000	135 000	150 000	50 000	–	20 000	55 000	90 000	53 100
1756	290 000	–	156 000	137 000	120 000	70 000	47 000	16 800	–	–	47 500
1760/61	347 000	59 000	201 000	130 000	165 000	70 000	53 000	20 000	–	36 000	99 000
1770	160 000	30 000	151 000	160 000	110 000	60 000	–	20 000	35 000	30 000	31 000
1789/90	136 000	85 000	314 800	195 000	106 000	74 000	47 000	20 000	24 000	36 000	38 600

Note

The table includes field and garrison troops but excludes militiamen and any colonial forces. Note that a sizeable proportion of most German (including Prussian after 1714) and Scandinavian establishments were given extended leave in peacetime. Regiments recruited outside the country but forming a permanent, integral element of the army are included, but foreign auxiliaries and subsidised allies, such as those hired by the British and Dutch, are excluded. Details for minor powers omitted from the table are patchy, but are as follows: (a) *Portugal*: official strength averaged 30 000 throughout the period, but only half were normally effective; (b) *Venice*: land forces averaged over 20 000 in 1650–1718 but many of these were foreign auxiliaries. Thereafter they declined to 6000; (c) *Naples–Sicily*: became an independent state after 1735, but most of its troops continued to be paid by Spain until 1748. Effective strength was around 25 000; (d) *Papal States*: apart from the brief war against Austria in 1708, strength rarely exceeded 5000.

However, the Dutch reformed their land and naval forces without abandoning their republican government.[14]

These developments were given an additional impetus in central Europe by the resumption of the Turkish threat. Already in 1681–82, the Austrians had taken the then rare step of augmenting their army in peacetime. The Turkish siege of their capital was repulsed by a truly international effort which included a large force of Poles, still organised essentially as they had been in the sixteenth century. The Polish contribution to the Christian victory on the Kahlenberg hill outside Vienna was considerable, but the refusal of their nobility to concede royal demands for war taxes prevented reform of the still largely decentralised system of defence. The crown's inability to integrate the various aristocratic contingents into its own, small royal army, was compounded by the structure of the Polish–Lithuanian commonwealth, with its high degree of political autonomy for powerful magnates and their right of armed resistance. Poland was already at a disadvantage by the 1690s as both Russia and Austria moved to exploit the decline of Turkish power. The next decade saw the transformation of this once powerful state to a battlefield of foreign ambitions during the Great Northern War (1700–21). Subsequent external interference, particularly from Russia, prevented military reform and deprived the commonwealth of the means to prevent the three 'partitions' (1772, 1793, 1795) by which it was removed from the map.[15]

The contrast with Austria and the German states could not be greater. Here, the combined French and Turkish threats resulted in almost continuous two-front warfare during the period 1683–1718, forcing the pace of German militarisation and legitimising the princes' demands for greater power at the expense of traditional representative institutions. Nonetheless, few of the German territories other than Austria and Brandenburg–Prussia had sufficient resources for an independent military role, a fact which compelled them to collaborate within the collective framework provided by the Holy Roman Empire. Even the Habsburgs and the Prussian Hohenzollern dynasties relied on the Empire's medieval constitution to sustain their authority and enhance their security. These political factors influenced the reform of collective defence, completed in 1681–82, primarily to halt French encroachments in the West, but soon utilised during the mobilisation against the Turks in 1683. The reform sacrificed the potential military advantage of a single German army for the sake of preserving the political compromise between the princes and the Habsburgs which underpinned the Empire's traditional structure. The decision confirmed that, in practice, the princes, not the Empire, created the German standing armies. Consolidated in the larger territories like Bavaria, Saxony, Hanover and Hessen-Kassel in the 1680s, these were used to defend German princely absolutism, particularly in the international context, by serving as auxiliaries for the English, Dutch and French, as well as the Habsburgs, in return for cash subsidies and political concessions.[16]

The military expansion which had accompanied the prolonged warfare since 1667 came to an end with the peace settlements of 1713–21. The major powers were not only exhausted financially, but the growth of their armed forces had in many cases outpaced their organisational capacity. Despite fielding powerful forces in later eighteenth-century wars, France never exceeded the maximum reached during the 1690s, while both the Swedish and Dutch establishments declined considerably. Apart from Russia, only Austria and Prussia continued to expand their armies, particularly as their political rivalry escalated into armed conflict after 1740. Their expansion was facilitated by a combination of internal administrative reform and greater resources, as both states acquired further territory at their neighbours' expense.

These general developments were also marked by a growing trend towards standardisation, as armies not only adopted a more formal and permanent internal organisation, but these structures became increasingly uniform across the continent. There was already a pronounced tendency by the 1650s for weaker states to orientate their organisation, tactical doctrine and even uniforms around those of the predominant regional power, especially if there was a religious affinity between their rulers and populations. Protestant Sweden and the Dutch Republic were the early influences on Britain and the north German territories, especially Brandenburg, while Catholic Austria provided a model for those of the south. The military legacy of Catholic Spain was still present amongst the Italian territories which had retained their independence, but was giving way to French and later also Austrian influence. Emulation of French practices grew with

Louis XIV's victories and political influence, and Spain reorganised its forces with French assistance after 1700. However, the expulsion of the dissenting Huguenot minority in 1685 also spread French ideas to Protestant powers, especially Brandenburg, and several states like Savoy–Piedmont and the Dutch Republic had separate regiments of refugees for a time. This pattern remained essentially in place until Frederick the Great's victories over first Austria in the War of the Austrian Succession (1740–48), and then also France in the Seven Years War (1756–63), made Prussia a continent-wide model. The employment of German officers, particularly by Russia, but also the American colonists in the 1770s, helped spread Prussian influence further beyond central and western Europe.

Given these developments, it is possible to discuss the detail of military organisation in terms generally applicable throughout the continent. The core element of all European armies was the company, the smallest formal unit and the basic building-block for all larger formations. The company was originally the body of men recruited by a mercenary captain, either under subcontract for a more powerful military enterpriser (or colonel), or acting directly on the orders of a prince or state government. Captains retained considerable autonomy in many countries until well into the eighteenth century in the recruitment, administration and economy of their company which could be transferred, in return for payment, to another individual. This practice, as well as the general internal administration of all military units, was subject to growing central supervision and control from the 1650s, but the extent to which captains had lost their autonomy varied considerably, even in the late eighteenth century. In many cases, particularly Austria, Britain and France, control of the captains passed, not to the state, but to the colonel commanding the regiment into which the companies were grouped.[17]

Later writers, particularly liberals and military men, castigated this system of privilege and commercial entrepreneurship as corrupt and detrimental to military and national efficiency. Though it was open to abuse, not least the defrauding of the state exchequer by the company commanders, it was nonetheless representative of the nature of the old regime, incorporating both its social inequality, but also the contractual nature of most economic relations. Not only did the captain enter into a contract with the crown or republic which employed him, but the soldier signed a similar agreement with his company commander, often specifying a fixed period of service, along with rights and duties on both sides. Even where the state resorted to limited forms of conscription, such as drafting men from militia rolls into regular formations, it often paid recruits a small bounty and promised them a discharge at the end of hostilities. In contrast to the general trend of the European economy, which moved gradually to more open forms of market capitalism, soldiers' service relations changed from economic to extra-economic coercion. Poverty and under-employment drove men to volunteer, or marked them as potential conscripts for the mercantilist-minded state before 1789, whereas the ideal of universal conscription propounded by the French Revolution ignored economic forces and compelled, at least nominally, all to serve.

Company size could vary considerably. The average in the mid-seventeenth century was still about 200 men for the infantry, but numbers were already declining by the 1670s, while France, England, and later, Spain, soon preferred much smaller units of 40 to 70 soldiers. The reduction in size reflected both contemporary tactical doctrine and the nature of old-regime armies. As greater emphasis was placed on precision and control of infantry firepower, the ratio of officers to men had to be altered in favour of the former. Meanwhile, the perennial problems of war finance forced most states to reduce their establishments, whenever possible, discharging large numbers of privates and retaining a core of experienced officers and men as a cadre to be filled out again when needed. By the early eighteenth century the European standard was about a hundred men per company, including the captain and two to three junior officers, around ten NCOs, a company surgeon and a couple of musicians. Only those states like Prussia and Austria which came to rely heavily on conscription continued to favour larger formations. Companies were grouped for tactical and administration purposes into regiments which also maintained their own small staff of senior officers, clerks, and often a musical band. Regiments varied considerably in size, with up to as many as twenty companies in elite guard formations. The battalion emerged by 1700 as an intermediate level of organisation, sometimes identical with the regiment, but often acting as a convenient smaller grouping of five to ten companies.

The company also formed the basic unit of cavalry organization, but was generally smaller, numbering only 30 to 100 men, so that horse regiments rarely totalled over 800 men, while those of foot could number 2500. The cavalry formed between one-sixth and a quarter of total strength, but weaker and poorer armies often kept most of their horse regiments dismounted in peacetime as an economy measure. This compounded the difficulties of cavalry training, already problematic, as most were scattered in rural billets where their horses had access to fodder, whereas infantry were usually quartered in company-sized detachments in major towns and fortresses. These problems contributed to the relatively slow mobilisation of most armies, already delayed by the need to incorporate untrained new recruits and to hire or purchase transport animals.

Perhaps the greatest area of change was in the artillery, which was completing the transition from its medieval, guild-like structure to become a fully professional, permanent element in all armies. The artillery encompassed a wide range of technical expertise, from the manufacture and repair of equipment and its storage, to its use in field and position (siege) warfare, in addition to associated engineering tasks, including the design and construction of temporary and permanent fortifications, bridging work, sapping and mining. Few armies had given these tasks formal organisational structure before 1650, instead distributing artillerymen amongst their key fortresses, and relying on additional expertise hired from the civilian economy when needed. The French military reforms, together with the prolonged warfare of the later seventeenth century, encouraged the evolution of distinct branches, creating separate units of field and garrison artillery, engineering, pontooner, sapper and mining corps, as well as logistical support and transport units. Though still poorly regarded socially, all were recognised as vital to any military organisation and were often at the forefront of the technical and professional training of officers.

INTERNATIONAL CONFLICT

These armies waged the great struggles for European political predominance which decided the nature of the post-Westphalian states system, as well as access to economic and colonial wealth.

Older notions of universalism, based on the combined spiritual and secular overlordship of the Pope and Holy Roman Emperor, had been undermined by the religious schism and wars of the sixteenth and early seventeenth centuries. Dutch and Swiss independence were recognised internationally in 1648, joined 20 years later by the Portuguese, who overthrew nearly nine decades of Spanish rule to regain a separate existence as a minor world power. Rivalry between France and the Spanish and Austrian Habsburgs continued, but now concentrated on pre-eminence within a hierarchy of sovereign states. Lesser powers fought to preserve their position as full members of this new European order, as well as for regional predominance.

The struggle for state sovereignty indicates the primarily dynastic nature of international conflict, since sovereignty was largely defined by kingship and personal rule. Even in the republican regimes of Venice, Genoa and the Dutch, political power was displayed through a court and hereditary nobility, alongside narrow representative assemblies. Similarly, the crown and royal and imperial titles of Polish king and Holy Roman Emperor symbolised the sovereignty of both these political commonwealths, despite the absence of hereditary royal rule. Position in the new international order was still associated with the prestige and status of the monarch, alongside his or her ability to enforce claims to disputed territory, which also derived primarily from dynastic inheritance rights.[18]

The role of territory, however, raises the question of whether material concerns, or even an underlying mode of production, somehow structurally determined the causes and nature of European wars.[19] Certainly, the primary objective of any conflict was the control of territory, and the capture and retention of strategic towns was the main measure of military success. The imposition of a particular religion on an opposing population which had formed an important goal before 1648 largely disappeared, though confessional affinity continued to influence international alliances into the early eighteenth century. Moreover, no major war was possible without the labour of millions of ordinary Europeans, most of whom were peasants with no formal political power. The geopolitical shifts of the period confirmed that territory, population and taxable wealth were vital to political prestige and military success. Small states like Venice, Sweden and the Dutch Republic, all once significant powers, were marginalised after 1648, while those like Brandenburg–Prussia and Savoy–Piedmont, poorly endowed with indigenous resources, had to resort to extreme measures to keep pace with their larger neighbours. The diffusion of enlightened philosophy, as well as mechanistic theories of the balance of international power, encouraged statesmen to see the world in more rational, material terms. Yet wars were never exclusively about material wealth, be it for personal or public gain. The use of dynastic claims and royal rights went beyond legitimising conflicts in the eyes of Europe's political elite, to form the core of why they went to war. Prestige and honour represented their 'symbolic capital', something which gave meaning to their lives and was as tangible to them as any material concern.

The presence of these factors, together with the socially exclusive world within which decisions were taken, should not, however, lead us to the common conclusion that war in this period was simply the 'sport of kings'; a sort of seasonal variation on hunting intended to give the nobility something to do. Monarchical rule did allow the foibles of a few privileged individuals to exercise great influence on events, and the decisions of headstrong kings, like Charles XII of Sweden, could plunge entire populations into disastrous conflicts. Nonetheless, few could go to war on a whim, as a host of practical and ideological constraints limited their freedom of action. Not only were the mechanisms of resource mobilisation cumbersome and inefficient, but peace, not war, was absolutism's chief goal. Its claim to supreme political power rested on its relative ability to preserve domestic tranquillity after decades of civil and religious strife. War, or even the costly preparation for it, threatened to disturb this delicate internal equilibrium and so could not be trifled with. This, in turn, explains the delays which accompanied the outbreak of hostilities and characterised most campaigns. Old-regime armies were no less capable of operating in winter than those of Gustavus Adolphus or Napoleon, but generally preferred not to in order to ease the logistical and financial burden, and to allow time to find a suitable peace with honour.

The exceptions to this appear be the Anglo-Dutch wars of the later seventeenth century and the protracted struggle of the northern powers to control the Baltic, where geography helped concentrate wealth at obvious strategic points, such as the Sound and the mouths of major rivers. Powerful interest groups were associated with trade in these areas, as well as oceanic commerce with the colonies, and there is evidence that some agitated for war to secure further economic advantages. English entrepreneurs, for instance, supported the republican Commonwealth's war against the Dutch in 1652–54, championing the mercantilist association of wealth with military power and the belief that force was necessary to acquire a greater share of world markets. However, the huge cost of the conflict, as well as the damage to trade, changed opinions by the time of the Third Anglo-Dutch War (1672–74), when commercial circles were accusing Charles II of cynically exploiting mercantilist rhetoric to justify a conflict intended to increase royal power.[20]

In fact, it was the narrow fiscal advantage accruing from trade and additional territory that influenced decisions for war, and it is not surprising that the leading mercantilist politician of the age, Colbert, was in the service of Louis XIV. Fiscal concerns also drove the debate over the state's military power. Attempts by those excluded from office, including bourgeois groups, to control the state monopoly of violence were not intended to exploit this for their own ends in external wars, but to redistribute the domestic burdens of its maintenance to their advantage. In contrast to the period before 1648, these political struggles remained relatively peaceful, except in areas of historic autonomy, like Scotland, Ireland and Hungary, which a centralising state was seeking to integrate into its fiscal–military structure. War was now waged primarily between states rather than within them, assisting in the consolidation of territorial boundaries and the sharpening distinction, marked more clearly in international law and diplomatic protocol, between both war and peace and war and revolt.[21]

TACTICS AND COMBAT EXPERIENCE

All wars involve more than the relative ability of states to mobilise resources and organise armies; they also include violent confrontation on the battlefield and the individual experience of combat. In keeping with absolutism's goal of peace, along with philosophical and practical reasons to conserve human life, old-regime strategy did emphasis the value of manoeuvre and deterrence to achieve political objectives. Ultimately, however, all armies prepared to fight and their tactical doctrine was intended to facilitate a decisive victory. In contrast to other periods, this did not necessarily mean the physical annihilation of the opposing forces, but simply the achievement of a clear margin of success sufficient to compel them to concede victory.

These concerns, together with the nature of contemporary military technology and the topography of the war zone, determined deployment and action on the battlefield. While commanders sought open terrain suitable for their cavalry and an effective field of fire, in practice most engagements took place near inhabited settlements, since these formed the principal objectives and were essential sources of money and sustenance. Many important battles, like Turin (1706), Belgrade (1717) or Prague (1757), were fought either to relieve or capture vital cities, and virtually every other action took its name from a village or larger settlement featuring prominently in the fighting. These settlements, along with natural features like rivers, woods and hills, were enhanced by earthworks and other field fortifications, where time permitted. German troops campaigning in the more open terrain of the Hungarian Great Plain even carried portable wooden obstacles to protect them from the Turks, whose armies always included a large proportion of cavalry.

Deployment was essentially linear, emphasising width rather than depth for both attack and defence. The 56000-strong Franco-Bavarian army occupied a frontage of nearly 5 km at Blenheim (1704); a ratio of manpower to physical space that remained roughly constant throughout the century. The better regiments were generally placed in the front line, with a second formed up about 300 paces[22] behind, a distance sufficiently close to permit effective support, yet far enough to prevent the accidental discharge of musketry killing those in the first line. The intervals between the second line units were generally double those in the first, and often greater, if the army was numerically inferior to its opponent.

Reserves were rare, partly because of the difficulties in ensuring they could reach the areas where they were needed. Indeed, the problems of command and control, often exacerbated by personal jealousies amongst the generals, proved the greatest inhibitor of tactical innovation and a major cause of battlefield defeat. These difficulties extended to the level of unit deployment and influenced the way commanders sought to use or avoid different types of terrain. Contrary to some later assumptions, linear formations were not overly rigid and could operate in broken or wooded country. The battles of Friedlingen (1702) and Lobositz (1756), to cite just two examples, both involved assaults by lines of infantry up tree-covered slopes against enemy positions. The fact that such action was generally avoided was not due to any fear that, once out of the sight of their officers, soldiers would desert.[23] All orders had to be communicated by oral and visual signals, which, in an age of black powder, had only a limited range and were open to misinterpretation. Moreover, the break-up of tight formations threatened unit cohesion and left individual soldiers vulnerable, particularly as their weapons were ill-suited for individual combat.

These factors limited the size of tactical units to about 150 cavalry or 500 infantry, designated squadrons and battalions respectively. The administrative organisation of regiments into companies was generally dissolved for tactical purposes, with those of the cavalry being combined into squadrons, while their infantry counterparts were broken up into fire squads called platoons or divisions. The grouping of regiments into brigades was for convenience of command only and generally had little permanence until some late eighteenth-century experiments in France and the German states.

As the emphasis on firepower grew in the late seventeenth century, the lines became more extended, reducing the number of ranks for the infantry from five or six to three or four by the 1740s; the Prussians' use of two rank lines in the Seven Years War was forced on them by lack of manpower rather than tactical advantage. Regulations varied considerably in detail, but most allowed no more than 50 cm frontage per man and only twice or three times that space between the ranks. The difficulty of maintaining such tight formations reduced their rate of movement to a maximum of 75 to 80 paces per minute.[24]

Both deployment and training were intended to maximize firepower, though individual regulations differed as to how this should be achieved. Most armies continued to use some form of firing by ranks by which an entire row of infantrymen discharged their pieces while the others levelled or reloaded. Firing by platoons involved individual sections of the line firing in turn, with the intention that at least one squad would be firing at any one moment. There is some debate as to which country invented this system, but it was certainly in use by the Dutch in the late seventeenth century and by Britain and Brandenburg soon after. Its principle advantage over firing by ranks was less the continuous musketry it was supposed to deliver, than the greater control exercised over the smaller platoons.

Even platoon fire was difficult to sustain under battlefield conditions. Significantly, the primary example of its successful delivery took place at the battle of Mollwitz (1741), where a Prussian army with years of drill but no battlefield experience met a smaller Austrian force which included a large number of untried recruits. Generally, musketry broke down into each man firing as soon as he had reloaded, making it difficult for the officers to direct it or even bring it to an end. Technical factors contributed to this. Late seventeenth-century muskets were still comparatively crude, and even the introduction of the flintlock and, later, the iron ramrod, did little to improve accuracy. Accordingly, drill emphasised the overall volume of fire, training men to deliver up to five shots per minute under ideal conditions. The switch to aimed fire was not encouraged until the 1790s, when further technical improvement made this a more realistic objective.

Close-range musketry could be deadly, as illustrated by one short exchange at Malplaquet (1709), where an Irish regiment in the English army killed one opponent for every 15 shots at 100 paces. However, most theorists reckoned the more usual rate was only one casualty for every 250 to 400 shots discharged; a factor less to do with technical limitations than the problems of fire control.[25] Few armies had the discipline to wait until their opponents came within the effective range of 160 paces, usually opening fire at 300 paces, or, as often proved the case in the Seven Years War, at the totally ineffective distance of 800 paces. Advancing units generally halted just within effective range, returning fire whether their officers ordered it or not. It was rare for an attack to converge to only 50 paces before the morale of one or other side gave way and precipitated a retreat. Despite periodic emphasis on battle-winning bayonet attacks in official regulations, hand-to-hand fighting generally occurred only in pursuit of fleeing opponents, or the assault of buildings or other fixed positions.

The cavalry's tactical role was more varied and reflected by the division of that arm into distinct types, each characterised by different training, equipment and style of uniform. Heavy cavalry, or cuirassiers, often still wearing metal breastplates and skullcaps, were trained as shock troops intended to defeat mounted opponents and charge disordered or fleeing infantry. Dragoons were usually given similar tasks, but were still trained and even deployed as mounted infantry, as at Guastella (1734), where three French regiments fought on foot in support of an infantry attack. A third type of horseman emerged by the early eighteenth century, often modelled directly on the Hungarian hussars who had served in the Habsburg forces for over a century. These were used for scouting prior to a battle, as well as for harassing the flanks of the enemy army.

All cavalry tactics were reliant on the physical attributes of horsepower. This made mounted units more mobile than the infantry, capable of covering 300 paces per minute at a trot, and up to 500 at full gallop. The sight and sound of a cavalry unit moving at speed had a considerable impact on morale, and, indeed, those who advocated the superiority of shock tactics relied in part on this being sufficient to break an opposing force. However, horses presented a large target to enemy musketry and artillery fire and were easily exhausted, particularly as they were often loaded with more than 100 kg of saddle and equipment. Cavalry generally had to rest after half an hour's movement at a trot, and the fact that the average life of a Prussian cuirassier horse was only four and a half years indicates the harsh realities of their existence.[26]

The use of artillery changed considerably across the time-span, reflecting both technical developments and organizational changes. The 12-pounder became the standard battle piece and had a maximum range of a least 2 km, but was effective generally only up to 680 m. Most armies attached smaller, so-called battalion guns to their infantry which had an effective range of about 500 m. These weapons generally fired solid roundshot at distant targets, switching at closer range to canister shot, a loose package of smaller projectiles which spread upon discharge, turning the piece into a murderous larger version of a shotgun. Explosive projectiles became more common from the 1650s, but were limited to specialist weapons like howitzers, used for lobbing shells over intervening obstacles and fortifications.

The mobility of artillery had improved considerably since the early sixteenth century as the use of different metals and lighter-weight gun carriages became more common. Horse-drawn cannon could cover about 300 paces a minute, about twice as fast as when manhandled, but even the latter rate compares favourably to the slow pace of infantry in formation. Artillery fire was most deadly when concentrated against stationary targets and when uninhibited by either smoke or physical obstacles. The practice of distributing cannon amongst the infantry reduced effectiveness, but this was compensated by a steady increase in the numbers of guns each army deployed, particularly from the 1750s. Austrian mobilisation plans in 1768 envisaged a ratio of one cannon for every 229 men of total strength, representing an increase of nearly 400 per cent on the average at the beginning of the century. Additional cannon contributed to the already difficult logistical problems by requiring further horse teams and transport vehicles. Considering that there were generally as many baggage and artillery horses as there were soldiers in any field army, these factors help explain the limited operational radius of most forces and their difficulties in operating outside the spring and summer months.

While the standard picture of two opposing lines closing on each other holds true in the basic pattern of most battles, there were numerous variations, especially due to different terrain and the presence of field fortifications. Most commanders were more imaginative than often supposed and sought, either by initial deployment or prior manoeuvring, to gain an advantage over their opponents. A famous example is the Prussian oblique order developed by Frederick the Great, where the bulk of the army was concentrated on one wing to make a decisive attack. However, this rarely worked in practice and in any case relied heavily on pre-battle manoeuvring rather than actual deployment for success.

Nonetheless, the French and Austrians, as well as the Prussians, developed new tactics from the 1740s, collectively forming the precursors of revolutionary and Napoleonic warfare. All three used converging columns of four or five short lines of units arranged in depth, for concentrated attacks against chosen points, most notably by the Austrians at Hochkirch (1758), but also by the Prussians at Freiberg (1762), and on several occasions by French generals. The latter also experimented with columns at the lesser tactical level of unit formation, while the Prussians developed faster horse-drawn artillery for rapid deployment. Austria's wars against both conventional European armies in the West as well as the Turks in the East also encouraged innovation, as did English, French and German experience in colonial conflicts, particularly the American War of Independence (1776–83). These innovations were not, however, fully developed or combined with the new ruthlessness and forms of organisation necessary to transform European warfare until after 1789.

Most engagements were not great battles, but minor skirmishes in the constant war of outposts and reconnaissance that accompanied all old-regime campaigns. Formal sieges were also important, particularly in the more highly urbanised and fortified regions of northern Italy and the Low Countries. Technical factors tended to induce considerable similarities in the course of sieges which involved the slow advance of protective trenches towards the fortified position and the reduction of the latter by cannon fire or mining.[27] The need to garrison important towns greatly reduced available field forces and, thus, also the likelihood of major engagements. The system of garrisons was often extended to include small detachments in villages, or along long lines of earthworks. This tendency seems to have become more pronounced, particularly in the last wars of the eighteenth century; the War of the Bavarian Succession (1778–79) between Austria and Prussia, and the Austro-Russian attack on Turkey (1787–92). In the latter, the Austrians deployed along a 1350-km line in 1787, probably the first use of such an extensive continuous front in military history. This strategy, sometimes known as cordon defence, inhibited troop concentrations and certainly contributed to the fragility of old-regime armies against the revolutionary French, who grouped their forces for specific attacks.

THE LEGACY OF THE OLD REGIME

The period 1648–1789 witnessed important developments in European warfare. The first of these was structural, and involved the decisive shift to the state monopoly of violence and the consolidation of its apparatus in permanent land and sea forces, along with the bureaucratic infrastructure necessary to sustain them. This changed both the nature of the army and of war itself. International and civil conflict became more distinct, with the latter also becoming less prevalent. The army now faced outwards against external dangers, while internal threats to the status quo were met by a variety of more peaceful diversionary tactics, most not fully developed until the mid-nineteenth century. War became more exclusively an instrument of state policy, though this was still frequently defined in dynastic terms. Political debate focused on the distribution of the burdens of defence, something which could provoke radical criticism of the entire social order, as in France by 1789.

Armies, meanwhile, became more professional and took on an internal organisation and forms of behaviour that were to characterise their structure well beyond 1789. Tactical innovations were slowly transforming the experience of combat and the conduct of war. This remained limited more by moral and practical restraints on violence than by lack of political objectives. The events following 1789 would indeed bring profound change, but they would also leave much substantially unaltered.

4. Naval Warfare 1453–1815

RICHARD HARDING

Between the fall of Constantinople in 1453 and the end of the Napoleonic Wars in 1815 the sea assumed an unparalleled importance to Europe. The political and economic impact of maritime commerce and war altered out of all recognition. The purpose of naval war is to secure the advantages of free passage across the sea. In 1453, this was of little consistent interest to anyone outside the city states of Italy or the Hanseatic League, but by 1815 naval warfare was built into the calculations of statesmen across Europe. European navies were capable of operating in all the world's oceans and having a major effect upon societies across the globe.

The means by which this was achieved is vital to our understanding of the emergence of the modern world. Many questions remain unanswered. The relationship between technological development and organisational change is obscure and technological diffusion across Europe is unclear. The social and cultural impact of naval war has only been partially explored and its economic significance to various states is imperfectly researched. As each generation adds to the questions it asks of the past, the list of queries grows rather than diminishes. The purpose of this chapter is to put some of these questions into the context of the broad development of naval warfare.

The Mediterranean has the longest history of organised naval warfare. From 3000 BC, the Egyptians used galleys to transport soldiers to Asia Minor.[1] Mediterranean civilisation, which depended so much upon maritime trade links and coastal states, with urban infrastructures of crafts and capital, quickly developed a specialised warship – the oared war galley. A galley fleet could not exercise distant or sustained sea control. Its large complement of oarsmen and soldiers and its small cargo capacity made long voyages impossible. Very seldom did galley fleets sail out of the sight of land. They relied upon local port facilities to refresh the crew and their main function was to support armies or defend merchant vessels along the coastal trade routes.

The gradual collapse of Muslim commercial and political power between the eleventh and thirteenth centuries enabled Christian powers to dominate the trade routes, although they were always exposed to both Christian and Muslim pirates.[2] The great Venetian trading empire was essentially a series of bases that dotted the coastline down the Adriatic and into the Levant. The crusades left a legacy of militant orders, such as the Knights of St John, that nominally protected the pilgrim routes to the Holy Land. The critical event that upset this balance of power was the fall of Constantinople in 1453. The study of Turkish naval power is still in its infancy. Somehow, this nomadic society organised and absorbed the skills of the Anatolian shipwrights and united them with a practical knowledge of artillery and the maritime fighting traditions of the corsair communities. Between 1453 and the 1560s Turkish naval forces supported the expansion of the Ottoman empire. The Turkish–Venetian War of 1499–1502 left the Turks astride the main Venetian trade routes. By 1503, the Turkish fleet numbered over three hundred vessels – enough to overawe all the Christian states of the Eastern Mediterranean. The conquest of Egypt in 1517 confirmed Turkish command of the Levantine trade routes.[3] This success was not achieved by technical superiority over the Christians. The key factor was the Sultan's ability to convert the diverse maritime resources of his empire into an overwhelming number of vessels. How it was achieved remains an important unanswered question. Equally important is the question of the decline of Turkish naval power. The reverse at Malta in 1565 and defeat at Lepanto in 1571 were not self-evidently decisive moments, yet they illustrate the difficulty of maintaining a maritime empire by galley forces. The length of the communication lines from Gallipoli and Constantinople to the Central Mediterranean, and the weakness of the Sultan's political control over his North African vassals, presented the Ottomans with precisely the same problems the Christian powers had faced in the Levant during the Middle Ages. The dominant galley technology and mechanisms of political control could not sustain maritime power over long distances in the face of local opposition.[4]

Long before this, the Venetians had come to rely upon Turkish protection of the trade routes, particularly the vital grain route from Alexandria. For the Venetians it was their fellow-Christians – Tuscans, Spaniards and particularly the English and Dutch, who were the greatest threat to their prosperity. In northern Europe, the nautical conditions of the Eastern Atlantic, with its strong tidal races and gales, made the galley unsuitable for trade or war. The sailing ship, or round ship, with its high freeboard, large cargo capacity and sail power, was ideal for both.[5] The evolution of these ships is critical to the development of naval might. From clumsy, single-masted vessels, they gradually developed into three-masted ships called carracks. They provided an efficient means of bulk cargo-carrying and they could easily be converted for military purposes. The principal naval tactic was to take the enemy by boarding. The high structure of the ship, which could be built up fore and aft by additional castles, was good for firing arrows into the enemy from above and descending on them in a boarding operation. It also made the defence of the vessel much easier. When monarchs required naval forces, ships could easily be mobilised from the maritime community. In England, the Cinque Ports on the South Coast periodically provided the monarch with ships for his purposes in exchange for local freedoms. Expensive arsenals on the Venetian or Turkish model were unnecessary. Occasionally, a more formal naval establishment came into being, such as the French king's yard, Clos des Galées, at Rouen in 1293, or the English roadstead in the River Hamble in the early fifteenth century, but they did not lead to large-scale investment in naval forces.

In the Mediterranean and northern waters, the basic skills required for war at sea were those of the soldier. Archers supported the decisive clash of infantry in boarding. Galley oarsmen did not require specialist nautical skills and the sea routes were overwhelmingly coastal. The ship required skilled men to handle the sails effectively and there was need for some navigational skills in the less predictable Atlantic waters, but naval warfare in both regions was predominantly a variant of land warfare in the confined conditions of ship-to-ship combat. However, major changes occurred between 1470 and 1570.

The first of these changes was the growth of oceanic navigation from the 1470s. Alongside the carrack, another type of ship, the caravel, was evolving. Originally a fishing boat, the caravel was lateen rigged, carrying fore and aft sails, and highly manoeuvrable in coastal waters. Portuguese caravels and carracks voyaged down the African coast in the last quarter of the fifteenth century, and, later, into the Indian Ocean. Eventually, the square-rigged sail plan of the round ship was merged with the lateen rig of the galley and caravel, creating a fairly standard pattern of square-rigged fore and main masts with a lateen-rigged mizzen mast. The development of the spritsail gave added manoeuvrability to the carrack. By the end of the century the Spanish voyages to America, and Portuguese voyages to the Indian Ocean, placed new demands on seamen. Oceanic voyages required much greater seamanship. Over time, the demands placed upon the men and ships brought about changes in the vessels and attitudes to life at sea. Voyages could last for years and men were confined to the vessels for months at a time. Very little is known about how the seamen responded to this change in their working environment, but it might have created new regional variations in how seamen viewed their lives. Atlantic seamen's lives were dictated by their lengthy absence from home and new social ties focused on the ships they sailed.[6] On long-distance trades, the distinction between peaceful commerce and piracy was inevitably blurred, as more ships meant unwelcome competition on established routes or newly discovered markets. The collapse of Mediterranean cloth production in the mid-sixteenth century encouraged English and Dutch vessels to enter the area. The grain shortage at the end of the century provided a further stimulus for Dutch, German and Scandinavian ships to trade there. These northern sailing ships played an important part in the legitimate commerce of the region, encouraged by the Grand Duke of Tuscany's decision to open up Leghorn to them in order to rival Venice as a North Italian entrepot.

The second important change was the introduction of cheap iron cannon on to ships from the 1570s. Cannons had been mounted on ships since the fourteenth century, but it was not until the 1470s that Venetian galleys began to carry powerful, heavy cannons in the bows. This gave the galley both firepower and manoeuvrability that the sailing ship could not match. Ships employed heavy guns at the bow or stern for protection, but it was not until the second half of the sixteenth century that cannon were cheap enough for the average private merchantman to be formidably armed to deter attackers. The development of naval gunnery placed a greater emphasis upon the skills of the professional seaman gunner. The ability to work the guns to deter boarding began to be valued as highly as skills in infantry combat. Whereas the latter could be exercised by any soldier, the gunnery skills could only be learned at sea.[7]

Third, an increasing role was played by the state or crown in providing finance for naval activities. During the sixteenth century, Sweden, Denmark, England and France, and later, the United Provinces of the Netherlands, all began to channel significant funds into the maintenance and development of naval forces. It is not easy to generalise about the reasons for this. The motive of the Baltic powers may have been the profit that could be extracted from control of the lucrative trades in grain, fish and naval stores. For Portugal the decision to maintain a royal monopoly of the Far Eastern spice trade might have been significant. For England the reason might have lain in her inability to compete with France on land, whilst for France, the only way that England could be attacked was by crossing the English Channel.[8] Whatever the causes of this development, the result led to a gradual, but significant change in the nature of navies. Permanent shore facilities, run by people experienced in sea affairs, were established. They were responsible for expanding royal fleets, the effective use of hired merchantmen and managing an increasing investment in maritime enterprises. They created a vital link of interest and knowledge between the royal court and the maritime community.

The combined impact of these three factors slowly changed the balance of power at sea. The city states and the crusading maritime orders, which had exercised significant economic power, were increasingly challenged. Denmark and Sweden overwhelmed the naval power of Lübeck, the dominant Hansa town, during the 1530s.[9] In the 1560s English naval power also wrung concessions from the Hansa.

In the Mediterranean, Spanish royal ships, predominantly galley forces, dominated the seas between Spain and the Habsburg Kingdom of Naples. Venetian trade fell prey to Spanish, Maltese and Tuscan ships, which swept through the Mediterranean. The defeat of the Turkish fleet at Lepanto in 1571 further weakened the Venetian economy, which depended on Turkish sea forces to control piracy in the Eastern Mediterranean. The final blow to the prosperity of the Venetian trading empire came from the well-armed square-rigged sailing ships from England and Holland, the *bertone*. They revictualled and traded at Leghorn and on the Barbary Coast, before travelling on the Aegean and the Levant to trade or plunder. The Venetian authorities believed the galley was a match for the *bertone*, but events proved them wrong.[10] Likewise, Turkish maritime domination of the Levant declined in the face of these interlopers. Although both Venice and Turkey built sailing warships at the end of the seventeenth century, neither power could reassert the domination of Levantine waters. The reasons for this still need serious investigation.[11]

By 1600, oceanic navigation by well armed, financed and supported sailing ships had created a distinct maritime community which had a major impact on European diplomacy. Habsburg Spain had become the most powerful state in Europe, largely owing to the wealth of American silver. The Dutch revolt (1567–1609) was financially sustained by maritime commerce. England, whose continental power had collapsed between 1453 and 1558, had re-established itself as a major force at sea. The English crown was able to mobilise an effective defence at sea against the Spanish Armada in 1588. English vessels, under men such as Sir Francis Drake, preyed upon Spanish shipping and settlements from the 1560s. Although by no means as decisive or damaging to Spain as the English often believed, the dramatic raids in the Caribbean during 1571–73, 1585–86, and on Cadiz in 1587, had a major impact on English thinking. By 1600, Spain had greatly improved her maritime defensive systems, but it was partly her failure to deal with foreign interlopers that led to bankruptcy in 1596. By 1609, several states had shown the ability to put large forces to sea by uniting royal and merchant vessels as common fleet. They had found ways to sustain offensive operations for long periods over great distances. Underpinning all these developments was maritime commerce. The customs duties and financial liquidity created by commerce were essential to many states.

However, the wars of the second half of the sixteenth century did not produce a clear blueprint for future development. It was

still unclear how best to organise and develop maritime resources
for war. There were two distinct trends – the more frequent
mobilisation of the merchant community, and the growing numbers of specialised warships owned by the crown or state. The
mobilisation of well-armed merchant ships enabled the state to
maximise the number of ships it had in its fleet. The Dutch and
the English, who possessed the world's largest mercantile sailing
fleets, were particularly favoured. Although fragile compared to
the specially built warship, merchant ships were manoeuvrable
and available in large numbers. While boarding tactics dominated, sheer numbers in a mêlée could be more important than
specialist fighting vessels. However, their particular value lay in
their role as privateers. Dutch, French and English privateers
played a more consistent part in the maritime war against Spain
than did the regular navy. They damaged trade and fractured
the Spanish supply lines. As privateers, coastal raiders and convoy escorts, the merchant fleet played an important part in naval
affairs well into the nineteenth century, but its role within the
battlefleet became more uncertain after 1650.

   Many questions remained unanswered about royal warships.
The growing number of cannons at sea led to questions about the
design of ships. Some favoured the carrack-type vessel, with its
high fore and aft castles, to provide an advantage to gunners and
boarders in a hand-to-hand battle. Others favoured the lower
'race-built' galleons, without the castles, which were more manoeuvrable, thus making it possible to bring the cannons to bear
from all parts of the ship.[12] By the 1620s, the galleon dominated
orthodox thinking across Europe, but the size of ships was another issue. The English had a preference for large, heavily
gunned vessels. Peter Pett's *Sovereign of the Seas*, carrying over
ninety cannons, was completed in 1637. Its power, size and
decoration made it a magnificent expression of royal power at
sea. In France, the *Grand Saint Louis* (1627), and the *Wasa*, in
Sweden (1628), made similar statements. Against this there were
still serious questions about their value. Their sailing qualities
were not impressive. The *Wasa* was lost on its maiden voyage,
before it had even sailed out of Stockholm harbour, and the
Sovereign had to be modified in the 1650s before it was considered to be a satisfactory warship. Apart from the propaganda
value, which must not be discounted, the major significance of

these large warships was to fight similar ships or to act as floating batteries at particular economic or political pressure points. The Sound was the principal point of this pressure between 1600 and 1650. All the valuable trades of the Baltic had to pass through this narrow stretch of water. Heavily armed warships could not be avoided for miles on either side and they could only be driven off by similar warships. Early on, therefore, Denmark became 'battleship dependent'. Elsewhere there was less call for such large vessels. The main threat to trade came from smaller, fast and very manoeuvrable 'frigate'-type ships. Spanish privateers cruised from Flemish ports. Barbary corsairs ventured as far north as the Irish Sea and Dutch warships infested waters as far apart as the Caribbean, Biscay and the Mediterranean. There were few harbours in northern Europe that could accommodate deep-draughted warships. Spain occasionally sent some of her larger galleons as escorts to troops and money destined for Flanders, but they never remained there for long.

The operational range of the large warships was also limited. Their power to interdict traffic was important and, in exceptional circumstances, could be decisive. Threats to blockade London in 1648 and 1660 were important features in English politics.[13] However, the supply bases for these fleets were only a few miles away in Kent. Likewise, the Danish and Swedish battleship control of the Western Baltic had local supply sources. Even fairly short sea distances made lengthy operations impossible for battlefleets. Irregular victualling and store replenishment and the threat of being caught on a leeshore made sustained operations very difficult. In 1653 and 1673 the English could not maintain their fleet off the Dutch coast. Likewise, the Dutch could not remain in the mouth of the Thames in 1667.[14]

The large warship was also vulnerable in confined situations. Loading and reloading cannon at sea was time-consuming and smaller merchant warships could approach, fire their cannon, retire and allow their companions to press home a similar attack, whilst the large warship was struggling to reload. In October 1639, a Spanish Armada of over seventy ships was confronted by over one hundred Dutch ships in the Downs. The Dutch cut in among them, boarding and capturing many. On several occasions during the First Dutch War (1652–54), powerful English warships were isolated and threatened by more numerous Dutch opponents. In these battles, the weight of metal fired by the two sides was not as different as a crude count of guns on given ships would imply. Large warships were also vulnerable to fireships. Restricted by large numbers of smaller enemy vessels, the large battleship could be entrapped by a fireship and burned. In 1638, the Spanish fleet was caught at anchor by the French at Gueterias, and suffered heavily from fireships.[15] In 1672, at the battle of Southwold, the Earl of Sandwich's flagship the *Royal James* was trapped by smaller Dutch ships and destroyed by a fireship. This mêlée tactic of charging into the enemy fleet was well suited to a fleet of converted merchantmen or light warships. It maximised the advantage of the lighter vessels and minimised the need for complex signalling and lengthy training. It relied upon the vigour of the seamen to press home the attack by boarding and was suited to the contemporary feeling that boarding and infantry combat were the honourable and effective way of warfare.

The English had an advantage in the maintenance of the large battleship. Their deep-water ports and well-developed maritime infrastructure made the building of these vessels practicable. They had been experimenting with ship designs that united the lower, finer lines of the frigate with the size of the old carrack-type Great Ship. The result was a long and heavily armed warship, with relatively good manoeuvrability. Ship for ship, these vessels were more than a match for the Dutch warships, frigates and converted merchantmen during the First Anglo-Dutch War (1652–54). The main danger was that the mêlée tactics eliminated the advantage of the more powerful gun batteries as the warships were brought to hand-to-hand combat by the Dutch. The large battleship would only realise its full potential when its superior strength and firepower could be exploited fully throughout the battle, rather than just in the approach.

The point at which these two trends – the mobilisation of merchant warships and the building of large specialised state vessels – were brought into sharp relief was in the three Anglo-Dutch Wars (1652–54, 1664–67 and 1672–74). The English had more of the large specialised warships, but both sides mobilised private warships and converted merchantmen. During the First War, both sides recognised the advantages and disadvantages of their fleets and tactics. The Dutch found that they could not overwhelm their more powerful opponents by numbers and bravery. They also recognised that merchant masters did not have the courage or interest to charge unconditionally with their weaker ships into the English. The English also saw that merchant masters could not be relied upon. Each side had come close to major disaster because their ships had been cut off or unsupported in mêlées. Both sides knew that a military discipline had to be imposed. One method was to replace merchant masters with naval officers. Another was to reduce reliance in combat upon merchant vessels. The Dutch also began a programme of building stronger and more heavily armed warships, which, for the first time, belonged to the Estates General, rather than the individual local admiralties, who might sell them off after the conflict.

The most important change to emerge from this war was the development of the single line ahead formation. Ever since heavy cannon had been put on ships it had been recognised that effective cannon fire could cripple an enemy vessel, if not sink it. Spanish galleons had used cannon fire effectively against smaller privateers. The problem was that the slow rate of fire might enable swifter enemy vessels to get around the warship to divide its fire and guncrews. With ships moving in line ahead, the vulnerable stern area was protected and the disciplined line presented the enemy with a long line of gun batteries. The line ahead was used in battles between anchored and attacking fleets in the 1630s, but may have been first used by two fleets under full sail, by accident, at the battle of the Gabbard in June 1653. Light winds made it impossible for the Dutch to come up from leeward to grapple with the English, who were satisfied to stay upwind, firing into the struggling Dutch force. A few weeks later, the line was used more aggressively at the battle of Scheveningen (August 1653). The English squadron, in line ahead, drove into the massed Dutch fleet, firing into the enemy on either side of it. It made three passes through the Dutch mêlée, keeping formation and making the superior firepower of the ships pay. The Dutch recognised that they needed to close with the English quickly, but were held off by cannon fire.[16]

At the outbreak of the Second War, the Dutch had built more powerful warships, and by 1666 they had adopted the line of battle as the basic tactical formation for approaching to the enemy. The ultimate objective of both sides was still to board their crippled enemy, but instructions prohibited falling out of line to achieve this while other enemy ships remained a danger. The major battles of the war, off Lowestoft, on 3 June 1665, the Four Days Battle, on 1–4 June 1666, and the St James Day Fight, on 25 July 1666, were not fought in strict fleet line of battle, but rather, squadrons moving behind each other in line. During the Third War, similar tactics were employed. However, the importance of the line was evident and it was not long before both theory and practice focused upon perfecting the line of battle. The merchant warships were gradually eliminated from the line as too small or weak to maintain themselves in the firefights that developed. At a time when officers' skills had not been honed by experience, the line was a simple tactic that required minimal signalling or initiative on behalf of the captains in the confused conditions of a battle at sea. It promised a sound defence for the fleet as a whole, presented the maximum firepower towards the enemy and still made possible the ultimate victory by boarding the enemy ships. Instructions for captains became more precise. The independence of junior flag-officers and captains, which had been jealously guarded in the days of the mêlée, was curtailed by stronger codes of discipline. The emphasis was on discipline in the approach, gunnery skills in the clash, and, if the admiral judged, vigorous boarding in the final stages.

Between the 1670s and 1690s, naval warfare became a more specialised form of military activity. The sailing battleship had become a vital part of the naval arsenal. Its use in large numbers required the discipline and some of the skills of the soldier, but many other skills that were unique. Around these ships, a whole social, technical and economic structure was gradually emerging. Precisely why the battleship became the dominant type of vessel at this time is unclear. Factors such as technology, the prestige of monarchs and the impact of war on the maritime community are involved. Since the sixteenth century, privateers and pirates had forced merchants to use convoys, escorted by light warships which were capable of combating the predators. These convoys presented tempting targets as they converged on the choke-points of the trade lanes – the Sound, the North Sea and the Straits. The large warship could push aside the escorts and devastate the convoys. Only similar battleships could combat their firepower and defend the merchantmen. The battles of the Anglo-Dutch Wars and the Danish–Swedish wars (1643–45, 1652–60 and 1675–78), around these choke-points, were the testing grounds for the new tactics and ship designs that created the line of battle.

Once established, the line of battlefleet placed new demands on states. The magnificent battleship had always been a major symbol of state power and was properly commanded only by the aristocracy in the name of the monarch. On the other hand, the handling of these ships required high levels of technical skill, not usually found in courtiers. States had to find ways of merging the social and technical requirements of the naval officer corps. Recent studies have deepened our understanding of this process in England and France. Some work has been done on the way the Russian navy managed the process, but this remains an important and much needed area of study.[17]

The new battlefleets needed more sophisticated and consistent infrastructures which placed fiscal pressures upon states and social tensions between the administrators and the naval officers. Louis XIV's decision to support Colbert's expansion of the French navy from 1661 led to one of the most remarkable administrative feats of the pre-industrial world. Between 1661 and Colbert's death in 1683, France created the largest navy in the world and put in place the structure of ports, arsenals and supply policies that were to support it. When the Nine Years War (1688–97) broke out, France was building a second generation of even stronger warships. In England the administration of the navy has probably received the most detailed study, partly because of the prominent role and prolific writings of Samuel Pepys. Until recently, Pepys's prominence has done a great deal to distort the history of the central administration of the navy and much more still needs to be done to clarify the workings of the yards and, particularly, the finances of the navy. Studies in English of Dutch, Spanish, Danish and Swedish administrative practices are minimal yet vital to an understanding of the diffusion of administrative ideas and the impact of local conditions.[18]

States developed their navies at different speeds and had to come to terms with local constraints. Traditionally, these constraints have been described as technological or political barriers. The inability of the Dutch to build the largest three-decked warship has been ascribed to the shallowness of their country's estuaries and coastal regions. The collapse of the French battlefleet is seen as an example of Louis XIV's misguided lack of interest in his navy. The persistence of the galley fleets in the Mediterranean has also been seen as a lack of political understanding of naval power. There is a degree of truth in all these statements, but they are often based upon the assumption that by the 1690s the line of battleship had made other types of vessel obsolete. This assumption is largely based on the work of Captain Alfred Thayer Mahan, whose *Influence of Seapower upon History* was first published in 1890. Mahan's objective was to demonstrate to the American people that seapower, and particularly the battlefleet, were keys to the growth and development of the United States in the twentieth century. His importance in the development of naval historiography must not be underestimated, as he did a great deal to condition successive generations to thinking about seventeenth- and eighteenth-century naval power in the terms of the late nineteenth century. Failure to develop the battlefleet was presented as political misjudgement, rather than a response to contemporary conditions. Subsequent historical interest in technology has also placed an emphasis on mistakes or incapacity rather than choice.

Neither of these approaches is necessarily wrong, but they do not make enough allowance for statesmen and monarchs making choices that appear rational to them. In the period 1660 to 1713, the battlefleet was highly effective in those regions where it had developed to serve a clear purpose. During the Anglo-Dutch Wars, the objective of both sides was to win control of the narrow waters. When a battle was decisive, or the strategic situation was generally favourable, battlefleets could cruise off the enemy coast and sometimes cause substantial damage to enemy shipping and villages. However, they could not stay long enough, nor spread themselves far enough, to have a decisive impact on the fighting power of the enemy. The long-term damage was done by the smaller warships and privateers, whose pickings were increased by the break-up of the convoys. Likewise, in the Sound and the Baltic, the Danish–Swedish wars were fought around the convoy choke-points, while in the shoal waters of the Eastern Baltic, privateers and later galleys played a more important part in stopping maritime traffic.

The important interaction between battlefleets and a variety of smaller warships continued during the Nine Years War (1688–97), the War of Spanish Succession (1701–13) and the Great Northern War (1700–21). English and Dutch control of the Eastern Atlantic seaboard and the North Sea was established by the end of 1692. Likewise, English and Dutch squadrons in the Baltic had a significant impact on Swedish and Russian policy in the Great Northern War. This did not mean that the allies had secured for themselves the advantages of free passage across these waters or denied them to the enemy. The battlefleet ensured that specific critical points were covered, such as the North Sea. It protected communications with the army in Flanders, prevented a French landing in Scotland in 1708 and covered vital convoys through the Baltic. The battlefleet could not, however, prevent the enemy making use of the sea in all cases. The French privateering effort between 1692 and 1698 contributed to a major financial crisis in 1696 and privateers continued to inflict serious damage upon English and Dutch trade throughout the War of Spanish Succession.[19] Likewise, the allies discovered that when they shifted their actions from convoy protection to attempts to hinder Russian inshore operations in the eastern Baltic, their capabilities were seriously limited.[20]

The battlefleet was only part of seapower. It forced an inferior enemy to break up concentrations of shipping, which made them prey to the smaller warships and privateers. For England and Denmark this was crucial, as the battlefleet made it impossible for an enemy easily to move large bodies of troops over the open seas. Thus the battlefleet was the key to their national defence. Conversely, their battlefleets enabled trade to be convoyed or armies to be transported without interference. However, as an offensive weapon the battlefleet had serious limitations. Battlefleets could position themselves off critical trade points, such as the Sound, the Texel, the Thames estuary or Cadiz. This was attempted many times between 1660 and 1713, but seldom succeeded, as the supply infrastructure was simply inadequate. The French and Dutch fleets found that their ability to influence land operations on Sicily between 1674 and 1678 were limited whilst they could not reach each other's galley forces. English naval forces gradually built up a supply network at Lisbon, Leghorn, Cadiz and Gibraltar in the 1670s and 1680s. Support from these sources made it possible to overwinter a large fleet in the Mediterranean during 1694–95. The capture of Gibraltar in 1704 and Minorca in 1708 finally provided the English with permanent bases for cruising in the Western Mediterranean. However, as convoys became less frequent and the enemy squadrons remained in port, the significant damage to the enemy had to be done by the smaller vessels, away from the trade termini.

The allied success in building a supporting infrastructure in the Mediterranean is usually seen as confirmation of Louis XIV's folly in failing to maintain a direct challenge to the allied battlefleets.[21] Within 50 years, the significance of this failure was apparent, but not in the 1690s or the 1710s. Battles at sea had not proved as decisive as land battles. The wars had demonstrated the power of the battlefleet in local waters and at critical points in the trade lanes. There were some important improvements to the victualling and supply administration, particularly in the Mediterranean, which had extended the operational range of these fleets. A *modus vivendi* between the emerging professional bodies of naval administrators and sea officers was emerging. However, the impact of these changes was less clear. The French victory at Beachy Head in August 1690 had not provided Louis with any significant advantage throughout 1690–91. Likewise, the defeat at La Hogue and Barfleur in 1692 did little damage to Louis's war plans in Flanders. William III's attempts to impose a blockade of France failed.[22] The battle off Malaga in August 1704 prevented France from reasserting control over the Western Mediterranean, and exposed the coasts of Provence to serious raids in 1707 and 1710, but did not have a major effect upon the campaigns in Europe. In sum, the expensive battlefleet had not done a great deal for France and the allied fleets had not inflicted serious damage upon her. On the other hand, the *guerre de course*, the privateering war, in conjunction with small royal squadrons, had shown some important results for very little cost to the hard-pressed royal treasury. The squadrons acted as powerful escorts, small expeditionary forces or raiding forces. They did not need to contest control of the critical points in the sea lanes, so long as they could evade the superior enemy fleets.

Nevertheless, important shifts in the balance of seapower became apparent during the next 50 years. After 1695, the permanent presence of English squadrons in the Mediterranean changed the balance of power. They disrupted the French campaigns in Catalonia throughout both wars between 1688 and 1713. They prevented Spanish attempts to recover Sicily by force in 1718. Later, they were a check on the movements of both the Spanish and French fleets in the Mediterranean during the War of Austrian Succession (1740–48). All Spanish attempts to remove the British from Gibraltar by diplomacy and force failed, but the British squadrons in the Mediterranean were never strong enough or provided with adequate numbers of small warships to maintain a presence east of Sicily or effectively interdict coastal traffic. However, they were large enough to spell the end of the galley as an effective force in the deeper waters of the northern Mediterranean coast. Along the shallower North African coast and the Aegean archipelago, galleys still had a role as cruisers, but the last galley campaign in the western Mediterranean was mounted in 1742 and by 1748, both Spain and France had abolished their galley corps.[23]

In the Baltic the emergence of Russia as a naval force equal to Sweden or Denmark changed the balance of power for good. From the 1650s Dutch and English intervention had undermined Swedish and Danish control of the Baltic, but these were temporary incursions. The Russian fleet was a permanent force and, although largely untested in battle, it made Swedish attempts to revive her fiscal and economic fortunes by control of the trade routes impossible.[24]

The third area where naval power had an increasing impact was in the Americas. Although both France and Britain toyed with the idea of a neutrality in America during the 1680s, it was impracticable. The temptation of the West Indian colonies or Spanish silver proved too much. Nine expeditions were sent to the West Indies during the Nine Years War and 19 during the War of Spanish Succession.[25] Two French expeditions went to Rio and one British expedition was sent to Quebec in 1711. They achieved very little, but contemporaries clearly believed that Spain's control over her American empire and their control over their own colonies was very fragile. In Britain, despite the lack of results, there was a growing feeling, partly fuelled by domestic political conflicts, that France and Spain were vulnerable in the Americas. The development of this 'Blue Water' strategy had major consequences for British foreign policy throughout the eighteenth century.[26] France and Spain were not convinced of the central importance of Americas, but nor were they able to create a coherent or consistent policy with regard to Britain in the wider context of their foreign policies. Once again, Britain was favoured. Despite fears of Hanoverianism, Britain had, by the mid-1750s, a clear strategy based upon its maritime strength. Neither France nor Spain achieved this, and for both these powers, the maritime dimension of the wars from 1733 to 1763 produced only confusion and disappointment.[27]

Between 1713 and 1739 Britain was in an exceptionally advantageous position. The battlefleet was the foundation of national defence and deeply engraved in the political consciousness of the nation. Britain was also fortunate in that it did not have to make such stark choices as its rivals. Seapower lay in the effective combination of battlefleet, privateers and the national maritime infrastructure. Although the fleet and the privateers were complementary naval forces, they were also significant competitors for the limited pool of seamen. Britain's maritime economy expanded dramatically between 1660 and 1689, and continued to expand more slowly during the eighteenth century. There was always great tension between the Royal Navy, the merchants and the privateers over seamen, but the population base of seafarers in Britain and North America was large enough for all. This was not so in the United Provinces, France or Spain, none of whom ever possessed adequate manpower to create a battlefleet to challenge Britain, whilst at the same time exploiting those aspects of naval power which the battlefleet was ill-equipped to carry out.[28]

Britain had both the motivation and the real maritime resources to develop her naval forces as a whole. British ministries were careful not to share their maritime conquests with their allies, the Dutch, thus laying the foundations for a permanent, national naval presence in the Mediterranean and North America. Although disputes over 'Blue Water' or 'Continental' strategies formed part of the political rhetoric of eighteenth-century Britain, the navy was never allowed to decay to a dangerous level. When war broke out again in 1739, British statesmen were not always sure in their handling of the navy, but they had the luxury of possessing a far superior force than their Bourbon enemies.

If the wars up to 1721 only hinted to the growing capability of seapower, the more peaceful years up to 1739 did not demand much spending on naval forces. The maritime economies of

Europe continued to expand, and with it there was a slow but sure development of the naval infrastructure. Tension and conflict between England and Spain in the Mediterranean and the West Indies ensured that naval facilities on Jamaica, Antigua, Minorca, Gibraltar and the Spanish cities of Havana and Cartagena de las Indias were developed. France built up a major fortress, Louisbourg, on Cape Breton Island. For the first time in nearly a century, the Spanish navy began to develop as part of Don José Patino's strategy for recovering the Italian lands lost at the peace settlement of 1713. In the Far East, European trading companies were developing their factories to support their large armed merchantmen.[29]

The wars between 1739 and 1815 demonstrated both the importance of seapower and its fragility. In 1739 the tensions between Spain and Britain erupted into war. The confident predictions of a rapid Spanish collapse, if Britain exerted its naval power in the Caribbean, disappeared during 1741–42. The Spanish fleet did not present a serious challenge to the British battle squadrons. However, its manoeuvrings and the movements of the French fleet did cause great anxiety. British and American privateers quickly swept up what little Spanish trade ventured to sea, but little was achieved against Spanish America. Spanish privateers hit the British merchant fleet hard. When the war finally merged into a general European war in 1744, Spain showed no signs of collapse. Naval power in the Mediterranean had played an important part in the Habsburg–Bourbon war in Italy since 1741, but British optimism concerning its naval power had been misplaced.[30]

Naval war with France from 1744 also produced no decisive results. French trade was hit by privateers and blockade. In 1745 the capture of Louisbourg produced a great deal of British rejoicing, but had little impact on French war plans. The naval war was carried to India, but without decisive results. In 1747, two battles off Cape Finisterre provided the public with naval victories, but did little to influence peace negotiations, which were, by then, well advanced. The war in Italy, Flanders and Germany concentrated minds at the French, Dutch, Austrian and Sardinian courts more than victories at sea.[31]

Seapower might have played a critical role in preventing a French invasion of England in support of the Jacobite rising in

1745. If so, it reinforced its defensive significance to Britain, but, as an offensive weapon, the navy had not proved itself. Yet the Seven Years War (1756–63) was a dramatic expression of the potential of seapower as an offensive force. By the end of 1757 French trade had largely disappeared from the seas. During 1758–59, the French empire in India, Africa, America and the West Indies began to collapse as British land forces, supported and protected by the navy, exerted increasing pressure. Without reinforcements, the French positions were doomed. French squadrons got to sea, evading the British forces on a number of occasions, but could not maintain consistent support for the overseas possessions. Privateers damaged British trade, but were increasingly driven into port by British warships and privateers. When Spain joined the war in 1761, Manila and Havana were captured by amphibious expeditions. Unlike 1748, this was a decisive defeat for the Bourbon powers, who could not make any counterbalancing conquests in Europe.[32]

   The story of the war is well known, but the reasons for this dramatic change in the effectiveness of naval warfare are still not clearly understood. Britain had achieved a significant comparative advantage over its rivals. Traditionally, this was ascribed to the vision and policies of individuals like William Pitt and Admiral Lord Anson. The longer-term factors of continuous funding, parliamentary support or a clear role for the navy have received less attention. Gradual improvements in the manning, victualling and storing of ships and the accumulated expertise that led to new frigate designs gave the navy additional capabilities in cruising and inshore work. The revised privateering law and practice made the war on trade more effective. Experience also improved the strategic disposition of the fleet, the tactical handling of the ships and the fleet's ability to work with the army in amphibious warfare. Most of all, its officers experienced a run of unbroken successes. The confidence with which they could engage the enemy gradually changed their outlook. In 1756, during the trial of Vice-Admiral John Byng, after the battle of Minorca, a great deal was made of the instructions to keep to the line of battle, but by 1759, Hawke's dramatically successful chase of the French squadron into Quiberon Bay revealed a confidence in the decisive advantages of close action that superior seamanship and numbers engendered. The line of battle had become

less relevant to the British, and the decisive results provided the
background to debates over the following decades as French,
British and Spanish naval thinkers tried to interpret the tactical
lessons of the war. Between 1763 and 1815, there was extensive
experimentation with the line of battle for offence and defence,
as navies tried to reproduce the dramatic results of the Seven
Years War in very different military conditions. It culminated in
the last great battle of the sailing-ship era, Trafalgar, in which
Nelson broke through the Franco-Spanish line in two columns
and devastated their fleets.

The impact of the Seven Years War on the contestants and
naval warfare generally is also in need of further exploration.
Although the French navy was bankrupt by the end of 1759, the
remnants of the fleet were maintained. Furthermore, by 1764,
the French court had begun a major rebuilding programme. The
French economy does not appear to have suffered significant
long-term damage as a result of the war. By 1778, the French
navy was in an excellent condition to challenge Britain again.[33]
Likewise, Spain suffered no permanent damage as a result of the
war, revived its building programme and made its fleet one of the
most powerful and well constructed in Europe.[34]

The war sharpened political, strategic and tactical ideas about
the operation of seapower. It had also led to important administrative changes within European navies. Britain's advantage,
built up over 50 years, made other nations aware that naval
power could be important and that the skills and resources required substantial, long-term investment. It was a lesson that
coincided with opportunities emerging from the revival of long-
distance maritime commerce and was underpinned by new
economic theories about free trade and fiscal policy.

Under the combined stimulus or commercial opportunity and
belief in the efficacy of naval power, naval competition grew
significantly during the last 30 years of the century. France,
Spain, Portugal, the United Provinces, Denmark, Sweden, Russia
and Turkey, besides Britain, developed their naval forces.[35] The
investment was large, but naval power remained as elusive and
fragile as ever. Britain's advantage vanished very quickly. By the
early 1770s it proved impossible to convince Parliament to fund
a superiority in naval forces over potential enemies that had been
decisive in the 1750s and had averted war over the Falklands in

1770. After 1776, the need to finance a large army in America and maintain a constant cruising war against the small American warships and privateers necessitated the laying up of the larger battleships. France entered the war in 1778, Spain in 1779 and Holland in 1780. The British navy was overstretched across the globe. Although victories in the West Indies restored the balance and the crisis was weathered by 1782, it was too late to prevent the loss of the American colonies and Minorca.[36]

The French and Spanish revival proved as ephemeral as the British domination. By 1785, the French navy was again bankrupt. By 1791, the Revolution had destroyed the officer corps, so that by the time war broke out with Britain in 1793, the French navy was a shadow of the force it had been ten years earlier.[37] By 1798, and Nelson's victory at Aboukir Bay, the French battlefleet had all but collapsed. The rebuilt Spanish navy gradually wasted away until its main strength was defeated at Trafalgar in 1805. The Dutch fleet was effectively reduced after the battle of Camperdown in 1797. This rapid collapse of naval power experienced by Britain, Spain, France and Holland in the last 30 years of the century was also experienced by Sweden and Turkey. Sweden had gradually built up its naval forces in the second half of the century, only to see them broken in a war with Russia between 1788 and 1790.[38] Turkey had built up a sailing fleet to support its operations in the Balkans, but in June 1770 a Russian squadron destroyed their main force at Chesme.[39]

By 1815, only the British navy remained as a major world force. Since 1756 naval warfare had had an unprecedented impact on the world. Events at sea had a major impact on the collapse of the British North American empire between 1778 and 1782 and British seapower had a great influence on the independence movements of South America up to 1825. Seapower was only one of many factors that shaped the wars of 1792 to 1815, but its significance cannot be neglected. British naval power exercised in the Baltic, Mediterranean and Atlantic had been important factors in Europe's relationship with Revolutionary and Napoleonic France. It formed the basis of an expanded British empire in the Far East. It secured the trade receipts of the Americas, India, and the Mediterranean, which enabled Britain to act as paymaster of the coalitions against France.[40]

Naval power remained extremely fragile and its cost was still excessive. It required a consistent minimum expenditure even in peacetime, which few powers were willing to maintain. In wartime the cost could be prohibitive. The complexity of maintaining a balanced fleet was also a major task of administrative and strategic foresight. The battlefleet was the symbol of seapower, but much of the effective work of using the advantages of free passage across the seas had to carried out by smaller, often private vessels. Besides what appeared to be uncontested control of the seas exercised by the mighty battlefleet, there raged the *petit guerre* between privateers, merchantmen, hired ships and small warships. Only Britain, for a short time in the 1750s and again, more permanently, from the late 1790s, possessed the maritime resources to maintain the battlefleet and the smaller warships simultaneously. Without this interaction between battlefleet and the rest of the maritime resources of the state, seapower was a very weak and limited tool. Attrition also rapidly took a cumulative toll of maritime resources. In the 1750s and 1790s the French maritime community was rapidly depleted by losses to British action. The greater the losses, the weaker were the replacements and therefore the quicker they perished. Spain and Holland suffered from a similar debilitating process.

Between 1453 and 1815 naval warfare came to play a major role in military events across the world. Many issues remain to be investigated. Although the belief in the predominance of the battlefleet as the source of seapower is no longer as strong as it was, much remains to be done to explain how seapower was exercised at different times, in different parts of the world and by different navies.

5. Ottoman Warfare in Europe 1453–1826

GÁBOR ÁGOSTON

INTRODUCTION

The Ottoman Empire was a determining world power of the sixteenth and seventeenth centuries; in modern terms the Empire was a superpower. It held this rank by virtue of its geopolitical situation, its enormous territory and population, its wealth of economic resources, and a central and provincial administration that was capable of mobilising these resources to serve the goals of the state. The efficient use of resources formed the base of the Ottoman army, which was one of the best armies in Europe at the time.

The devastating force which in 1453 occupied Byzantium, a state once believed to be invincible, arrived in Anatolia in the course of the second great wave of Turkish migration. Although considered by the Europeans to be Turks, the leaders of this great new conquering force named their country *Osman eli* (after the first ruler of the new state, Osman, ?–1324) and called themselves *Osmanlı*. Osman's immediate ancestors, who belonged to a group of Turkish tribes speaking the Oguz dialect, had been driven out of their central Asian homeland by the Chingisid Mongols. They were granted new territories in north-west Anatolia on the Seljuk–Byzantine borderlands by the Seljuk sultan of Rum, who was ruler of the area. Osman was a near-contemporary of Rudolf of Habsburg (1218–91) and of Sheik Safi al-Din (1252–1334), whose descendants were to build two of the major empires of the sixteenth century, the Habsburg and the Safavid Empires, and were to become the Ottomans' main competitors in international politics.

Just as sixteenth-century European history is incomprehensible without a proper knowledge of the Ottoman–Habsburg–Valois confrontation, many of the issues surrounding the development of European warfare may only be understood in the light of Ottoman military expansion. It can hardly be denied that the Ottoman challenge served as a motivating factor in the modernisation of the anti-Ottoman defence system (from the North African coast to the Hungarian border-fortress lines, and the steppes of southern Russia), the development of the military–administrative system of the Austrian Habsburgs, and the appearance of many of the manifestations of the military revolution in the central and eastern European region at this time. Similarly, it is no coincidence that the first phase of Ottoman expansion in Europe occurred in the fourteenth and fifteenth centuries, for it was in the course of these two centuries that Europe was plagued by a series of military and social crises which culminated in the dissolution of the *Respublica Christiana* and the expiry of the common anti-Ottoman foreign policy of the European powers.

An examination of Ottoman military successes and failures becomes more effective if we employ the methods and approach of the 'new military history'. Instead of offering an explanation based on one single factor, this new approach seeks for the causes of the military successes and failures in the underlying social, economic, financial and military structures of the states in question. Employing such an approach, we may explain not only the Ottomans' military successes of the fifteenth and sixteenth centuries, but also their failures of the seventeenth century on the European front. In order to explain these issues correctly, we need to acquaint ourselves with the changes that took place in the social, economic and military fields among both the Ottomans and their enemies. This is particularly important in the case of the European enemies of the Ottomans, for it is precisely in the sixteenth and seventeenth centuries that the Europeans – thanks to advances that were occurring as part of the much disputed military revolution – gained a military superiority that could be felt by both sides.

After a brief introduction, this short chapter seeks to explore the history of Ottoman military warfare between the fifteenth and nineteenth centuries by employing the above approach. The chapter is divided into three parts: the Islamic Gunpowder Empire, 1453–1566; the Empire on the Defensive, 1566–1699; and Retreat and Reform, 1699–1826. I shall focus on the European front, but I shall not ignore events on the eastern front – events which from time to time played an important limiting role in the western expansion of the Ottomans.

The unprecedented Ottoman expansion, the unparalleled legitimisation of the Ottoman dynasty, and the survival of the Ottoman Empire over a long historical period, raise numerous questions to which there are as yet few universally accepted answers. This is not the place – nor am I the author – to discuss 'the causes of the Ottoman success'. Still, it is worth referring to some of the possible factors and circumstances that were decisive in the development and expansion of the Ottoman state and which, in varying proportions, played a significant role in its success.

A decisive factor in the Ottomans' early success was without doubt their geopolitical location. The Ottoman principality was a true frontier principality, which served as a magnet for the mighty warriors of the neighbouring Islamic and Christian states and provided space and opportunity for acculturation and for the mutual transfer of state and military institutions, military technology and tactics. All of this was facilitated by the following factors: a syncretistic understanding of Islam among the peoples of the marches, the convergence of heterodoxy, the universal nature of the state – a state in which there were various religions, traditions and institutions and in which the common spirit of the *gaza* (which, rather than being a holy war against the infidels, was more often a 'predatory raid' launched jointly by Muslims and 'infidels' – both sharing in the booty) and the frontier ethos of the 'other side' coexisted, and in which alliances could, and did, cut across religious and ethnic lines.

Marriage alliances with the influential Muslim and Christian families of the frontier region and the tolerance exercised by the Ottomans in their relations with the non-Muslim populations of the Balkans were two further factors which helped to consolidate Ottoman power.[1] The basis of this tolerance was a belief on the part of the Ottoman leaders that the supreme means of state power was the army, whose relative strength was, in turn, dependent upon the welfare of taxpaying subjects. This approach divided society into two functional groups: the first group comprised the taxable *re'aya*, whose task was the production of the goods that were needed in order for the state to operate. The second social group consisted of administrators and soldiers, whose task was the redistribution of the goods. Given that their most important function was connected to the military, members of this second group were called *askeri* (military).

The system of military slavery

The Ottomans recognised from the start that they needed to establish an independent army, a force that would stand above the various religious, cultural and ethnic groups in the area. Such a force was provided by the Janissaries, the new army (*yeni çeri*). It is hardly a coincidence that the Janissary forces, which represented the cornerstone of the centralising political technology of the Ottomans, were established during or immediately after the crisis of the 1370s, when the threat posed by centrifugal tendencies to the power of the Ottomans was greater than ever before. It was also around this time (in the 1380s) that the *devşirme* system was introduced in order to ensure replacement generations of Janissaries. Under this system non-Muslim children were levied and then Ottomanised. Subsequently, they were trained for government service or became members of the salaried central corps of the Sultan. The institution of military slavery (the *kul-devşirme* system) created the highest and most loyal pillars of support for the House of Osman. In periods of greatest crisis, it was these elements that prevented the break-up of the state, and indeed it was they who, acting out of their own interests, pressed continuously for renewed conquests. This saved the Ottoman state from destruction at the end of the great period of expansion and during the decade-long interregnum after the battle of Ankara in 1402. In the course of this decade, territories stretching from the Danube to the Euphrates, which had been conquered during the reign of Beyezid I (1389–1402) but not yet properly integrated into the Ottoman state, had begun to fall into pieces.

The early Ottoman army

In this first period the main constituent elements of the Ottoman army were: the ruler's military entourage, the cavalry troops of the tribes which had joined forces with the Ottomans, and those peasants who had been called up as soldiers for military campaigns. The members of the military entourage, who were designated by the word *kul* or *nöker*, were the forerunners of the Sultan's salaried troops.

The troops of the Turkmen tribes that were in alliance with the Ottomans received a share of military booty and were granted the right to settle on occupied land. In return, they had to provide men-at-arms in proportion to the amount of benefice in their possession; later they became the *timar*-holder *sipahi*s, another pillar of the Ottoman army.

Since the salaried troops of *kul*s and the *timar*-holder cavalry proved too few in number to fulfil the needs of a growing state, young volunteer peasant boys were taken on. These youths later formed the infantry *yaya* and cavalry *müsellem* units. The numerous campaigns and predatory raids required that this third component of the army be made permanent: the voluntary nature of the force was therefore abandoned and compulsory enlistment was introduced during the military campaigns.

In the second half of the fourteenth century, numerous changes were made in the organisation of the salaried troops. These changes did not, however, affect the *timar*-holder *sipahi*s. The *müsellem* were replaced by the palace horsemen, who were also called *spahi*s, and the *yaya*s were replaced by *azab*s and the Janissary corps. The *yaya*s and *müsellem*s became auxiliary forces. The infantry *azab*s, who were equipped with bows and arrows, constituted a *militia portalis* rather than a real group of mercenaries, because they received their military kit from – and were sent to the campaigns by – a certain number of taxpaying *re'aya* families. The most significant measure was the establishment of the Janissary corps, the first standing army in Europe, which was financed by the treasury and stood under the direct command of the sultan.

The artillery unit was another mercenary corps formed at this time – also the first of its kind in Europe. Although many would question whether the Ottomans really did use firearms against the Karamanids in 1386 and in the course of the first battle of Kosovo Polje in 1389, and whether they used cannons in Bursa in 1364, it is nevertheless highly probable that the Ottomans were already acquainted with firearms in the fourteenth century. Independent and unrelated European, Bulgarian and Turkish sources all point out that cannons were used by the Ottomans during the siege of Constantinople (1394–1402).[2]

The early years of the Ottoman state were marked by spectacular expansion but also by similarly spectacular retreats and setbacks. The military setbacks did not, however, lead to the complete destruction of the state. The survival of the Ottoman state was largely due to the fact that the main pillars of the state – including the institution of military slavery – had been established during the reigns of Murad I (1362–89) and Bajezid I. After the interregnum of 1402–13, Mehmed I (1413–21) and Murad II (1421–51) actively reconstructed the Ottoman state, the territory of which grew in size to cover more than 560 000 square kilometres.

THE ISLAMIC GUNPOWDER EMPIRE, 1453–1566

In the early modern period, much of the known world lay under Muslim rule. During the reign of Sultan Süleyman (1520–66) the Sunnite Ottoman Empire became the determining world power in the region. The land possessions of the Empire extended from Buda to Basra and from Algiers to Tabriz, a territory of 2.5 million square kilometres. The Black Sea became an 'Ottoman lake', and the Empire also controlled the eastern basin of the Mediterranean. The Ottomans' eastern neighbour was the Safavid Empire of Persia (1501–1732), which experienced its golden age during the reign of Shah Abbas I (1588–1629). From time to time the Shi'i Safavids played a role in maintaining the balance of power in Europe by virtue of the fact that, through their many wars against the Ottomans, they tied down the Ottoman military potential in the east. Even further to the east, the Great Mughal Empire was flourishing (1526–1720). This empire covered much of the Indian subcontinent, an area of 3.2 million square kilometres. It is generally accepted that artillery and gunpowder technology played a decisive role in the rise of these three empires. For this reason, they are commonly called 'Gunpowder Empires'.[3]

Islamic attitudes towards military technology

Scholars of European military history have traditionally held the opinion that the Islamic empires were reluctant to use firearms and European military technology, because these forms of weaponry had not been attested to in the time of the Prophet Mohammed and therefore counted as innovations that were incompatible with Islam (*bid'a*).

While it is true that such Orthodox views did (and do) exist within Islam, the political and religious leaders of the Islamic empires always managed to find a way around this dilemma. The Ottomans were pioneers in this. The Ottomans were far from being prisoners of the 'extreme conservatism of Islam' – as suggested by the traditional Eurocentric secondary literature – for they were quick to adopt western military technology and knowhow, and did so with a remarkable thoroughness. They also transmitted knowledge of these modern weapons and military techniques to their fellow Muslims and justified their use. A group of Ottoman religious scholars who supported the adoption of the eighteenth-century military reforms, for instance, elaborated a special ideology, the so-called theory of reciprocity (*mukabele bi'lmisl*), according to which the use and adoption of the enemy's modern weapons was allowed if such weapons were to be used to defeat the enemy. Meanwhile, during the reign of Shah Abbas, the Safavids were compelled by the Ottomans' military superiority to undertake radical military reforms, including the introduction of new infantry units equipped with muskets and the establishment of the corps of artillerymen. During the reign of Akbar (1556–1605) the Mughals, partly with the help of Ottoman military experts, also broke with the strict rules of Islam and established the most formidable artillery and army in the region. Military experts sent by the Ottomans acquainted both the Safavids and the Timurids with the *destur-i Rumi*, i.e. the Rumi or Ottoman order of (battle). This defensive arrangement, which consisted of wagons that were chained to each other and armed with guns and arquebuses, served as protection against cavalry attack. The arrangement was a version of the *Wagenburg*, and the Ottomans called it *tabur cengi* or 'camp battle'. This phrase was derived from the Hungarian *(szekér) tábor*, or 'wagon camp', which underlines the fact that the Ottomans learned the arrangement from the Hungarians in the course of their campaigns against János Hunyadi between 1441 and 1444.[4] Later, in the middle of the sixteenth century, Lazarus von Schwendi, the commander of the imperial forces in Hungary during the years 1564–68, observed that the Ottomans used the *Wagenburg* system very successfully against the Imperialists and that they owed their military success to the *tabur*. Consequently, he urged the Imperialists to use the *Wagenburg* constructed from war-chariots and furnished with double arquebuses as well as with small cannon.[5]

Although it would surely be a mistake to exaggerate the role played by military technology in a historical period in which temporary technological advantages seldom proved to be crucial in the longer run, it can hardly be denied that the Ottoman artillery and the devastating fire power of the Janissaries were crucial elements in the Ottomans' struggle against neighbouring states which possessed none or few of these means of military violence.

Army size, weaponry and tactics

The campaign of Mehmed II against Uzun Hasan in 1473 mobilised 100 000 men-at-arms, a body of men which included 64 000 timariot *sipahi*s, 12 000 Janissaries, 7500 cavalry of the Porte, and 20 000 *azab*s. The central imperial budget dated 1528 numbered some 120 000–150 000 members of the regular units, including 38 000 provincial *timar*-holders, 20 000–60 000 men-at-arms brought to the campaigns by the *timar*-holders, and 47 000 mercenaries (including 24 000 members of the salaried troops of the Porte and 23 000 fortress guards, *martalo*s and navy). These figures do not include the various auxiliary troops, who were the following: the *müsellem*s, who repaired the roads and bridges in front of the marching armies; the *yaya*s, who helped to transport the cannons; the *Yörük*s, who collected the draught animals and cast the cannon balls in the mines; the *cerehor*s, who performed various engineering work; the *akıncı* raiders; and the Tatar troops.[6]

Scholars of European military history continue to argue that the Ottoman artillery missed out on developments in European artillery from the mid-fifteenth century, and that whereas in

Europe emphasis was increasingly laid on the more mobile light field artillery, the Ottoman ordnance continued to be characterised by giant cannons. Recent research based on the unpublished accounts of the Ottoman state cannon foundry (*Tophane*) has shown that the Ottomans did possess all types of cannons that were available to their Christian enemies, and that the majority of the Ottoman cannons were small and medium calibre. Direct military conflicts, the employment of European renegades, and prohibited trade in weaponry all played a role in the transmission of Western military technology and created similarity in heavy weaponry.[7] The Ottomans started to employ hand firearms during the reign of Murad II, but they became widely used only under Mehmed II. By 1500 the Janissaries had become experts in the use of this new weapon. Bayezid II further increased the number of Janissaries and provided each of them with a considerably more effective weapon. The Janissaries used two types of guns. In siege warfare they employed the eight-sided or cylinder-barrelled heavy matchlock musket (*fitilli tüfek*) with a 130–160 cm-long firing tube. On the other hand, in field battles they used muskets of 120–135 cm in length, weighing 3–4.5 kg, which could be fired in a kneeling or standing position and did not need to be propped up, as is visible in a miniature depicting the battle of Mohács in 1526.[8] From the seventeenth century the Ottomans preferred to use flintlock fusils with the miguelet-lock (*çakmaklı tüfek*), which had been developed from the Spanish wheel-lock. Since early flintlocks were not as reliable as the matchlock (the flint became worn, hit the pan at the wrong angle, or fell out of the finger piece, and therefore failed to strike enough sparks to ignite the powder in the pan), the Ottomans also used combination locks, used also in European armies and known commonly on the continent as the 'Vauban lock' after about 1688. The Ottoman government attempted to provide other units of the Ottoman military with firearms, but the timariot cavalry began wearing pistols only in the mid-seventeenth century. The only provincial regular soldiers who employed firearms were the *tüfenkçi* horsemen and the infantry *müstahfiz* and *azab*s serving in the fortresses.

Both European and Turkish historians are generally of the view that the peculiar crescent-shaped Ottoman formation, the pretended flight, and the two-sided outflanking of the enemy were the significant factors in the victories of the Ottomans over their enemies. Nevertheless, we now have a growing literature suggesting that there were other factors (which varied from battle to battle, and were of varying significance) and causes (e.g. desertion, recognition and exploitation of topographical advantages, imbalances in the size of armies and their weaponry) which should also be taken into consideration. Indeed, it would seem that the role of these factors in determining the outcomes of battles was often equal to, or greater than, that of the mystified Ottoman tactics.[9]

The core zones

The period between 1453 and 1566 is usually called the classical age of the empire. It was during this era that the patrimonial world empire came into being and that the institutions of the Empire were formed and established. Although it had already been one of the props of the Ottoman state, the unigeniture first became commonplace during the reign of Mehmed II. The system of *kul-devirşme* continued to be one of the main supports of the Empire – particularly in times of crisis (e.g. in 1481 and in 1512), but the negative aspects of the system were also becoming apparent.

This was the period in which the Empire was able to consolidate its power in the core provinces and achieve its greatest expansion. The core provinces were the Balkan peninsula and Anatolia. Attached to this core was the so-called outer zone, which comprised the Asian provinces in the east and the Ottoman territories in Hungary located beyond the Danube and Sava rivers, two rivers which together formed the natural northern border of the Balkans. The next era was to be characterised by efforts made to retain this outer zone.

The natural centre of the core provinces was the new capital, Constantinople, a city which had been the seat of imperial traditions for more than a thousand years. After 1453 the new capital became the military and logistical centre of all military campaigns. The taking of Constantinople permitted a consolidation of earlier, uncertain conquests in both halves of the core zone. These areas were to remain integral parts of the Empire for many centuries. Crucial stages in this process were the occupations of

Serbia in 1459, of Bosnia in 1463, of the Morea peninsula in 1464, of Albania in 1468 after the death of Skanderbeg, and the occupation of Karamania in Asia Minor, also in 1468. As many historians have suggested, it is perhaps symptomatic that the collapse of the Empire came with the loss of its core areas in the Balkans in the late nineteenth and early twentieth centuries, and at the same time as the collapse of the former great rival of the Ottomans, Austria. Both conquest of the core zone and further conquests in Central Europe would have been unthinkable without a complete consolidation of power in the Black Sea region and in the Danube delta. These areas were brought under Ottoman control between 1454 and 1484.

Ottoman sea power

These achievements were closely related to the establishment of the Ottoman navy during the reign of Bayezid II (1481–1512). Without such a navy, both logistic support for subsequent campaigns against Central Europe or Iran and the supply of food and military hardware to the troops would have been impossible. It was their recognition of the importance of the sea and the decision to establish a navy which set the Ottomans apart from the other Muslim empires: the Ottoman Empire became a maritime power. The first steps towards transforming the Black Sea into an 'Ottoman lake' were taken during the reign of Mehmed II: in the south, the Ottomans had occupied the northern coastal region of Asia Minor by 1461 (Amasra in 1459, Isfendiyar and the Empire of Trebizond – the last Christian state in the East – in 1461), and in the north, they conquered Caffa and the Crimea by 1475. Ottoman naval supremacy in the eastern Mediterranean helped to eradicate piracy and to establish favourable conditions for maritime trade. At the same time, the Ottomans used their naval power to subjugate the Mameluke Kingdom even before they occupied Cairo. Indeed, the existence of a navy facilitated the Ottomans' conquest of a vast area that extended from Syria through Egypt to Morocco; they were also able to expel the Portuguese from the Red Sea. According to a report submitted by the *Bailo* of Istanbul, Andrea Gritti, Bayezid II had at least 150 ships of different types at his disposal in ports across the Empire (Galata, Gallipoli, Avlonya in the Adriatic and Volissa on the western side of Chios). At the beginning of the sixteenth century, apart from the Ottoman Empire, only Venice and the Knights of Rhodes possessed regular fleets in the Mediterranean.[10] But in the Indian Ocean the Ottoman effort to counter the Portuguese and to help Muslim rulers in their fight against the Westerners met with only limited success, because their Mediterranean galleys designed for close-in fighting proved vulnerable to the long-range weapons of the heavy-gunned Atlantic ships, and because the Mediterranean style of naval warfare, of which the Ottomans were experts, was becoming obsolescent in open waters.[11]

Expansion on all fronts

This was the period of spectacular expansion: the area of the Empire increased from 560 000 square kilometres under Murad II to 860 000 square kilometres under Mehmed II. On 23 August 1514, at the battle of Çaldıran, Selim's artillery and Janissary musketeers routed the Persian army. In 1516 his forces occupied Diyarbekir and annexed eastern Anatolia. In the same year an Ottoman artillery force routed the Mameluke army at Marj Dabık, north of Aleppo. In 1517, at the Battle of Ridaniyya near Cairo, Selim defeated the last Mameluke ruler, Tumanbay (1516–17), and proceeded to establish his rule over Egypt and Syria. Meanwhile the sharif of Mecca, fearing a Portuguese invasion, recognised Selim's authority over the Hejaz.

In 1521 Süleyman occupied the key to the Hungarian defence system in the south, Nándorfehérvár/Belgrade, and in 1526 he completely defeated the obselete Hungarian feudal army at the Battle of Mohács. In 1541 Süleyman occupied the capital of Hungary, Buda, and annexed the central part of the country to the Empire. In the campaign of 1534–36, the sultan occupied Tabriz and Baghdad. In 1546 the governor-general of Baghdad occupied Basra, and thus the Ottomans gained access to the Persian Gulf and the Indian Ocean. In 1555, in the year of the Peace of Augsburg between the various Christian confessions, a peace treaty was signed at Amasya by the highest leaders of Sunni and Shi'i Islam. Iraq, Kurdistan and the larger part of Armenia fell under Süleyman's rule at this time. Selim's conquests increased the area of the Empire to 1.5 million square kilometres. Under Süleyman, the total area of the Ottoman state reached 2.3

million square kilometres. A population of 12–13 million at the
beginning of the sixteenth century grew to perhaps 20 million
(others suggest 30–35 million) at the close of the century.[12] At that
time the Empire's total population was certainly above the 15–17
million threshold which Julius Beloch and Fernand Braudel have
suggested was a necessary condition for great power status in this
period.

Military self-sufficiency

The Empire was an *'économie monde'*, and, unlike many of its
rivals, was self-sufficient in the production of weaponry and
ammunition. With the exception of tin, the Ottomans possessed
all the necessary raw materials to cast ordnance and to supply the
artillery with cannonballs and gunpowder. Iron was excavated in
large quantities at three locations: Bilecik, Kiği near Erzurum
and Keban. In the European part of the Empire, there were iron
mines in Samakov (present-day Bulgaria), in Kamegrad (Bosnia),
in Novo Brodo and Rudnik (Serbia), and in Praviste near Kavala
(present-day Greece). There were important copper mines at
Küre in the district of Kastamonu and at Ergani, Keban and
Gümüşhane in Anatolia. There were further copper mines in
Rumelia (Ustovo, Petkovo, Skopje, Prištine, Sarajevo, Čiprovic,
Kratovo and Majdanek). Next to these mines, furnaces were in
operation making hundreds of thousand of cannonballs.[13]

Wood and charcoal needed to operate the war industry plants
and used in the construction of ships and fortresses could easily
be obtained from the wooded areas of the Empire. Most of the
wood came from the forests along the Black Sea coast. Wood for
the workshops in Istanbul came from a section of the European
coast that extended from Istanbul to Varna and from a section of
the Asian coast from Istanbul to Samsun.

The Empire also disposed of plentiful applies of the raw mate-
rials needed for the manufacture of gunpowder. Large quantities
of saltpetre were to be found in Egypt (especially in Old Cairo),
in Syria, in Lebanon, in Palestine and in Iraq (especially in the
Basra area). Saltpetre was also to be found in Asia Minor
(Karaman, Malatya, İçel and the region of Van) and in the
European part of the Empire (Thessalonica, Plovdiv, Monastir,
Skopje, Temesvár, the Morea, and Karasu in the Crimea). The

main sources of sulphur, which was the other main constituent of gunpowder, were located in the vicinity of the Dead Sea, in the region of Van, at Hakkari, in Moldavia and on the island of Melos. There were gunpowder factories in Istanbul, Gallipoli, Thessalonica, Izmir, Belgrade, Buda, Temesvár, Bor in the province of Karaman, Van, Ercis, Cairo, Baghdad, Aleppo, etc. These powdermills were capable of manufacturing the required quantity of gunpowder. In short, the Empire did not have any 'difficulty in mass-producing', and was not dependent on the import of European weaponry and ammunition, as has been suggested by many European historians.[14]

European observers clearly understood that the strength of the Ottoman military lay in the abundant material and human resources of the Empire. After Lepanto, Spanish and Venetian military experts therefore proposed the burning of forests used by the Ottomans in the construction of their navy. During the Cretan wars the Venetian secret service employed some of the means of chemical and biological warfare (e.g. they poisoned wells and pasture lands) and elaborated a plan to spread the plague among the Ottoman army stationed at Candia and in other parts of the Empire. The incredible wealth of the Empire's natural and human resources is well demonstrated by the speed of Ottoman rearmament after Lepanto, including the rapid construction of a fleet of 200 new galleys armed with a total of 20 000 arquebusiers within a period of six months. 'I should never have believed the greatness of this monarchy, had I not seen it with my own eyes', wrote François de Noailles, Charles IX's ambassador to the Porte.[15]

THE EMPIRE ON THE DEFENSIVE, 1566–1699

Scholars of Ottoman history used to portray the century and a half after 1566 as a period of both decline and decentralisation, and of the collapse of the 'world order' (*nizam-i alem*) of the Süleymanic 'golden age', that is, as a period in which the classical institutions of the Empire, above all the army and the system of ownership and taxation on which this army was based, were degenerating and cracks were beginning to appear in the functional stratification of society, and as a time of increasing

favouritism and corruption. Military defeat suffered at the hands
of the troops of the Holy League, and the loss of the Hungarian
territories at the end of the seventeenth century were seen as
direct consequences of the general economic, social and military
decline. More recently, historians have tended to use the words
crisis or change instead of decline, emphasising factors such as
the economic, financial and military changes, as well as the
cautious reforms which enabled the Ottoman Empire to endure
for at least three hundred years despite the shifts in power.[16]

In military terms, the period was characterised by the defence
of earlier conquests rather than by territorial expansion. The
main aim of the campaigns and wars of this era was to defend the
Empire or to restore the *status quo*. In contrast to the wars of
earlier periods, these campaigns did not result in an increase in
territory. The conquests of the Köprülü grand viziers represent
an exception to this rule, but of these conquests only Crete
remained in Ottoman hands in the longer term (nominally until
1913).

Power relations on all three fronts became more balanced in
the course of this period, and on all fronts the Ottoman army
reached the furthest extent of its *action radius*. From the second
half of the seventeenth century, owing to the advances of the
'military revolution', the European adversaries of the Ottomans
were capable of putting up an army that was similar in size to the
Ottomans'. In addition, these European troops were of a higher
quality than the Ottoman troops. The situation of the Ottomans
was rendered more serious by the fact that these changes were
accompanied by the ending of Ottoman conquests, a series of
economic and social problems associated with the end of expansion, and a decline in the quality of the Ottoman army.

As in Western Europe, wars became longer and increasingly
exhausting: on the Danubian frontier, the 'Long War' of 1593–
1606, the war in Transylvania (1658–60), and the war fought
against the Holy League (1683–99); on the eastern frontier, the
Iranian wars of 1570–92, 1603–11, and 1623–39; and in the
Mediterranean, the Cretan wars of 1645–99.

The cost of the frontier zone

The conquered territories did not increase the resources of
the state treasury; on the contrary, these territories required

subsidies from the centre. Everywhere the border zones were loss-making. A large part of income from the provinces of Aleppo, Diyarbekir and Erzurum was spent in neighbouring, former Iranian territories which had been occupied by the Ottomans. The largest expenses were incurred on the Danubian frontier, where the Habsburgs, after establishing the Aulic War Council (*Hofkriegsrat*) in 1556, strengthened and modernised the Hungarian defence system according to the new mode of *trace italienne*. This action effectively prevented any further Ottoman expansion. As a consequence, the Hungarian frontier became rigid, and the Ottomans were required to station a disproportionately large number of soldiers in Hungary to defend their positions.[17] By the second half of the sixteenth century, no less than 25 000 soldiers (including 18 000 garrison soldiers and 7000 *timar*-holder cavalry) were stationed in the two Hungarian provinces; in the 1520s, a similar number of soldiers had defended the fortresses of the entire Balkan peninsula. By 1613 some 73 per cent of an estimated 38 000 Ottoman garrison troops were stationed in Hungary and Bosnia.[18]

Only a fraction of the cost of providing for such a disproportionately large army could be covered by the province. In the fiscal year 1558–59 the revenue of the province of Buda covered just 28 per cent of salaries paid to the soldiers stationed on the Hungarian frontier, and only 38 per cent in the following year. By the 1570s, owing to the extension of the Ottoman administration and territorial expansion, revenues had been increased. In the province of Buda local revenues now covered 90 per cent of the soldiers' pay, and a subsidy from the neighbouring province of Temesvár rendered the Hungarian frontier self-sufficient. This was a substantial achievement, considering that, on the other side of the frontier, the local revenues received by the Habsburgs covered just 30–40 per cent of the salaries of the soldiers serving in the Hungarian border fortresses.[19] Still, the Long War of 1593–1606 radically altered the economic and financial situation on the Hungarian frontier. Before the war 70–90 per cent of Buda Treasury income was of local origin, but during the war this figure dwindled to just 17 per cent. Of the revenue of the province of Kanizsa (established in 1600), almost 90 per cent came from the central Treasury. In the seventeenth century the Hungarian provinces were provided for by the Balkans.[20]

*The Long War of 1593–1606; the challenge of
the European military revolution*

Unlike the majority of the European wars (but similarly to earlier
Habsburg–Ottoman conflicts in Hungary), the Long War was
largely a war of sieges. Neither of the warring parties made
substantial territorial gains in the course of the war. The
Ottomans did occupy Eger (1596) and Kanizsa (1600), with these
two towns becoming the centres of two new Ottoman provinces.
Meanwhile, in 1598, the Christians reoccupied Győr, the 'gateway to Germany', which had been captured by the Ottomans in
1594; they also successfully defended Várad, the 'gateway to
Transylvania'. In 1606 a peace treaty was signed 'in a camp
located between the Danube and Zsitva rivers' between the
Ottomans and the Habsburgs on the basis of the *status quo*. Unrest
on both sides of the frontier – the Celali rebellion and the Bocskai
uprising (1604–06) – were factors that encouraged both parties to
sign the Peace of Zsitva-torok.

Recent research has revealed the logistical strength of the
Ottoman army during the Long War. Owing to an efficient
supply system, the army continued to receive food, fodder and
provisions during the war. There were few shortages of supplies
even when Transylvania and the two Romanian principalities
were temporarily annexed by the Habsburgs. Two rivers, the
Danube and the Tisza, which both flow from north to south,
greatly facilitated the transport of provisions, weaponry and war
materials. The movement of goods along these rivers was supervised by the Ottoman river fleet. Heavy weaponry, gunpowder,
shots and *matériel* were transported across the Black Sea to
Varna. From there the supplies was taken in wagons or on
draught animals to Belgrade or to any other port on the Danube,
where hundreds of *şaykas* waited to forward the consignments on
water. In contrast to soldiers in the service of the Habsburgs or
the other European powers, the Ottoman soldiers received their
salaries on time.[21]

The war did, however, expose the weaknesses of the Ottoman
army. In the winter of 1593–94, exploiting the 'Turks' incapacity
to fight in the winter', an incapacity which had been revealed by
Hans Rueber, captain-general in Upper Hungary (1568–84) as
early as 1577, the Christians succeeded in reoccupying a large

and connected piece of territory, including the castles of Nográd county. The only major field battle of the war at Mezőkeresztes (1596) clearly demonstrated the firepower superiority of the Christian troops. As early as in 1577, at a military conference gathered in Vienna to discuss the strategy to be employed against the Ottomans in the decades to come, counsellors were of the opinion that 'for the time being, hand firearms are the main advantage of Your Majesty's military over this enemy' (i.e. the Ottomans). Research in recent years has shown that during the war the armoury of the imperial Habsburg legions, as well as their composition, were very similar to those of the forces fighting in Flanders, and that the proportion of infantry soldiers carrying firearms (this figure is usually considered to be one of the main indicators of the so-called military revolution) was as high as in the Netherlands (in some units this figure reached 75 per cent). This firepower was further strengthened by the Hungarian Heyducks and garrison soldiers, who were also equipped with firearms. In addition, it has been shown that the tactics of these troops were already based on firepower. The firepower superiority of the Imperialists was noted by the Grand Vizier himself and by other Ottoman contemporaries.[22]

The Ottoman government attempted to counterbalance in two ways. First, they increased the number of arms-bearing Janissaries. Second, they established formations of arms-bearing infantry generally known as *sekban*. However, the increasing numbers led to a rapid fall in standards. In addition, the salary burden was a source of financial distress in an empire that already suffered from a cash-flow problem.

Table 5.1 *Increases in the number of Janissaries, 1567–1680*[23]

Fiscal year	Number of Janissaries
1567–68	12 798
1609	37 627
1660–61	54 222
1665	49 556
1669	51 437
1670	49 868
1680	54 222

The establishment of the *sekban* troops was to have other draw-backs in the longer term. As a result of the economic and social changes of the sixteenth century, details of which will not be covered here, thousands of peasants became deprived of home and country, and many of these became outlaws possessing fire-arms – despite all efforts on the part of the state to ban or restrict the use of firearms. During the Iranian and Hungarian wars the government welcomed with open arms soldiers who knew how to use firearms and who could be recruited for a campaign or two and then discharged. However, these *sekbans* did not return to their villages after the campaigns. Instead, they joined the bandits or supported the uprisings in Anatolia. Ottomanists used to see a connection between the Celali rebellions and the Long War in Hungary; they considered the war to have been a major cause of the unrest. It is now known that the Anatolian rebellions began some time before the Long War, and that the vast majority of *sekbans* taken on in the war were not from Anatolia, but from Bosnia and from Albania, and therefore could not have been involved in the Anatolian rebellions. Nevertheless, the war did have an important indirect effect on the Ottoman military: the Habsburg firepower superiority increased the demand for fire-arms and for men-at-arms able to use them. In the end these measures led to a weakening of the army. The government used the Janissaries to put down the rebellions and, with this action, set the two main elements of the Empire's armed forces against each another.[24]

Growing sizes, growing expenses

Human and material resources that had once seemed inexhaust-ible were no longer enough to finance the increased number of salaried units and the drawn-out wars: from 1592 the imperial treasury finished each year with a deficit.

Table 5.2 reflects the results of consolidation measures intro-duced by the Köprülü grand viziers, Mehmed Köprülü (1651–61) and Köprülüzade Fazil Ahmed (1661–76). These measures did succeed in reducing the deficit, while also permitting the construction and arming of the fleet and financing of the Cretan war. What followed – the suppression of the rebellion of Abaza Hasan Pasha (1658), the conquests in Hungary (Jenő, Karánsebes, and Lugos in 1658, Várad in 1660 and Érsekújvár/

Table 5.2 *Deficit in Ottoman budgets in* akça, *not including* timar *revenues, 1565–1701*[25]

Fiscal year	Revenue	Expenditure	Difference
1565–66	183 088 000	189 657 000	−6 569 000
1567–68	348 544 150	221 532 453	+127 011 697
1582–83	313 744 645	277 578 755	+36 165 890
1592–93	293 400 000	363 400 000	−70 000 000
1597–98	300 000 000	900 000 000	−600 000 000
1608	503 691 446	599 191 446	−95 500 000
1643–44	514 467 015	513 817 970	+649 045
1650	532 900 000	687 200 000	−154 300 000
1652–53	517 271 470	528 862 971	−11 591 500
1654	537 356 433	658 358 459	−121 002 026
1661–62	581 270 828	593 604 361	−12 333 533
1666–67	553 429 239	631 861 656	−78 432 417
1669	612 528 960	637 206 348	−24 677 388
1687–88	700 357 065	901 003 350	−200 646 285
1690–91	565 751 408	812 878 365	−247 126 957
1691–92	818 188 665	950 246 521	−132 057 856
1692–93	828 373 518	919 012 036	−90 638 518
1693–94	797 446 775	922 173 910	−152 799 750
1694–95	946 680 191	1 114 192 325	−167 512 134
1696–97	938 672 901	1 096 178 240	−157 505 339
1698–99	1 147 718 378	1 211 379 266	−63 560 888
1700–01	1 173 142 514	1 109 781 204	+63 361 310

Neuhausel in 1663), and the conquests of Candia (1669) and Podolia (1672–76) – were successes on a scale not seen for over half a century.

Encouraged by these successes, the grand vizier, Kara Mustafa (1676–83) launched his campaign against Vienna. He undertook this action even though, as the limited achievements of the 1678–81 Russian–Ottoman war had demonstrated, he did not possess the fortune or skill of his predecessors. The events of the Holy League War of 1683–99 were proof that the Köprülü grand viziers were not capable of performing miracles, and that the Christian armies, which had been reformed in the course of the Thirty Years War, were now able to defeat the Ottomans. The Ottomans were at a disadvantage because in the course of the Hungarian siege wars they had been given little opportunity to acquaint themselves with the reformed warfare and military tactics of the Europeans – the battle of Szentgotthárd (1664) was

Gábor Ágoston

the only exception to this. And yet knowledge of these reforms soon became essential, for after 1683 siege warfare was superseded by field battles; indeed, fifteen major field battles took place in the fifteen years between 1683 and 1697. The Ottomans won just two of these battles; one battle ended in stalemate and all others were won by the allies. The Ottomans suffered their greatest defeats at Nagyharsány in 1687 – a battle referred to as the Second Mohács because it took place just 25 km from Mohács, at Szalánkemén in 1691, at 'the most bloody battle of the century', and at Zenta in 1697. Troops of the *Liga Sacra*, which had been formed in 1684, were victorious in all three battles. The allied forces proceeded to reoccupy Érsekújvar in 1685, Buda in 1686, Kanizsa in 1690 and Várad in 1692.

The war required the mobilisation of larger amounts of material and human resources than ever before. Owing to the peculiarities of the Ottoman fiscal administration, it is impossible to estimate the Ottomans' military expenses. The Ottoman central imperial budgets contain only the cash revenues and cash expenses, and therefore exclude the soldiers paid by the provincial treasury, the *timar*-holder cavalry, and major items relating to the provision of food, fodder, weaponry and war materials. The majority of these latter expenses were not paid for in cash, but were financed out of various tax-farm incomes and through the *ocaklık* system.[26] Nevertheless, the central imperial budgets do provide some data which can be used to demonstrate the increasing military expenses (see Table 5.3).

Table 5.3 *Army size and military expenditure, 1687–1701*[27]

Fiscal year	Central troops	Garrison soldiers	Total number of soldiers	Soldiers' pay (in akça)	% of total expenditure
1687–88	58974	–	–	440431988	48.88
1690–91	69247	–	–	458474172	56.40
1691–92	59956	74280	134236	495379604	52.13
1692–93	62593	70351	132944	503172351	54.75
1693–94	79786	–	–	527255974	57.17
1694–95	114012	75971	189983	648013576	58.15
1696–97	107403	77168	184571	60399096	55.09
1698–99	103913	86395	190308	668041167	55.14
1700–01	81853	87310	169163	636569460	57.35

The exhausted empire suffered its first major loss of territory at Karlowitz in 1699: reoccupied Hungary (excluding the Temes region) and Transylvania were handed over to the Habsburgs. Meanwhile Venice received the Morea; Poland was granted Kaminiecz; and Russia, which had joined the Holy League in 1686, was awarded Azov.

RETREAT AND REFORM, 1699–1826

Eighteenth-century Ottoman military history is characterised by the Habsburg–Russian–Ottoman confrontation, the slow but continuous loss of territory and cautious and insufficient reforms. The wars fought against the traditional enemies of the Ottomans (the Venetians, Habsburgs and Persians) in the first half of the century brought mixed results, while the wars against the Russians in the second half of the century ended in a series of devastating defeats. In the first half of the century, failure on the battlefield led to domestic political unrest; there were two rebellions, resulting in the dethronement of two Ottoman sultans (Mustafa II in 1703 and Ahmed III in 1730). In the second half of the century, the price of failure was even higher: exploiting the absence of the army – which was weighed down on the Russian front – various provincial notables (*a'yan*), whose power rested in part on their public function and in part on land ownership (*çiftlik*), detached themselves from the centre. By the end of the century some of them, including Ali Tepedelenli Pasha, the 'Lion of Yanina', Pazvantoğlu of Vidin, and the Karaosmanoğlu family of western Anatolia, were in possession of their own private fiefdoms and armies and had even begun to pursue their own foreign policy and foreign trade. At the beginning of the nineteenth century the central administration lost control of many of the outer zones: e.g. the Wahhabit religious sect, led by the Saudi emirs, took control of Medina (1804) and of Mecca (1806). Meanwhile Ottoman power in Egypt was challenged by the Mamluk emirs and by the invasion of the French (1789–1802). Finally, in 1805, Mehmed Ali, an Albanian mercenary of the Porte, seized power in Egypt. Relying upon his European-style army, Mehmed was to remain in power for 40 years. Even in the core provinces the power of the Empire was under threat. The Serb uprising of

1804 marked the beginning of a series of wars of national liberation. By the 1820s both Serbia and Greece, as well as Egypt, had become, in effect, independent.

In their first major war of the century, the war against the Venetian–Habsburg Alliance in 1716–18, the Ottomans suffered a great defeat at Pétervárad. Subsequent territorial losses included the Banat of Temesvár, the western regions of both Wallachia and Serbia, Belgrade and most of Bosnia. On the other hand, the Ottomans did succeed in reconquering the whole of Morea from Venice. Furthermore, in a new war against the Habsburgs in 1737–39 they won back Belgrade and the northern Balkan territories. Thereafter the Habsburgs retreated behind the Military Frontier which had been built along the southern border of Hungary.[28] Subsequently, the two empires attempted to avoid open war. The Habsburg forces were preoccupied with the War of Austrian Succession (1740–48) and the Seven Years War (1756–63), while the Ottomans, who had fortified their own fortresses on the other side of the Military Frontier in the first decades of the century, were engaged in increasingly hopeless and costly wars against Russia, a country which had become their main adversary (the wars of 1736–39, 1768–74, 1787–92 and 1806–12).

By the second half of the eighteenth century, Russia, whose territorial gains at the end of the Holy League war of 1683–1699/ 1700 had been disappointingly few, was rapidly turning into one of the great European powers. The Russian army, which had been thoroughly reformed under Peter the Great, was superior to the Ottoman army in terms of numbers of soldiers and weaponry. Whereas the Ottomans were still able to defeat a Russian army at Prut in 1711, they could not prevent a more skilful Russian army, which was nevertheless hampered by poor supplies and epidemics, from penetrating the Crimea in the war of 1736–39. Indeed, it was only French diplomatic intervention which saved the Crimea from Russian occupation at this time. Under the terms of the Peace of Belgrade, Russia, which had lost 100 000 soldiers in the war, was allowed to keep just Azak/ Azov; for the time being, Russia had to forgo its main ambition – namely, a fleet on the Black Sea. It was not until the Peace of Kucuk Kaynarca that this ambition was fulfilled. This treaty – signed following the catastrophic defeat of the Ottomans in the war of 1768–74 – was the most humiliating in Ottoman history.

THE RUSSIAN–OTTOMAN WAR,1768–74

This war demonstrated both the strength of the Russian army and the weaknesses of the Ottomans. It saw an unprecedented mobilisation for both empires: Russia stationed 100 000 men in the Danube region and 60 000 in Poland. The Ottomans mobilised some 60 000 Janissaries, 145 000 *toprakli* cavalry and 100 000 undisciplined Tatars. Russia, which was maintaining Europe's largest standing army (about 450 000 in the 1760s) on revenues which were equivalent in amount to just one-fifth of those of France, relied upon conscription. All male Russians were subject to the draft, and in the course of the century approximately 2.4 million were actually conscripted (24 000 per year on average). The Ottomans maintained two armies: the standing army located in Istanbul and in the fortresses, and the *miri levendat*, 'a combination of volunteerism, village conscription and bribery'. The transition to a system of conscription was still incomplete at the end of the century. A lack of leadership and problems of discipline continued to plague the Ottoman army.[29]

By European standards both empires were making war on the cheap; but the burden was still a large one for their weak economies. The Ottoman soldiers were better fed than the Russians, and the supply of provisions was, in general, better among the Ottomans than among the Russians – although neither empire was immune to famine and disease. The Ottomans' state commissioners bought grain and transported it to the battlefront. These men were the equivalents of the French munitionaires, but they often bought cheap, poor quality grain, and filled their own pockets with the money that was left over. The Ottomans were fighting out of their own territory; the soldiers and supplies were brought from the neighbouring provinces in the Balkans and increasingly from eastern Anatolia. In general, military supply was of good quality.[30] Nevertheless, the traditional Ottoman system was wasteful and by the 1770s production in the industrial workshops could no longer keep pace with ever-increasing demand; gunpowder, for instance, had to be imported. A further problem was the transport of supplies ever great distances. Between 1769 and 1773, 8500–9000 oxen, 9500–14000 camels and 6500–7000 horses and mules were hired by the state annually.[31]

War and Economy

In the first half of the eighteenth century, all sectors of the Ottoman economy were growing. At the centre for iron production in the district of Sofia-Samakov, 80 furnaces were in operation around 1720. In the 1730s a whole series of new furnaces were brought into use. By 1760 the local authorities were even requesting that the government withhold licences for further furnaces, because soon all forests in the area would be exhausted. Similar progress was achieved in the agricultural sector, and prohibitions on the export of certain goods (e.g. grain, leather, cotton and wool) were lifted.

The economy was exhausted by the Russian wars. In the 1790s production at the Samakov furnaces came to a halt owing to the outbreak of epidemics, which habitually accompany wars and cause greater destruction than weapons. The forsaken mines fell into the possession of the 'mountain rebels', who were the peculiar creation of war and disorder in the Balkans, and the centre lost the furnaces for good. The export of raw materials was once again prohibited, and new prohibitions were placed on the export of dressed leather and various fabrics. Price increases between 1760 and 1800 reached 200 per cent.[32]

Annual state expenditure rose by 30 per cent between 1761 and 1785 (from 14064788 silver *guruş* in 1761 to 18693336 in 1785), but in the war years there was a 100 per cent increase. Soldiers' salaries comprised 75 per cent of expenditure in 1784 and 74 per cent in 1785. Meanwhile state revenues remained at much the same level, and efforts to increase revenue failed owing to the general economic stagnation. The lack of financial resources prevented the Ottomans from reacting immediately when the Russians annexed the Crimea in 1783. The Ottoman leaders fully understood that new troops were needed for the war, but the treasury was unable to finance the payment of additional salaries. The senior accountant at the treasury stated that 15 million gurus were needed to begin the war, an amount equal to the treasury's total annual revenue. Meanwhile the Grand Admiral estimated the costs of building a battle fleet at 6–7.5 million *guruş*; he also considered the drafting of 36 000 troops necessary.[33] Under such circumstances, it is no surprise that the Porte waited until 1787 before launching its campaign.

Reforms

Ibrahim Müteferrika (1674–1754), the Hungarian renegade and founder of the Arabic letterpress in the Empire, began urging for reforms as early as in 1732. In his work, he revealed those characteristics which, in his opinion, ensured the strength of the European armies, and argued that it was precisely the absence of these elements which lay at the root of Ottoman military weakness. He praised the structure of the Christian armies, the balanced proportions of infantry, cavalry and dragoons, and the excellent co-operation between these groups. Other lauded qualities included superior methods of training and drilling soldiers, discipline, the high proportion of officers (at least 25 per cent), the competency of the high command, the order and defence of the camps, military intelligence and counter-intelligence, 'geometric' troop formations, 'la manière de combattre' and volley technique to maintain continuous fire. Muteferrika regarded the Petrine military reform as an example worthy of imitation, and he also drew attention to the construction of the Russian fleet, which had enabled the Russians to bring the Caspian Sea under their control.[34] His evaluation repeated many of the conclusions of other contemporary European observers, including Luigi Ferdinando Marsigli or Maréchal de Saxe. In 1732 the latter had claimed that 'it is not valour, numbers or wealth that they (the Ottomans) lack; it is order, discipline and technique'.[35] The secrets of success, in Müteferrika's opinion, were military organisation and the transmission of order and discipline, in other words, the introduction of a new order (*nizam-i cedid*).

The reforms that followed were nevertheless limited to the Bombardier Corps under the leadership of the French renegade Pasha Ahmed Bonneval. The Ottoman leadership declined to implement widespread fundamental reforms, fearing that such reforms would endanger the entire social fabric. Drastic reforms were attempted only after the disastrous failures of the Russian war of 1787–92. Selim III put forward a plan for the establishment of a new type of army on the European model. These plans met with the resistance of the traditionally privileged *askeri* class (particularly the Janissary–*ulema* alliance). The New Model Army (which had been established with one regiment of 2536 men, but had grown to some 25 000 men by 1808) was dissolved. True reforms had to wait until after the liquidation of the Janissary Corps (1826). As had been predicted, these reforms sparked off profound and unforeseen social changes.[36]

6. The Development of Russian Military Power 1453–1815

BRIAN L. DAVIES

I

Until the middle of the fifteenth century the grand princes of Moscow had directly controlled only a small household military force (*dvor*), consisting of their boyar retinue and their boyars' own retainers (the *dvoriane* and *deti boiarskie*). During emergencies, this could be augmented by forming an improvised peasant militia, and by invoking treaty obligations to call up the retinues of the princes of cadet lines of Moscow's Danilovich house and those of the other clans of princes ruling their own independent principalities. But the grand prince did not yet possess the power to force allied princes to come to his aid, even when it might be politically inconvenient for them; hence the boyar oligarchs of Novgorod and Pskov and the princes of Tver', Riazan' and Suzdal' gave no assistance to Dmitrii Donskoi when he faced the Golden Horde at Kulikovo in 1380.[1]

It was the civil war of 1425–53 that finally enabled Moscow Grand Prince Vasilii II to acquire a near-monopoly of armed force. The war destroyed Vasilii's most powerful rivals for the title of grand prince and led to the annexation of their patrimonies and the takeover of their retinues. Other princes, already weakened economically through generations of partible inheritance, now found their lands so devastated they had no choice but to seek survival as his vassals. The few remaining independent princes were forced to pay Moscow a heavy tribute that left them too little revenue to maintain sizeable military retinues; Tver' principality, once Moscow's most serious rival, was left unable to field more than 600 men.[2] As the grand prince's *dvor* expanded and the number of alternative centres for magnate allegiance

145

dwindled, Vasilii II and his successors Ivan III (r. 1462–1505) and Vasilii III (r. 1505–33) gradually transformed vassalage into a less reciprocal and more servile form of subordination by abolishing the right of a vassal to leave service and seek another lord; and once a prince's or boyar's departure could be equated with treasonable defection, it became possible to immobilise in turn the entire network of his kinsmen and clients by forcing them to sign collective surety bonds on his loyalty, pledging to pay large fines or even forfeit their lives if their lord should try to flee the grand prince's service. Meanwhile, the accelerated territorial expansion of Moscow principality – which more than tripled under Ivan III, to an area of 600 000 square miles – made available greater means for co-opting other princes and boyars, who could be assigned the temporary right to collect cash and provender 'feedings' from the provincial taxpayers they now governed as vicegerents (*namestniki*) on behalf of the grand prince. Muscovite expansion beyond the Volga and westward into the Smolensk and Seversk regions also encouraged many Tatar and Lithuanian nobles to defect and enter the service of the grand prince.

Since so many of these new members of the grand prince's *dvor* were formerly independent princes of exalted and even foreign lineage, some way had to be found to fit them within the same service hierarchy as the less genealogically exalted but longer-serving Moscow boyar retainers, without injuring the clan honour of the former or denigrating the service loyalty of the latter. By the early sixteenth century an elaborate system of precedence ranking (*mestnichestvo*) had arisen to integrate the status claims of these two groups. It sometimes led to complicated precedence litigation over regimental command appointments that might slow campaign mobilisations, or resulted in command assignments that owed more to seniority than to actual military experience, but on the whole *mestnichestvo* proved essential to the construction of Muscovite autocracy. It rewarded the Moscow boyars for their generations of loyal service while simultaneously giving enough recognition to clan honour to reconcile the titled princes to the service of the grand prince, offering the latter status and offices in exchange for the surrender of their sociopolitical autonomy. In fact it made use of clan honour to reinforce the service ethos, by holding that an individual's demotion in rank or failure to serve lowered the precedence of his kinsmen and descendants. *Mestnichestvo* thereby transformed the *dvor* into a more cohesive and loyal upper service class whose members' social status derived far more from the performance of state service than could be said of any European nobility. Remembering the chaos of the first half of the fifteenth century, and largely satisfied with the way in which *mestnichestvo* distributed the greater political spoils made possible by Muscovite expansion, this upper service class saw little reason not to collaborate with the grand prince in the construction of an 'autocratic' court culture.[3]

The transformation of the provincial petty nobility into a middle service class – which would provide the bulk of the grand prince's army – began in 1478, when Ivan III took advantage of the 'treasonable' political resistance of Novgorod's boyars and archbishop to carry out a mass confiscation of their estates, which were redistributed as *pomest'ia* to 2000 of his junior retainers. The *pomest'e* was a new form of land tenure – service-conditional, unlike the larger allodial estates of the upper service class. *Pomest'e* service landholding spread through Riazan', Pskov, Smolensk and the other territories annexed by Moscow over the next few decades; those assigned *pomest'e* grants in exchange for their military service to the grand prince included many formerly independent but now impoverished princes and boyars and their manumitted slaves and former free retainers (*deti boiarskie*).

This extension of the state service principle from the metropolitan nobility to the petty provincial nobility gave the grand prince the ability to field armies that were significantly larger and more politically reliable. The remaining great appanage princes like the Vorotynskiis and Bel'skiis continued to bring their own private detachments into the grand prince's host, but these were comparatively small. From the 1450s we typically find the grand prince's army taking the field in either a Small or Large Array of three or five *polki* or regiments: his *dvor* turned out as the Great, or 'Sovereign's', Regiment (about 2700 men by the early sixteenth century), while the middle service class formed Advance, Rearguard, Left-Wing and Right-Wing regiments commanded by the leading service princes and boyars; the huge baggage train was in turn guarded by large numbers of their slaves and peasants. On particularly major campaigns the army could be further enlarged with cavalry auxiliaries provided by service Tatars and other non-Russian tributary peoples, and by a peasant militia serving as irregular infantry and sappers.

The reigns of Vasilii II, Ivan III and Vasilii III saw fewer full-scale mobilisations and less protracted campaigns than the reign of Ivan IV, however, and until 1512, when the practice of annually stationing regiments along the banks of the Ugra and Oka began, Muscovite defence strategy found large force concentrations along a broad front unnecessary; it was considered enough to deploy small forces near a few fortified points athwart the roads traditionally used by the invading Crimean Tatars or Lithuanians, to slow the enemy's advance and give Moscow time to mobilise. Therefore, the enhanced resource mobilisation power of the grand prince did not immediately lead to huge field armies, despite the claims of Soviet historians, who uncritically accepted the estimates made in Russian chronicles and the accounts of foreign observers. It was highly unlikely that Vasilii III could mobilise 175 000 men in 1517 as the Pole Maciej Miechowita claimed, even with auxiliaries and baggage-train personnel thrown in. The earliest Muscovite military deployment records are not of much help in assessing army size; they list only command appointments and do not report regimental strengths. But A. N. Kirpichnikov and Dianne Smith are probably correct in arguing that logistics and the structure of command kept Muscovite field armies to a maximum of 35 000 men throughout the sixteenth century, and the total strength of the Muscovite armed forces under Vasilii III was probably considerably less than what it would become (110 000) by the end of the sixteenth century.[4]

This may be why there is so little surviving documentary evidence to support the contention of Gustave Alef, A. V. Chernov, V. I. Buganov and others that already under Ivan III the increasing size and complex organisation of the army, together with *mestnichestvo* litigation and the spread of *pomest'e* land tenure, had made it impractical for the grand prince and his Boyar Duma to manage military affairs without the assistance of a central secretariat specialising in military record-keeping. It is true that some fifteen to twenty secretaries and twice as many clerks can be identified as working in the grand prince's court by the last decades of the fifteenth century, when the first military deployment books were produced; but Marshall Poe has more recently argued that it was actually not until the 1550s that the army was of sufficient size and complexity to require certain court scribes to undergo formal and permanent functional differentiation into a secretariat specialising in military administration. In other words, it was premature to speak of a prototype of the Deployments Chancellery (*Razriadnyi prikaz*) already existing in the 1470s, the functional differentiation of central government at that time having proceeded no further than the division of labour between the court treasurer and the major-domo responsible for managing court properties.[5]

In this period the ability to mobilise provincial cohorts to join the *dvor* on major campaigns therefore depended more directly upon increasing the accountability of local officialdom. Before the late fifteenth century the vicegerent system of local government must have been of limited administrative effectiveness; although responsible for nearly all aspects of local administration, the vicegerents received only oral working orders and made infrequent reports to Moscow, while the fact they were remunerated only by the 'feedings' they collected from the district population could lead to extortionate imposts. But the vicegerents at least had military expertise (those assigned to strategic frontier districts system had considerable prior campaign experience), they cost the treasury nothing, and it was of enormous political advantage to Vasilii II's successors that they could place so much local government authority in newly annexed territories in the hands of their most trusted courtiers – and replace them after a year or two so they could not turn their feedings into sinecures. Under Ivan III and Vasilii III a series of measures rendered vicegerent administration more accountable and efficient: the 1488 Beloozero Charter established the precedents of limiting certain feeding requisitions and requiring community representatives to witness legal proceedings; the 1497 *Sudebnik* law code introduced standardised judicial procedures and prohibited bribery; and after 1510 the secretaries responsible for military record-keeping were placed in central supervision of the vicegerents. A sign of the further militarisation of local government under Vasilii III was the appearance of a new kind of local official, the 'fortifications steward', who assumed some of the fiscal and policing duties of the vicegerent in addition to supervising the town artillery and fortifications corvée.[6]

These reforms were encouraged by Russia's demographic and economic recovery after the 1470s. By the end of the century the government was able to conduct cadastral surveys of the recently annexed Novgorod region, thereby enhancing its ability to collect taxes, mobilise peasant militiamen, and balance the campaign service obligations of its *pomeshchiki* against their land and labour resources. Together with the St George's Day restrictions on peasant right of departure, cadastral registration also helped to initiate the long process of the enserfment of the peasantry to maintain the military service capacity of the middle service class.

It would still be another half-century before cash tax revenues began flowing into the central treasury on a significant scale, but it was also the case that the army did not yet demand much treasury expenditure. The largest military investment in the reigns of Ivan III and Vasilii III was probably in fortress construction on the frontiers, the burden of which fell upon taxpayers, primarily in the form of corvée. The campaign army was still predominantly a cavalry army, armed with bows or cold steel weapons rather than firearms, and it was largely responsible for outfitting and feeding itself. Herberstein observed that the cash stipends paid to the middle service class were meagre and infrequently paid, and that only the wealthier cavalrymen had sabres and cuirasses, with the greater number clad in thickly padded hemp *tegilai* coats and armed with bows.[7]

Gunpowder warfare was introduced into Russia in two stages. One cannot eliminate outright the possibility of its introduction by the Tatars; the first surviving reference to Russian use of guns (1382) calls the cannon or mortar Moscow's defenders fired against the forces of Tokhtamysh a *tiufiak*, which probably derives from the Turkish *tüfeng*. But it is more likely that the first guns (small-calibre guns of rolled sheet iron reinforced with iron bands) entered Russia in the 1380s from Livonia and Lithuania, and until the mid-fifteenth century the grand princes of Moscow had less access to this technology than the princes of Tver' and other western Russian lands. The second stage (1470s) had a far greater impact on Muscovite military development: with the Livonian Order's blockade making it difficult for Moscow to obtain sulphur, saltpetre and metals from northern Europe, and aware of what Mehmet II had been able to accomplish at

Constantinople using large-calibre bronze cannons of Italian model, Ivan III took advantage of his bride Sofiia Paleologa's connections with the Papal court to invite Rudolfo Fioraventi degli Alberti and other Italian masters to Moscow.[8] By 1494 a Cannoncasting Yard and Powder Yard had been established near the Kremlin to produce for the grand prince's arsenal. Most of what was produced was mounted on town walls; given the great size of these guns and the difficulties of road transport, it was not economical to use them in the open field until the 1520s, when horsedrawn wheeled gun-carriages came into use. Vasilii III is said to have used 2000 guns in his 1514 siege of Smolensk. but most of these were small falconets. Infantry use of handguns was also still very limited, one of the few exceptions was in 1521–22, when 1500 Lithuanian and German mercenary footsoldiers and one mobile field gun stood with the cavalry regiments along the Oka defence line against the Crimean Tatars.[9] Archers, not arquebusiers, provided most of the firepower repulsing the Tatars on the Ugra in 1480.

Yet Muscovy's military fortunes in the late fifteenth and early sixteenth centuries suggest the increased size and cohesion of its cavalry army – combined with shrewd diplomacy – was at this stage enough to make it more competitive against its northern European neighbours. The diffusion out of Novgorod region of the new *pomest'e* system of mobilising middle service class cavalry in the Novgorod did much to secure and then enlarge the western frontier; Moscow's wars with Lithuania (1492–94, 1500–03 and 1512–22) forced the Lithuanian grand princes to renounce their claims upon Pskov and Novgorod, caused many Lithuanian princes and boyars to defect to Moscow, and ultimately resulted in Muscovite annexation of the regions of Smolensk, Briansk, Novgorod-Severskii and Chernigov. Moscow successfully defended Pskov against the Livonian Order in 1480–81. A 1495–96 Finnish campaign against the Swedes was less conclusive: the Russian army took many prisoners but failed to capture Vyborg and the Swedes sacked and burned the recently built Russian fortress of Ivangorod.[10]

The ability to conduct larger operations along the western and north-western fronts was also made possible by the reduced danger in the south and east. The disintegration of the Great Horde had enabled Moscow to establish the client Khanate of Kasimov

(1452), intervene in succession struggles in the new Kazan'
Khanate and ally with the Crimean khans against Lithuania,
Livonia and the Great Horde (1480–1512). Crimean raids in
Lithuania deprived Khan Ahmed of the Great Horde of the
Lithuanian reinforcements that might otherwise have embold-
ened him to cross the Ugra and attack Moscow in 1480.

II

Almost immediately after Ivan IV took the title of Tsar in 1547,
his government embarked upon a series of major reforms that
systematised and expanded the service obligations of the metropolitan and petty nobilities, created new military formations, and
strengthened the ability of central and local government to mobilise revenue and manpower. The most immediate stimulus for
these reforms seems to have been the decision to undertake the
conquest of the Kazan' Khanate, made possible after 1549 by the
revolt of the Khanate's Cheremis tributaries and by Shah Ali's
readiness to become a Russian client in order to win the throne
of Kazan'. The reforms were also warranted by the need to
defend against the Crimean Khanate, which had been raiding
Russian frontier towns since the 1520s, and less immediately by
the recognition of the opportunities for territorial aggrandisement present in the weakening hold of the Livonian Order over
the townsmen and peasants of Estonia and Latvia.

Given the Ottoman Empire's reputation for the fullest autocracy and most powerful army in Europe, it is not surprising
that much of the reform programme of Ivan IV should seek to
create Russian analogues of certain Ottoman institutions. It
implemented several of the measures recommended in 1549 by
Ivan Peresvetov, who was familiar with Ottoman military and
political practice from his years of service under Prince Jan
Zapolya of Transylvania, Moldavian Gospodar Peter IV Rares,
Lithuanian Hetman Fedor Sapieha and Habsburg Emperor
Ferdinand I.[11]

Peresvetov's call for Ottoman-style meritocracy in the promotion of military servitors could not be fully implemented because
of the political necessity of *mestnichestvo*, but the government did
take steps to make command appointments in particularly im-

portant campaigns exempt from precedence challenge and to make service more equal to birth in determining precedence. In 1550 Ivan IV ordered that 1000 provincial servitors – mostly *deti boiarskie* – should be resettled on *pomest'e* allotments of three standard sizes, according to rank, within 60–70 versts of Moscow so that they should be immediately ready for service. The creation of this Chosen Thousand may have been politically motivated – to inject fresh blood into the *dvor*, or serve as a counterweight to the more powerful princely and boyaral clans – or may have been simply an attempt to form within the *dvor* a more effective palace cavalry guard (comparable to the *sipahi* of the Porte, only remunerated with service lands as well as salaries). A reform of far greater significance was the promulgation in 1556 of an Ordinance on Service, which systematised the relationship between landholding entitlements and military service obligations for all members of the upper and middle service classes. It required every holder of a *pomest'e* or an allodial *votchina* to provide one mounted man in full kit (with an extra mount, if called up for distant service) from every 100 *chetverti* (about 400 acres) of land held. Only those who continued to meet these service norms were entitled to receive the Sovereign's cash allowance, to retain right to their *pomest'ia*, and to hope for eventual promotion with a higher *pomest'e* entitlement rate; by the end of the century even the allodial lands of the upper service class became subject to confiscation in part or in full for non-performance of military duty. The Ordinance on Service thereby completed the process of binding the metropolitan nobility to compulsory state service alongside the provincial petty nobility. It also made it possible for the government to know in advance how many cavalrymen and their slave and peasant retainers were available for mobilisation; in that regard it functioned somewhat like the Ottoman *timar* system, which established the ratio between *çift* allotments and the number of *sipahi* cavalrymen and their *çelebi* retainers they were to support.[12]

Peresvetov had also recommended the creation of a standing infantry palace guard, decimally organised as in the Ottoman army, and a 20 000-strong infantry corps, equipped with firearms and paid out of the treasury, to defend the southern frontier against the Tatars. Under Vasilii III the fortifications stewards of certain frontier towns had sometimes carried out temporary levies of urban taxpayers equipped with arquebuses, but these had not been standing units. In 1550, however, the tsar created a standing palace infantry guard of 3000 Select Musketeers (*vybornye strel'tsy*), each of whom was paid four roubles a year, and by 1552 thousands of musketeers were participating in the siege of Kazan'. At Polotsk in 1563 the besieging Muscovite army included 12 000 musketeers. Their resemblances to the Ottoman janissary corps have been remarked upon by several historians, as well as by Peter I himself. Although not of course of *kapikulu* origin, the musketeers were recruited from life from plebeian backgrounds and were eventually allowed to supplement their treasury pay by engaging in duty-free commerce. Their tactical role was very similar, and they made no use of pikemen for defence. In dress and armament they most closely resembled Ottoman *tüfekçi* musketeers.[13] The army also now used field artillery on a far larger scale, and the regimental artillery became a distinct tactical unit, with its own officers, some of whom had gained technical expertise during prior service at the Cannoncasting Yard in Moscow.

While the campaign army continued to follow the Small or Large Array order of battle, the *polki* now became larger corps of mixed composition as a result of the creation of the *strel'tsy* infantry and expansion of the artillery; and starting with the 1552 Kazan' campaign, the army mobilised according to pre-existing rolls assigning contingents from particular districts to particular corps, with officers permanently assigned to each unit. The introduction of a regular force structure under continuing command enhanced discipline and tactical specialisation. The record-keeping involved in this, as well as in the supervision of *pomest'e* and salary entitlements and service obligations necessitated by the 1556 Ordinance on Service, finally brought about the permanent functional differentiation of the court's secretariat. There now existed a staff of secretaries and clerks permanently responsible for listing appointments and deployments, supervising inspections, processing promotions and setting new cash and land entitlement rates; from 1566 it had its own office, the *Razriadnaia izba*, and by the end of the century was referred to as the Deployments Chancellery (*Razriadnyi prikaz*). A Musketeers' Chancellery (which also supervised the registered cossacks) existed from 1577, as did an Artillery Chancellery. The formation of specialised central chancelleries was further promoted by the annexation of Kazan' and Astrakhan' (the Chancellery of the Kazan' Court), by the need for a central organ to supervise the allotment of service lands at entitlement rate (the Service Lands Chancellery), and by the decision in 1555 or 1556 to allow many communities the right to exempt themselves from vicegerent rule and elect their own officials. This last measure, called the *zemskii* reform, was actually a means of increasing the flow of revenue out of the provinces into the central treasury, to pay for the army campaigning in Livonia; what the communities once had to pay in 'feeding' maintenance to their vicegerents they now remitted to the treasuries of newly created territorial chancelleries at Moscow, and some of these feeding quitrents were of considerable value (the 1400 roubles paid by the inhabitants of Dvina, for example, was enough to cover the annual cash service subsidies of over 200 cavalrymen).[14]

Contrary to historiographic tradition, vicegerent rule did not everywhere give way to *zemskii* self-government. Nor did the emergence of a central chancellery apparatus at once necessitate a single reformed system of local government. Through the rest of the century different local government formats prevailed in different regions, in part due to the division of political authority during the Oprichnina terror (1565–72), and because the selling of self-government rights in certain regions conflicted with the need to militarise local authority. The smaller and less militarily vulnerable districts in the north and centre of the realm tended to be placed in the hands of elected criminal justice elders, *zemskii* officials, or middle service class fortifications stewards; Novgorod's strategic and economic importance was reflected in the transfer of many responsibilities from its vicegerents to special secretaries able to conduct more regular and detailed correspondence with Moscow; and some frontier districts remained under vicegerents. But of greatest significance for the future militarisation and bureaucratisation of provincial government was the increasing tendency along the Oka defence line, in the regions of Riazan', Briansk and Seversk, and in Russian-occupied Livonia, to entrust civil administration as well as military matters to regimental commanders who thereby evolved into military 'town commandants' (*gorodovye voevody*). Government by town commandant would be universalised after the Time of Troubles and would prove crucial to the fiscal and military reconstruction of Muscovy.[15]

Russian military power was also enhanced by the greater use now made of the independent hosts of Don, Volga and Zaporozhian cossacks as light cavalry auxiliaries. By the 1590s the government had found it possible to take advantage of economic and political divisions within the cossack hosts and to follow the Polish example of registering cossacks as crown servitors. Many cossacks were registered as 'town cossacks', garrisoned in the southern frontier towns and required to serve in exchange for small annual cash and grain subsidies and grants of ploughland. These land grants, like those of the southern musketeers, were smaller than middle service class *pomest'ia*, carried no rights over dependent peasant labour, and were held as personal shares of a collective allotment. The town cossacks thereby took their place alongside the musketeers and cannoneers as members of a distinct lower service class.

The lower service class gave the campaign army greater firepower and mobility, but it also played a key role in local defence duty along the southern frontier. By the end of the century the fortifications of Tula and other strategically sited towns south of the Oka had been linked up into a single fortified defence line, the Abatis Line (*Zasechnaia cherta*), running for 600 versts from Pereiaslavl-Riazan' to the forests of Briansk, thereby creating a new outer perimeter defence beyond the regimental deployments along the Oka. The gunners and musketeers provided greater firepower to protect the garrison towns and their interconnecting earthen, palisade and forest abatis defences, while the cossacks and middle service class cavalry performed steppe reconnaissance duty (systematised in 1571 by Prince M. I. Vorotynskii) beyond the line, or rode in pursuit of the smaller Tatar raiding parties. By intercepting smaller Crimean and Nogai forces and providing early warning of larger incursions, the garrison forces along the Abatis Line enabled the government to begin redeploying the regiments farther south of the Oka. This in turn encouraged the projection of military power deeper into the steppe – through raids down the Don and Dnieper in 1556–59, but especially through the construction in the 1580s and 1590s of new garrison towns (Belgorod, Voronezh,

Livny, Oskol', Valuiki and Elets), considerably beyond the Abatis Line.[16]

In 1585 the overthrow of the Kuchum Khanate at the hands of a small expeditionary force of mercenary cossacks in the hire of the Stroganov merchant family opened up Siberia to Russian colonisation. Gunners, musketeers and cossacks (until 1635, mostly men transferred from the north of European Russia) subsequently played the leading role in the agricultural colonisation as well as the garrisoning of Siberia; the lower service class remained the largest social group in the Siberian population throughout the seventeenth century.[17]

It is a commonplace that Russian expansion to the south and east was facilitated by the Russians' enormous advantage over Asian peoples in gunpowder technology. This is overstated. Some of the larger Crimean armies invading Muscovy (such as the army of Khan Safa-Girei in 1541) were accompanied by artillery and Turkish Janissaries. If the Tatars made infrequent use of artillery and handguns against the Russians, it was not because of their technological backwardness but for a logistical reason: the difficulty of moving and feeding forces with large artillery and baggage trains across hundreds of miles of empty steppe. This same logistical consideration long protected the Crimea against Russian firepower – though it did not apply to the Kazan' Khanate, which fell to Ivan IV in 1552 largely because the Russians were able to make use of Volga river transport on a large scale. Russian use of handguns and artillery did initially intimidate some of the aboriginal peoples of Siberia, but proved less decisive against the more numerous nomadic horsemen of south Siberia, while the Iukagirs and other peoples were apparently able to obtain enough guns through theft, illegal purchase or plunder to begin using them against the Russians soon after their initial military encounters. Above all, the scarcity of gunpowder greatly limited Russian firearm use in Siberia; as on the southern frontier, logistics prevented the maximum exploitation of the gunpowder revolution.[18]

Even on Muscovy's northern and western frontiers the tactical consequences of the new military technologies were more limited than one might think. Cavalry armament changed: shields disappeared and body armour became simpler and lighter, the pro-

portion of sabres to bows increased significantly, and a few cavalrymen carried matchlock muskets. But cavalry tactics had not
appreciably changed from the preceding period, with the exception that dense formations gave way to more extended echelon
deployment in response to artillery fire; the emphasis remained
on keeping to the defensive, relying on numerical superiority,
and waiting for the opportunity to make a sudden and short
flanking attack Commanders preferred to use the *strel'tsy* infantry
to assault or defend fortified places, being reluctant to deploy
them in the open field unless they were well protected by cavalry
and artillery, by a *tabor* (an imitation through the Turks of the
Wagenburg used by the Hungarians since the fifteenth century),
or by the *guliai-gorod*. This last was a kind of adaptation of the
Wagenburg inspired by Peresvetov's observations of Polish and
Hungarian tactics against the Ottomans; Giles Fletcher described
it as a kind of 'moving castle' of great interlocking loopholed
wooden shields mounted on small carts. It is only by the 1590s
that we find reference to Muscovite musketeers occasionally following the new Dutch style of line tactics, the most effective (but
still probably atypical) instance occuring at Dobrynichi in 1605,
when the musketeers doubled their files and fired by rank upon
the Polish and cossack cavalry.[19]

It is tempting to assume that the Russians ultimately lost
the Livonian War (1558–83) because of the slowness of their
infantry to adapt to the new line tactics. But Russia held the
upper hand until 1578, perhaps because the war to that point
was largely one of sieges and raids, on terrain unsuitable for the
new tactics, and with Sweden unable to prevent her small mercenary forces from mutinying over pay arrears. The largest sieges
and battles occurred in Lithuania, their result a stalemate
between Poland and Muscovy. The war certainly did turn against
Ivan IV after 1578, but this was probably due less to Polish and
Swedish tactical innovation than to other developments: Poland's
new alliance with Sweden, the considerably greater revenue
which the 1569 Lublin Union of Poland and Lithuania provided
to the new king Stefan Batory, and the fact that the need to
deploy more troops along the southern frontier after the
Crimean Khan's sack of Moscow (1571) left only 35 000 Russians
holding the Polotsk theatre against the 51 000 advancing Poles
and Swedes.[20]

The Livonian War was above all a war of sieges, but its sieges provide little indication of a technological or tactical advantage accruing to either side. Giles Fletcher remarked upon the tsar's ability to deploy great numbers of guns against the Poles, and in sieges of enemy towns and castles the Russians set great store by the enormous calibre of their 'wall-crusher' guns. But with the exception of Polotsk (1563), strongholds more often fell to them through long blockade than through bombardment and storm. The same could be said of Polish and Swedish sieges of Russian fortresses. Despite an army of 40000 men and the services of German and Italian engineers, Stefan Bathory was unable to capture Pskov in 1581–82 even after seven months of heavy bombardments and 30 assaults; Gustavus Adolphus also failed to take Pskov in 1615.[21] The new fiscal resources available to the Muscovite government allowed a greatly expanded scale of fortress construction in the second half of the sixteenth century, and one of these projects, Smolensk (refortified in 1595–1602), was by far the most imposing Muscovite stone and brick fortress, a truly gigantic citadel. It is true that the Russians did not yet build according to the principles of the *trace italienne*, but the fortresses they besieged in Lithuania and Livonia were no more advanced than their own, and it ought to be remembered that it was only from the 1550s that the *trace italienne* was taken up by the French, English, Dutch and Germans.

It was in the scale of its engineering operations and logistical operations that the army of Ivan IV had become more effective. The construction of the Abatis Line and the military colonisation of the southern frontier was but one example. It was also demonstrated in the successful 1551–52 Kazan' campaign – in the prefabrication of a wooden fortress at Uglich, which was then shipped 1000 kilometres down the Volga and assembled at Sviiazhsk to serve as a magazine and forward operations base; in the use of river transport to move and provision much of the army; in the huge network of trenches, log stockades, gabions and siege towers with which engineer Ivan Vyrodkov surrounded Kazan'; and in the sapping and mining of Kazan's walls.[22] In the west it was illustrated by the army's ability to endure far more protracted campaigns in Livonia (where most operations took place in winter to allow troops to cross the frozen marshes), and especially by the sophistication of the

Fortification Chancellery's military administration of occupied Livonia.[23]

But by the 1580s the government's fiscal machinery and the *pomest'e* system of service mobilisation were no longer able to meet the costs of such undertakings. The situation was especially critical in the Novgorod region and the north-west, once one of Muscovy's wealthiest regions and a large reservoir of middle service class cavalry manpower; here the devastation wrought by the Swedes, Lithuanians and the tsar's own Oprichnina guard was exacerbated by the near-doubling of tax rates; fields became wasteland; the flow of revenue to Moscow fell sharply, and the surviving middle service class cavalrymen found themselves too impoverished to perform military service.[24] Moscow attempted to re-establish community fiscal solvency and revive *pomest'e* landholding by suspending peasants' right to leave their land-lords in districts undergoing cadastral updates (1581–82) and then abolishing the right everywhere in 1592. But the recovery following these 'Forbidden Years' decrees was negligible, and a more concerted response to these problems was prevented by the increasing political factionalism that followed the death of Ivan IV in 1584 and eventually led to the near-total collapse of central government authority during the Time of Troubles (1605–13).

III

After many of Tsar Vasilii Shuiskii's generals and chancellery officials defected to the Second False Dmitrii's camp at Tushino in 1608, the task of defeating the rebels and re-establishing strong central authority fell by default to local officials. The *zemskii* officials of Vologda and other northern districts had been the first to place themselves at the head of this campaign, raising and provisioning militias largely on their own initiative. After the deposition of Shuiskii and the Polish occupation of Moscow (1610) it became the cause of certain energetic town comman-dants, like P. P. Liapunov of Riazan' and especially D. M. Pozharskii of Zaraisk, who were able to mobilise resources on a larger regional scale; it was Pozharskii who finally negotiated the coalition with other towns, with boyar clans, and with the cossack hosts that succeeded in driving the Poles from Moscow and restoring the Russian monarchy under the new Romanov tsar Mikhail Fedorovich (r. 1612–13).

Tsar Mikhail's advisers saw this as a vindication of the town commandant system of local government that had emerged in certain frontier regions six decades before; only the town commandants had possessed the breadth of authority, the military experience and the local bureaucratic machinery necessary to defeat the tsar's enemies and re-establish the autocracy. Town commandant rule was therefore now universalised; courtiers were no longer appointed as vicegerents, and the fortifications stewards and *guba* and *zemskii* officials – everywhere but in certain parts of the north – were converted into deputies of the town governors. After the tsar's father, Patriarch Filaret, returned from Polish captivity in 1619 the government (which was to remain in Filaret's hands until his death in 1633) made use of the more militarised and bureaucratised form of local authority provided by the town commandants to re-establish central chancellery authority over the provinces and rebuild the fiscal system and the army. Banditry was finally suppressed, and the criminal justice system not only restored but recodified; considerable coercion was used to collect tax arrears and return fugitive peasants and townsmen to where they were registered in the cadasters and tax rolls; and from 1619 the town commandants assisted surveyors and inspectors sent from Moscow in a general cadastral survey, returning and reregistering taxpayers, reinventorying the town granaries and treasuries, and registering lands that had been distributed as *pomest'ia* and *votchiny*. The central chancellery apparatus, its fiscal foundations re-established, expanded dramatically from 37 chancelleries in 1610 to 68 by 1630. Functionally differentiated bureaux arose within the larger chancelleries, and the Deployments Chancellery assumed greater co-ordinating authority over the operations of 12 other specialised military chancelleries. By mid-century the town commandants were keeping the chancelleries so much better informed of the condition of the provinces that the tsar no longer needed to convene the Assembly of the Realm (*Zemskii sobor*).[25]

The Time of Troubles had further reduced the effectiveness of *pomest'e*-based military service, which might have experienced the same fate as the Ottoman *timar* system if the governments headed by Filaret and Cherkasskii (1633–42) had not taken several measures to revive it. They gave servicemen special short-term cash subsidies and temporary tax immunities, obtained additional land reserves to distribute to service novitiates, and permitted some gradual juridical fusion of *pomest'e* and *votchina* tenure rights. Two policies in particular reinforced the service capacity of the middle service class. The first – which would profoundly shape Russian sociopolitical development over the next two centuries – took the form of the state reassuring the middle service class it would help them recover their fugitive peasants by gradually extending the recovery time limit. In 1649 the time limit was abolished altogether, thereby finally enserfing the peasantry for the benefit of the middle service class.[26] The second policy occurred in the south, where fertile black soil offered higher yields but where the middle service class traditionally had far fewer dependent peasant tenants; here military colonisation and frontier defence were made to rely increasingly upon the cheaper service of *odnodvortsy* – middle service class cavalrymen who appeared in service without retainers, having few or no peasant tenants, and holding smaller *pomest'ia* as shares in collective allotments, in much the same manner as the service cossacks.[27]

Filaret's reconstruction campaign was effective in reviving the *pomest'e*-based cavalry, even in the Novgorod region, where muster data indicate that the middle service class cavalrymen of the 1630s were better equipped and mounted and able to bring more retainers along on campaign than their counterparts of the early 1620s.[28] Not counting the peasant militias and the auxiliaries provided from independent client polities (the cossack hosts and the Great Nogais), the total strength of the Muscovite armed forces by 1632 reached 104 718, of whom 24 714 were middle service class cavalrymen, 33 775 musketeers, and 11 471 service cossacks; 60 000 of these men were available for active duty on the western and southern frontiers (40 000 of them in the field army, 20 000 in garrison duty). The French army of the 1630s may have been larger, but Muscovy had only about a third of France's population – and its armed forces cost only about 275 000 roubles a year to maintain.[29] By the eve of the Smolensk War the government had also succeeded in expanding arms production at the Cannoncasting Yard and Armoury, pressing the nation's smiths into compulsory service making projectiles, and chartering a large new iron foundry at Tula under the Dutch entrepreneur Andries Winius to produce cannons and musket-barrels on government contract. Over the next 30 years the total strength of the artillery would reach 4000 or 5000 guns, the field artillery would shift to more mobile smaller-calibre bronze guns, and part of the new formation infantry would receive snaphaunce muskets.[30]

The government resumed building new garrison towns on the southern frontier in 1635, and their success in blocking Crimean Tatar and Nogai raids soon inspired an ambitious project (1637–58) to found even more towns and link up their fortifications in a new defence line hundreds of kilometres farther south from the old Abatis Line. This new Belgorod Line consisted of 25 garrison towns linked by wooden and earthen fortifications and forest abatis extending 800 kilometres across most of the southern edge of the forest–steppe zone, from the Vorskla River to Chelnavsk, where it joined the Simbirsk Line running to the Volga, another 500 kilometres away. At this time the Abatis Line was repaired as well, but as a secondary or inner defence perimeter, for after 1646 the field army that had been annually stationed along it was shifted down to the new Belgorod Line. The steppe town of Belgorod became the station of the Great Regiment. By 1658 the commanding general of Belgorod's Great Regiment had become marshal over several frontier regiments (perhaps in imitation of the organisation of Polish–Lithuanian forces at Chocim in 1621), and by 1663 his headquarters was serving as the command centre of the Belgorod *razriad*, a far more integrated regional defence and resource mobilisation network. Its ability to sustain more co-ordinated operations across broad fronts would be demonstrated in the Thirteen Years War. In the 1677–81 Russo-Turkish War the deployment of the regiments of the Belgorod and Sevsk *razriady* and the construction of a new 440-kilometre Iziuma Line deterred a Turkish invasion of left-bank Ukraine. The southern frontier districts also performed a remarkable achievement in provisioning the two 112 000-man armies V. V. Golitsyn led across the Dnieper steppe against the Crimean Khanate in 1687 and 1689.[31]

During the Troubles Tsar Vasilii Shuiskii had hired at Novgorod several thousand Swedish musketeers and pikemen, known as 'the Black Dogs' because of their lacquered armour. But when they proved too expensive and politically unreliable, General M. B. Skopin-Shuiskii replaced them with a peasant militia equipped with muskets and pikes and trained 'in the Belgian manner' by mercenary Swedish officers. They proved effective against the main rebel camp at Tushino in 1610 but were disbanded after Skopin-Shuiskii's sudden and mysterious death.[32] The next Muscovite experiment with troops equipped and trained in European fashion began in 1630, in preparation for the campaign to recover Smolensk from the Poles. Large cash bounties were offered to European mercenary officers willing to train a new force of 'foreign formation troops' – six regiments of infantrymen (*soldaty*), a regiment of heavy cavalry (*reitary*) and a regiment of dragoons (*draguny*) – formed from Russian peasant militia conscripts, cossacks, novitiate middle service class cavalrymen and free volunteers of varying social origin. The foreign formation troops were outfitted and salaried at treasury expense, in contrast to the *pomest'e*-based traditional cavalry. They would account for 51 per cent of the 33 980-man Russian army at Smolensk. Here they faced a Polish infantry of more experienced European mercenaries, defending the largest fortress the Russians had ever built, now refortified by the Poles with bastions and earthworks in the Italian and Dutch manners. Under the circumstances the Russian force performed creditably in the Smolensk War (1632–34); it resorted to all the latest European principles of siegecraft, and Polish observers praised the 'Dutch skill' of the Muscovite *soldaty*. But the campaign failed. Traditionally, blame has been placed upon the generalship of M. B. Shein and A. V. Izmailov (courtiers with little recent campaign experience, appointed for largely political reasons), as well as upon the fatal feud between mercenary officers Lesly and Anderson, although William Fuller has recently argued that Shein would have captured Smolensk before the arrival of the forces of King Władysław if poor logistical planning and bad roads had not kept him from bringing up his heavy siege guns in time.[33] Moscow could not afford to redouble its efforts at Smolensk because of Tatar raids on central Muscovy, the outbreak of the Balash rebellion, and above all the expense of arming and paying the foreign formation troops: merely to maintain 6610 *soldaty* in 1633 cost the treasury 129 000 roubles.[34] After the war the foreign formations were therefore disbanded and their mercenary officers deported.

While the government would not be ready until the turn of the century to assume the costs of remodelling the entire army along foreign formation lines and maintaining it as a standing army paid entirely at treasury expense, it did continue to search for ways to raise foreign formation units on a less expensive basis. In the late 1640s the peasants of several villages along the Karelian front and the Voronezh River in the south were turned into tax-exempt self-supporting 'settled' *soldaty* and dragoons, their military colonies in some ways analogues of Swedish *indelning-sverket* or Austrian Grenzer colonies.[35] Furthermore, its strategic objectives in the south and the west soon convinced Moscow it had to spend what was needed to maintain quite large foreign formation forces over protracted periods. The Belgorod Line had to be protected and the southern army kept ready against Turco-Tatar revanchism for the Don Cossack capture of Azov, for example, and it seemed possible to entrust this to foreign formation troops, given that in the south there was less potential for conflict between peasant infantry levies and the rights of serf owners, while the middle service class was mostly *odnodvortsy*, more adaptable to new forms of service. Therefore several thousand volunteers and veterans of the Smolensk War were ordered back into foreign formation units for temporary duty along the southern frontier in 1637–39 and 1642.

Then the Khmel'nitskii Revolt presented Moscow with the opportunity for territorial aggrandisement in eastern Ukraine, for which campaign the Belgorod Line was the ideal staging-ground. In late 1652 Moscow prepared for war with the Commonwealth by raising 8000 *soldaty* from 18 districts on the Belgorod Line, and when the Thirteen Years War broke out in 1654, 16602 of the 20000 campaign troops of the Belgorod Army Group were foreign formation infantry and cavalry. By 1663 foreign formation troops (24522 cavalry and 24958 infantry) accounted for 79 per cent of the Muscovite army. The cavalry units could be expanded by enrolling novitiates and transfers from the middle service class and even some peasant militiamen, cossacks and veteran *soldaty*. But the government had to rely primarily upon peasant conscription on a huge scale in order to maintain the desired proportion of infantry to cavalry while compensating for heavy losses at the front. Over a hundred thousand peasants would be taken into the *soldat* regiments by the end of the war, the largest number coming from the villages of the southern frontier, which also had to carry the largest share of the increasingly onerous burden of paying and provisioning the infantry. In 1663 it cost a million rubles to pay the active duty army, both traditional and foreign formation; this was four times what it had cost 30 years before.[36]

While Ivan Pososhkov, Ivan Mazepa and other contemporaries commented on the declining combat-readiness and rising desertion rate among the traditional formation middle service class cavalry in the last half of the century, it took some time before Russian commanders learned how to use the foreign formation troops with any greater effectiveness. There was no ordinance for the cavalry; the ordinance used for infantry evolutions, firing systems and tactics, the *Uchenie i khitrost' ratnogo stroeniia pekhotnykh liudei* (1647), was a translation of a 1615 manual by Johann von Wallhausen, but it sold only 134 copies in its first decade of use. Because a true standing army was not yet affordable, most infantrymen were sent home at the end of campaigns and probably spent no more than a month each year in town drilling under their colonels; and even the two elite Moscow Select Infantry regiments stationed in special settlements outside Moscow drilled intensively only just before the beginning of a campaign, the rest of the time being preoccupied with their ploughland or trades. Patrick Gordon described his Russian infantrymen as 'not especially well-trained', and other observers complained that the provincial infantry did not seem to know how to maintain formation and advanced 'like cossacks'.[37] In the Thirteen Years War their fire was inaccurate and they required more than their pikemen and the cavalry to protect them, showing real discipline and resolve only when protected by a *tabor, guliai-gorod*, or field fortifications (Cudnowo, the Basia River and Mścibów, 1660), like the *strel'tsy* of the preceding century.

But at the end it made little difference that Muscovy's foreign formation infantry was undoubtedly less well trained than the Swedish infantry or the Polish–Lithuanian *wojsko komputowe*, for the infantry line tactics associated with the Military Revolution did not play a decisive role in the Thirteen Years War. What continued to matter more was the ability to provision one's forces through a long siege (Mogilev, 1655; Riga, 1656), to overwhelm the enemy with masses of light cavalry – dragoons and especially cossack or Tatar irregulars (Konotop, 1659) – and above all the ability to recover from enormous losses and resume the campaign. It was in only in regard to this last that Muscovy's investment in foreign formation infantry was finally vindicated, for through peasant conscription on a great scale the infantry regiments could be rebuilt more easily than the old middle service class cavalry units. This became decisive after 1659 when territorial losses, military confederations on strike for their pay arrears, and the Diet's increasing fears of royal 'military absolutism' deprived the Polish crown of the means to pay, provision and discipline its army.[38]

By the time of the Russo-Turkish War we do find signs that the foreign formation infantry was better able to undertake complex manoeuvres under heavy fire and hold formation against overwhelming odds (Buzhin Ford, 1677; Strel'nikov Hill, 1678), and the state believed enough in their potential superiority to reorganise the *strel'tsy* into regiments and companies of the same structure and prescribe for them comparable evolutions and tactics in 1681. A series of reforms during and immediately after the Russo-Turkish War made it possible to support even larger foreign formations and attempted to rationalise the structure of command authority: state service obligations were redefined so as to shift more of the middle service class into the foreign formations; all of European Russia was subdivided into nine territorial *razriady* for resource mobilisation and army group deployment; the assessment of direct taxes was simplified and a Great Treasury and the first semblance of a state budget were introduced; and *mestnichestvo* was finally abolished. In 1681 the total strength of the Muscovite armed forces reached 214 000, of whom 81 000 were foreign formation infantry and 45 000 foreign formation cavalry.[39]

IV

While it no longer ignores the extent of Muscovite commitment to the foreign formations, historical convention continues to emphasise how little the *soldaty* and *reitary* of the late seventeenth century had in common with the army built by Peter I during the Great Northern War (1700–21). The humiliating rout of the Russian army at Narva is seen as the shock that awoke Peter to the necessity of a truly regular standing army, the creation of which required the final repudiation of Asiatic for European principles, not only in military organisation but in statecraft and elite culture. These principles are thought to have been mastered with remarkable rapidity; hence Russian victories after Narva are attributed to significantly improved training and new tactics and equipment, and great attention is paid to identifying Russian innovations that contributed to the further development of European military science. The revolutionary character of Petrine military change is illustrated as well in the extent to which the rest of Peter's reform programme was designed to develop from it and serve it (although how effectively certain new institutions and policies achieved this is not always explored). Above all, the historical convention stresses the enormous social costs of military reform for subsequent generations, especially in the form of the soul tax and conscription. But how much of his convention is in need of revision?

The process of constructing a regular standing army predated Narva. Several developments had already led to Peter's conviction of its necessity: the 1694 Kozhukhovo manoeuvres of his 'toy' regiments; his disappointment that undertrained foreign formation infantrymen actually performed less effectively than cossacks and musketeers in the Azov campaigns of 1695–96; the European military practices he observed on his tour abroad in 1697–98; the necessity of dissolving the politically unreliable *strel'tsy* units in 1698–99; and above all the recommendations A. A. Weide presented to the tsar in 1698 to prepare the Russian army for war with Sweden. In November 1699 the government began forming three divisions (27 regiments) of regular infantry and two regiments of dragoons, trained by foreign and Russian officers according to German ordinances introduced by Weide and Golovin; by May 1700, 32000 men had been placed in the new regiments, either by enrolling volunteers from the free population, levying house serfs at the rate of one recruit from every 25–50 households (depending on the social estate and service calling of the landlord), or by allowing landlords to pay 11 roubles' cash substitute for each recruit. In only one important respect did this depart from the recruitment methods of previous decades, and the innovation was one that had not even been announced in the mobilisation decrees: this time those taken into the new regiments would not be sent home after a few months but were to remain in the army for life.[40]

The débâcle at Narva in November 1700 occurred for a variety of reasons – poor intelligence, divided command authority and the decision to keep the Russian forces crowded together behind their earthworks. But Peter was also correct to blame the Russian army's lack of 'regularity and good order'. It was not only Sheremetev's old middle service class cavalry which fled in panic; the new regiments formed the year before were also routed, a shortage of qualified officers having left them inadequately trained. The only units standing their ground were the Preobrazhenskii and Semenovskii Guards regiments (founded in 1692) and the Lefortovskii Regiment (formed in 1642).

We tend to assume the deficiencies displayed at Narva must have been quickly addressed because the army went on to perform so much more impressively in Ingria, Estland and Livonia in 1702–04. Certainly there were more levies to rebuild the army, new infantry and dragoon ordinances were issued, nine more dragoon regiments and an artillery regiment were formed, the production of artillery and muskets was significantly increased, and the plug bayonet gave way to the ring bayonet (at least in the elite Guards regiments). But the government was unable to meet its promises on pay and provisioning: a national census to update the old 1678 household enumeration for tax assessment was authorised in 1704 but would not be carried out for several more years, and the new War Chancellery (*Voennyi prikaz*) founded in 1701 would not show itself logistically competent before 1706. The desertion rate therefore continued to rise. What kept the army intact in these years was an improvised mix of extraordinary levies in cash and kind, requisitions from the civilian population of the Baltic theatre, and foraging. Peter's commanders complained that the regiments remained undertrained and officered by underqualified men. Russia's battlefield victories in the years 1701–04 did not yet offer clear evidence that the tsar had succeeded in creating a regular army, for most of these victories were achieved only through overwhelming numerical superiority – much of which was still provided by middle service class cavalrymen, cossacks, Kalmyks and Tatars.[41]

In 1705, closer co-ordination of the old Service Land Chancellery with the new War Chancellery finally provided the cadastral data and administrative machinery necessary to shift over to a more systematic Swedish-style recruitment system. The new recruiting system took one infantry recruit from every 20 taxpaying households and one cavalry recruit from every 80 households. By 1709 another 75 000 men had been recruited into the army – considerably fewer than the numbers once claimed by Kliuchevskii and other historians, but enough to cover the army's heavy losses and increase its size from 60 000 to over 100 000.[42] Whether the great Russian victories at Kalisz (1706), Lesnaia (1708) and Poltava (1709) indicate the army's years of training and combat experience were now bearing fruit is debatable: William Fuller doubts that the great number of fresh recruits could have received much training before they were thrown into these battles, while L. G. Beskrovnyi and P. P. Epifanov stress the greater combat readiness of the army by 1708–09 resulting from the emphasis on personalised training at the hands of veteran corporals, the elimination of the officer shortage, Peter's firm insistence on the meritocratic promotion of officers after 1707, and the standardisation of infantry regimental structure (set at nine companies of musketeers and a company of grenadiers, with the companies now divided into platoons to allow platoon firing, and battalion and brigade organisation introduced for greater flexibility in battle deployment). Above all, Soviet historians tended to attribute the army's heightened effectiveness to Peter's readiness to depart from 'stereotypical' line tactics in order to adapt to the often forested or marshy terrain of the Baltic front and to the mobility and shock of Swedish *gå-på* tactics; for this reason they make much of Russian use of the *corps volant*, horse artillery, 'impulse' deployment by broken line and separated redoubts, and aimed fire and the bayonet charge, treating these as brilliant anticipations of Suvorov and ignoring the extent to which such breaks with tactical orthodoxy were occurring elsewhere in Europe in the period.[43] It does seem likely, however, that the Russian army was able to improvise to the special circumstances of the Great Northern War in part because European tactical thinking was still too unfamiliar to the Russians to have already become an unchallengeable orthodoxy.

The contribution of technological change and bureaucratic rationalisation before the final phase of the war (1710–21) may also be exaggerated. The artillery showed impressive development, but infantry firearms were not standardised until 1715, and until then many units were still armed with small-calibre fusées of already antiquated design. A shortage of muskets made it necessary to increase the proportion of pike to musket in 1707. It was not until 1712 that Russian industry could meet the army's need for muskets, and production costs remained high for some time thereafter.[44] Political rhetoric emphasised the necessity of a regular state for the maintenance of a regular army, yet systematic restructuring of central administration was postponed until very near the end of the war. Peter first tinkered with the old Muscovite *prikaz* apparatus, gradually replacing the Deployments Chancellery with a War Chancellery responsible for the recruitment system, a General Commissariat to arm and pay the army, a Proviant Chancellery responsible for food provisioning, and an Artillery Chancellery. In 1711 their functions were placed under the supervision of the new Senate and its Commissariat, although artillery administration was excepted. Further confusion derived from the division of the central government apparatus between Moscow and St Petersburg. In 1718 a Swedish-model apparatus of nine 'colleges' was created, but the Krigskollegium (*Voennaia kollegiia*) was not fully formed until the following year and did not acquire full authority over the artillery and the supply services.[45]

There was indeed a crucial connection between administrative change and the increased effectiveness of the army, but this administrative change was not of the centralising and bureaucratising character Petrine political discourse would lead us to expect. Ultimately Russia defeated Sweden through superior resource mobilisation power and more flexible strategic planning, and these capabilities were maximised by regionalising authority and transferring it from state officials to generals and favourites. Hence the *guberniia* reform of 1708–18: because of the tsar's prolonged absence from the capitals and the Swedish incursion into Ukraine in 1707–09 it became necessary to reroute most

authority for recruiting tax collection and provisioning away
from the *prikazy* and into the hands of eight of the tsar's most
powerful intimates, who served as governors with broad and ad
hoc military and civil authority over vast new superprovinces
(*guberniia*), modelled upon the territorial *razriady* of the seventeenth century. Only when the war was largely over did it become
possible to reverse this by creating colleges at St Petersburg,
breaking up the *guberniia* into smaller provinces (*provintsiia*) and
re-establishing central government control over the provincial
and district *voevody* (1717–19). Russian war planning was also
less centralised and bureaucratised under Peter than in the seventeenth century, when commanders sometimes found their
freedom of action constrained by campaign plans issued months
before back in Moscow by the tsar and the Deployments Chancellery. Peter held councils of war several times a year, often near
the front, and these worked out plans of campaign through
collegial consultation. This allowed the tsar to identify and per-
sonally quash destructive personal rivalries among his generals
and to encourage Russian commanders to consider the advice of
the army's foreign officers. Such collegiality (reinforced by fear of
Peter's wrath, of course) was well suited to a high command
which was still schooling itself in European military science.[46]

There can be no doubt that the construction of a regular
standing army carried great social costs, but they were made
more bearable by their temporary character. For the nobility
military modernisation required acceptance of a much greater
regimentation than had been known before: Petrine legislation
beginning in 1707 and culminating in the Table of Ranks (1722)
revived the compulsory state service principle and re-educated
the nobility for onerous new forms of service; it placed far more
stress upon meritocratic promotion and opened up at least the
junior officer corps to non-nobles; and it regulated land tenure
and inheritance rights in new ways in order to strengthen the
nobility's economic capacity to serve. But several factors combined to reconcile the nobility to these terms – the increasingly
militarised political culture, the state's readiness to preserve and
even expand serfdom, the far richer spoils (especially in the form
of bribes and kickbacks) now available to higher-ranking nobles,
and above all the realisation that much of this regimentation
would have to be relaxed after Peter's death. The taxbearing

population of course carried a far heavier burden. About 300 000 recruits had been taken into the army by the end of Peter's reign, perhaps half of whom were killed or died of disease in the course of the war. In 1680 annual military expenditure had been 750 000 roubles (half of the total state expenditure), but by 1724 it had risen to 5.4 million roubles (63 per cent of the state budget). Since P. N. Miliukov, historians have tended to see the introduction of the soul tax (a capitation) in 1718 as raising fiscal exploitation to intolerable levels, threatening peasant subsistence and leading to massive arrears that seemed a harbinger of social revolt. Actually the great increase in taxation occurred in 1705–15 and took the form of extraordinary levies, especially levies in kind. In replacing other taxes the soul tax actually lowered the tax burden, as had become possible with the end of the war in sight.[47] Resentment focused on the soul tax because this single new tax replaced a host of smaller exactions, because it further monetarised tax obligations, and because new categories of the population were subject to it and thereby enserfed.

With the exceptions of the 1799 Dutch campaign and the War of the Third Coalition (1805–07), the Russian army performed creditably in nearly every one of its major wars between Peter's death in 1725 and the final defeat of Bonaparte in 1815.[48] The army's increased effectiveness does not seem to have had much connection with new developments in military technology; the army generally kept pace with the period's few significant changes in armament – adopting rifled muskets with improved locks in the 1760s, for example – but no specifically Russian innovations or technological leads are discernible except for new types of artillery (the 'secret howitzer' and multi-purpose 'unicorn') introduced during the Seven Years War.[49] One might think that the Russian Enlightenment and the relaxation of the compulsory service obligations of the nobility over the period 1725–62 might have made a difference by promoting greater military professionalism and dignifying military science as an intellectual pursuit, but for most officers after Peter's reign promotion came through political patronage, and mastery of the art of war remained mostly a matter of field experience and drill, not theoretical study. Whether discipline and *esprit de corps* among the ranks significantly improved after 1725 is also open to debate. The ability of the Russian infantry and gunners to hold their ground under withering fire at Zorndorf, Paltzig and Kunersdorf (1758, 1759) could certainly be cited in evidence, and Walter Pintner and William Fuller stress that the Russian desertion rate after the 1730s was lower than that of other European armies, a difference attributable to at least three factors: the Russian army relied less on mercenary manpower; peasant recruits were allowed to form *artels*, strengthening small-group solidarity within the regiments; and even a soldier's life seemed comparatively privileged when contrasted with the condition of a private serf. But to J. L. H. Keep the desertion rate was high, considering the conscript nature of the Russian army and the severity of sanctions against desertion.[50]

The dominant voice in Soviet military historiography, L. G. Beskrovnyi, maintained that the army's successes mounted whenever the War College and the Generalitet awoke from their enchantment with 'Prussian' orthodoxy in military science and returned to the flexible 'national' empiricism that had served Russia so well in the Great Northern War. During periods of Germanophile hegemony at court (the Bironovshchina in Anna's reign, the reigns of Peter III and Paul I) the military establishment fixated upon traditional line tactics maximising firepower, expanded the clumsy cuirassier squadrons at the expense of the more mobile dragoons, and neglected manoeuvres for parade drill. But under Elizabeth Petrovna, and especially Catherine II, talented innovators like Rumiantsev and Suvorov achieved remarkable victories by breaking with this orthodoxy. They retrained their troops for deployment in divisional or regimental squares, or in loose formation with jaegers providing flanking support with aimed fire, and they made greater use of the bayonet charge, lighter artillery, forced marches over great distances and attack columns in order to obtain the advantage in shock and mobility. Beskrovnyi saw these innovations as rooted in Petrine precedent (in the 1716 Ordinances for War, for example), yet as also anticipating the new 'impulse' tactics later associated with the army of Revolutionary France.[51]

Such a dialectic is apparent in Russian military doctrine over the course of the eighteenth century – but so is it apparent in the military doctrine of the other great powers of Europe, particularly from the Seven Years War. Only in the later Turkish Wars do we see the Russians achieving crushing victories through new variable formation tactics – especially through the chequerboard deployment of mutually supporting hollow squares, used so effectively by Potemkin at Fokshany in 1770 and subsequently refined by Rumiantsev and Suvorov. At Larga it cost the Turks and Tatars 3000 casualties, the Russians less than a hundred; at Kagul 20000 Turks were killed or captured while Russian casualties totalled 1471.[52] Once again the more significant military innovations of the period had developed out of the struggle on the Turco-Tatar frontier rather than from operations against European powers. In fact Russian commanders, including veterans of the Turkish Wars like Kutuzov, were subsequently reluctant to apply the lessons of the southern frontier to the struggle against France; even Suvorov had written, 'Against regular forces the linear order as in the Prussian War, against irregulars as in the last Turkish War.'[53]

Logistics were slow to show much improvement. After mid-century there was recognition of the need to reduce the size of unwieldy baggage trains, but administrative shortcomings and the distances separating the theatre of war from Russia's agricultural heartland made it difficult to establish adequate forward magazines during the Seven Years War. One can point to improved logistics as a factor in victory in the Turkish Wars of 1768–74 and 1787–91, when larger reservoirs of manpower, grain and money were established closer to the front as a result of pre-war progress in military colonisation, the revival of cossack service, and fiscal reform in the Hetmanate under Governor-General Rumiantsev and in New Russia under Governor-General Potemkin.[54] But it is harder to identify institutional changes on the national level making military administration and resource mobilisation more efficient. Munnich's attempts to centralise military administration in the War College were defeated in 1741. The prevailing tendency over the next six decades was once again to personalise rather than bureaucratise authority over military affairs, and this time the monarch was less able than Peter to override factionalism among the oligarchs this empowered. The War College – indeed, the collegial apparatus in general – saw its powers transferred into the hands of cliques associated with the Senate. In wartime ultimate authority over operations was concentrated in special court councils; the closer co-ordination of war plans with domestic and diplomatic policy which resulted was sometimes offset by the over-centralisation of command authority in St Petersburg, and even its subjection to veto by diplomatic representatives of Russia's allies. The *guberniia* reform of 1775 did permit some streamlining of local government, leaving more revenue available for army expenditure, but it also reduced central supervision over the governors-general; this permitted innovation by governors-general like Potemkin, but for others it was an opportunity for greater corruption that did considerable damage to the interests of the army.[55]

How, then, is the growth of Russian military power over the period 1725–1815 to be explained? Arcadius Kahan concluded that a crucial factor was the nation's ability 'to carry continuously a fiscal burden that was of considerable magnitude for the population and economy of Russia'. Although the administrative machinery for conscription and taxation remained inefficient, its claims upon the nation's resources at least went largely undisputed because centuries of autocracy and compulsory state service had so limited the sociopolitical autonomy of the estates. It is true that after Peter's death the state did not dare increase the soul-tax rates for fear this would undermine the ability of private serfs to meet the rent demands of their landlords; but no such restraint applied to the government's ability to obtain revenue for war from the money rent (*obrok*) paid by Russia's numerous state peasants. Hence revenue from the soul tax rose from 4 million to 10.4 million roubles over the years 1726–96, while the yield from state peasant rents increased from 700 000 roubles to 14 million roubles over the same period.[56] Above all the supply of recruits, money and grain grew with the demographic and territorial expansion of the Empire. In this respect the Russo-Turkish Wars were of even greater significance than the partitions of Poland or the conquest of the Baltic region, for in liquidating the Crimean Khanate and driving the Turks from the northern coast of the Black Sea they opened up the rest of Ukraine to the spread of larger-scale manorial agriculture, employing *barshchina* to produce grain for the Russian and world markets (the resources of Ukraine would play an important role in the rebuilding of the Russian army after Borodino). The economy expanded sufficiently to assure that the per capita tax burden in the eighteenth century never exceeded 12–15 per cent of average taxpayer per capita income. As for the burden of conscription, recruitment rates, though rising briefly in wartime, on the whole remained steady over the course of the century; in nominal terms the cost of household labourers lost to conscription rose sharply in the 1780s, but remained fairly steady in real terms (when translated into the market price in rye of a young male serf).[57]

The size of the regular army tripled between the 1760s and the 1790s, and annual army costs rose from 9.2 million roubles in 1762 to 21 million roubles in 1796; yet the share of state revenue consumed by the army and fleet actually declined from 63.1 per cent to 35.4 per cent of gross expenditure over this period.[58] This was made possible in great part by the economic growth resulting from imperial expansion. In this sense the resources mobilised for war were reinvested in growing the national economy, though this growth strategy was of course of an extensive rather than intensive nature, reflecting the continued backwardness of the Russian economy.

V

Russia lay far outside the heartland of the sixteenth-century 'Military Revolution', at least as this revolution was originally conceptualised by Michael Roberts and Geoffrey Parker, the technological and organisational innovations Roberts and Parker saw as revolutionising the conduct of war and creating absolutism in Western Europe were not unknown to the Russians, but they were less immediately adaptable to the physical, economic and geopolitical landscape of Eastern Europe and so, until quite late, had a less transforming effect than other factors on Russian military doctrine, army size and state-building. A kind of military revolution did occur in the sixteenth and seventeenth centuries, but in response to challenges other than the *trace italienne* or Dutch line tactics. For example, Russia responded to the gunpowder revolution by pursuing an ambitious programme of fortification in the sixteenth century, the scale of which helped promote the development of new organs of central and local government and the expansion of the army's infantry and cavalry elements, even though these construction projects involved forms of military engineering more traditional than those required by the bastioned artillery fortress. In the seventeenth century Russia committed considerable resources to the maintenance of large foreign formation forces, but these forces made ineffective use of line tactics until late in the century, their real advantage residing in their social character rather than their tactical potential: through peasant conscription *soldat* regiments could rebuild more quickly after heavy losses than could the traditional cavalry regiments of the provincial petty nobility. Russian military practice really converged with that of Western Europe in terms of technology, tactics, administration and army size only from the middle years of the Great Northern War, when Peter's army underwent what Jeremy Black consider the more decisive Second Military Revolution of the 1660s–1720s. Thirty years later some differences in tactics still remained, but mostly as necessary adaptations to the special circumstances of steppe warfare; the Russian army's continuing logistic deficiencies were hardly uniquely Russian, and no significant Russian 'lag' behind Western Europe in technology and organisation was now discernible.

To a striking extent the early stages of Russia's military emergence built upon military and political institutions of non-European provenance. It has become a cliché that the Muscovite cavalry army of fifteenth and early sixteenth centuries was better adapted to steppe warfare against the Tatars than to war with European powers; actually it was not all that outclassed by the Swedes, Lithuanians and Poles, and this was because the Ottomans were becoming an equally important model for early Russian military development. Ivan IV's ability to conduct larger and more protracted operations, making greater use of infantry and artillery, derived in large part from his commitment to developing Russian equivalents of Ottoman military and political institutions; this was motivated not only by anticipation of an eventual war with the Porte (which became unavoidable only considerably later) but also by admiration – of the superiority of the Ottoman army to the armies of Europe, and of the superiority of Ottoman patrimonial autocracy to European monarchy. While the Second Military Revolution replaced most of these Ottoman-model institutions, the need to adapt to the Ottoman challenge continued thereafter to shape Russian tactical development as profoundly as did Russia's struggle with European powers.

It is difficult to separate cause from effect in the relationship between military change and political change in early modern Russia. Military development and state-building became interconnected, but the notion that changes in military technology and organisation 'created' Russian absolutism does not fit the narrative, which instead supports Jeremy Black's contention that the enhanced resource mobilising power of the state derived first from consensus politicking and only later from command. What made the establishment of Muscovite autocracy possible in the fifteenth century was neither the grand prince's national monopoly over military force nor his *prikaz* apparatus; for these emerged only after the political settlement with the nobility that reconciled the nobility to collaboration with the grand prince in return for their delivery from impoverishment and from a civil war that, while destructive, had been fought by traditional means, by small *dvor* retinues. Thereafter, resource mobilisation for the army could certainly be a major impetus towards political centralisation and bureaucratisation, but this was most clearly seen in the 1550s–1570s and in 1613–42; in other periods (the 1470s–1530s, 1699–1708) the size and complexity of the army increased, but the state was surprisingly slow to develop new central administrative machinery to manage it. The ruler continued to place more reliance on informal, ad hoc and personal authority for resource mobilisation than the rhetoric of absolutism has prepared us to expect. In fact, institutional change at the centre was ultimately less crucial to military resource mobilisation in territorially vast Russia than the development of effective provincial government, especially when the latter was harnessed to imperial annexations and colonisation campaigns enlarging the Empire's resource base.

7. Warfare and Society in the Baltic 1500–1800

KNUD J. V. JESPERSEN

THE BALTIC AND EUROPEAN WARFARE

In the early spring of 1628 the Swedish forces in Livonia suffered a series of minor defeats in their current, intractable war with Poland. This temporary setback prompted the Swedish king Gustav II Adolf to contemplate the situation in general and the ongoing war in particular. In a letter of 1 April to Axel Oxenstierna, his loyal chancellor, he reflected on the general pattern of conflict in Europe:

> things are come to this pass, that all the wars that are waged in Europe are conmingled and become one, as is shown by the actions of the Papists in Germany, and the help given by the Spaniards to Rochelle, and last summer against us in Prussia, as well as by sundry consultations holden at the Emperor's court, where, as it is certainly reported, it was resolved to press on, by the occupation of these Scandinavian lands, to that tyranny over body and soul which they lust after. . . .[1]

In this passage Gustav Adolf made clear what had been obvious to many thoughtful observers for some time, that all the wars in Europe were in the process of running together and becoming fused into one great conflict, whose single elements formed interconnected parts of an overall, comprehensive European conflict-pattern. The Baltic wars – previously fought in splendid isolation – were now becoming integral parts of the ongoing great European showdown, the Thirty Years War, which, like a whirlpool, successively sucked in most of the European states, and in the end brought about many fundamental changes in the international system, in the power structures of the European states and in societies, thus signalling the end of old, medieval Europe and

180

the beginning of the modern world. As correctly observed by the Swedish king, the Baltic wars now formed a small, but – not least, of course, to the region directly affected – important part of this great and violent process of modernisation and Europeanisation. The nature of this particular part will be in the focus of this chapter.

The Baltic wars in early modern times have already been given a brief, chronological overview by Dr Stewart Oakley and, in a somewhat broader context, are discussed in a few recent books covering the region.[2] For that reason the finer details of the history of Baltic warfare, as well as the broader context, will be left out here except for a brief introductory sketch. Instead, this chapter will focus upon the changing nature of warfare and, on a more principal level, the role that the changing format of war played in the modernisation of the Baltic region and its eventual integration in the European world. This emphasis explains, too, why the focus here is laid on the early modern period while the late eighteenth century is treated more lightly.

THE BACKGROUND TO DANO-SWEDISH RIVALRY IN THE BALTIC

Of the 158 years which elapsed from the beginning of the Northern Seven Years War in 1563 to the conclusion of the Great Northern War in 1721, the two leading powers in the Baltic, Denmark and Sweden, were at open war with each other for 29 years – or about a fifth of the time. These years were distributed over seven separate wars, dispersed evenly over the period. Even the intervening years of nominal peace were marked by an antagonism so strong that they are best characterised as years of cold war. It is therefore not greatly inaccurate to describe the entire period 1563–1721 as one of continuous conflict between the two countries.[3]

Regarded in a long time-perspective, this state of conflict between the two Scandinavian kingdoms was really the exception rather than the rule – even if the populations of Denmark and Sweden must of necessity have regarded the incessant warfare at the time as almost the normal state of things. However – apart from a solitary and unimportant skirmish in the 1780s – the fact

is that relations between the two countries have remained peaceful since 1721. And furthermore: for a long span of years in the
later Middle Ages the two countries even belonged to the very
same state-formation, the Union of Kalmar, bound together in
a personal union under the regency of the royal house of
Denmark.

This Union, lasting for the entire fifteenth century, was
equipped only with embryonic governmental machinery and,
moreover, lacked inner cohesion. It was kept together, however,
mainly by the force of the then dominant powers in the Baltic
region, the Teutonic knights in East Prussia and the North German Hanseatic towns on the south coast of the Baltic Sea, headed
by the flourishing city of Lübeck. This rich commercial centre,
with its huge resources, completely dominated the economic and
political life of the backward Scandinavian countries and effectively locked them away from the European continent. Being the
region's most important commercial centre, Lübeck, of course,
had a vital interest in keeping her hinterland, the Baltic region, at
peace and politically stable. For this reason, the city effectively
discouraged political conflict within its sphere of influence, including the Scandinavian Union. Hence the relative
political stability in the Baltic during the late Middle Ages, and the
extreme state of isolation of the region from continental Europe.

With the waning of Hanseatic power in the course of the
fifteenth century, however, Lübeck's control over Scandinavia
also loosened, thus creating an unstable political situation in
the region. Deprived of Lübeck's support, the Danish king was
unable to exert authority and to keep the Union together. The
unavoidable result was the eventual emancipation of Sweden in
the 1520s under the skilful leadership of Gustav Vasa. He thus
became the founder of the independent kingdom of Sweden
which, after the final collapse of the ancient feudal power of the
Teutonic Knights by the mid-sixteenth century, initially competed with the old leading power, Denmark, over supremacy in
Scandinavia and the Baltic, and would even come to threaten the
very existence of Denmark as a sovereign state.

This persistent competition for supremacy between the two
neighbours – an important pivot of Danish as well as Swedish
policy during the sixteenth and seventeenth centuries – was
caused mainly by three factors. The Danish government, in the

first place, tended to regard the Swedish defection from the old Union as something like a violation of the natural order. Consequently, the political efforts of the Danish government were from the beginning directed towards attempts at forcing Sweden back into the fold. Later on – as Sweden's military superiority became apparant from about 1630 – the Danish political aim was gradually reduced to trying to secure the country's survival as an independent state in the shadow of the rising great power of Sweden.

Second, the legitimacy of the new royal house of Sweden was doubtful. It had achieved its position by usurpation. Being a new state-formation, the Swedish Vasa-state thus had an almost insatiable need for security. And the nearest and greatest threat to her independent position was the twin kingdom of Denmark–Norway, surrounding her on three sides and locking her away from the vital naval routes to the rest of the world. Hence, according to Swedish strategical thinking at the time, better security for Sweden could only be achieved by weakening Denmark, which in Swedish conciousness thus became the chief enemy and the main obstacle to the emerging Swedish state.

The third factor was the above-mentioned breakdown of Lübeck's hegemonial power. As Lübeck's ability to exercise control in Scandinavia finally came to an end in the 1530s, the problems of administering the balance of power in the Baltic were left mainly to the two Scandinavian powers themselves. This left the way open to the many armed conflicts between the two countries over the next two centuries.

THE WARS

The first serious clash came in 1563, when a seven years' war between the two countries began. The war was nominally about the right to display three crowns in the royal coat of arms – the symbol of the old Union – but it was obvious that Denmark's real aim was to re-establish the Kalmar Union while, on the other hand, the Swedish goal was to reduce the Danish threat to the Vasa-state by taking advantage of the power-vacuum left in the eastern Baltic by the final collapse of the Order of the Teutonic Knights. As could be expected – taking the limited resources into account – this conflict eventually deteriorated into an exhausting war of attrition. The war simply ebbed away as resources on both sides came to an end. The issues at stake were not settled.

Precisely the same outcome was achieved when, in 1611, the Danish king, Christian IV, ignoring his government's advice, entered a new war against Sweden. Notwithstanding the initial high-flying plans on the Danish side of conquering the Swedish mainland in a single sweeping pincer operation, this war ended, just like the previous one, as an exhausting war of attrition. The modest outcome of the peace negotiations in 1613 was a Swedish promise to pay a considerable war indemnity. No borders were moved, however, and no Swedish land conquered by Denmark. The result was the status quo ante bellum.

This war, called the Kalmar War, after the main theatre of hostilities, proved to be Denmark's last serious attempt at forcing Sweden back under Danish supremacy. From then on the question of Sweden's existence as a sovereign state was removed from the agenda. Instead another problem – which of the two powers should exercise the *dominium maris Baltici*, that is, maintain the leading position in the Baltic – came to the fore.

Supremacy in the Baltic was conditioned mainly by three decisive factors. In the first place, the ability to control the exits from this inland sea, that is, the Danish straits and the Sound; second, the relative strength of the navies operating in the Baltic Sea; and, third, the degree of control over the coastal lands bordering it. It was consequently in these fields that the struggle between the two countries took place, and the shifting relative weight of those factors finally decided the long trial of strength in favour of Sweden.

The Danish government considered the command of the straits and a strong navy in the Baltic to be the best means of maintaining Danish supremacy. Danish military measures were consequently directed towards those ends. The Swedish government, on the other hand, chose to put the emphasis upon command of the coastal areas beyond the Baltic Sea. This Swedish strategy eventually became apparent in the 1620s, but Swedish troops had in fact already, since the mid-sixteenth century, carried out a methodical campaign of conquest in East Prussia and Poland, thus taking advantage of the collapse of the Teutonic

Knights – with the result that the Swedish king, by the 1620s, had obtained de facto control over the southern coast of the Baltic Sea from the Gulf of Bothnia to Poland.

This successful Swedish strategy of methodical conquest had two decisive consequences for the struggle for supremacy in the Baltic. Sweden was now, in the first place, quite within her right of disputing the Danish claim of the *dominium maris Baltici* and raising a claim of a divided Baltic, regardless of the strong Danish navy. Second – and perhaps even more important – the permanent Swedish engagement on the Continent eventually gave rise to a growing internationalisation of the so-far highly localised Baltic conflicts. After 1625 the scene of the Scandinavian rivalry was in fact temporarily removed from the Scandinavian peninsula and the Baltic Sea to northern Germany.

This escalation materialised for the first time when, in 1625, the Danish king – following English and Dutch pressure and once again disregarding his government's warnings – engaged Denmark in the Thirty Years War and declared war on the Emperor. The king's motive for this ill-fated engagement was presumably first and foremost a fear that Sweden should otherwise forestall Denmark and succeed in placing troops immediately on the southern border of his kingdom. Fighting for the Protestant cause was probably only of secondary importance for his decision, even if his position as Duke of Holstein obviously gave him some direct interest in German affairs, including the religious issue.

The king's involvement in the great European war proved most unfortunate for Denmark. After four years of fighting and two years of partial occupation by Wallenstein's troops, Denmark had to withdraw from the war and seek peace. Only a favourable international situation saved the kingdom from total humiliation at the peace negotiations in Lübeck in 1629.

At precisely this point Sweden, under the charismatic leadership of Gustav II Adolf, stood ready to proceed where Denmark had failed. In the summer of 1630 the Swedish expeditionary force, headed by the king, landed in Pomerania, thereby making a Swedish military presence in northern Germany a grim reality and, at the same time, paving Sweden's road to her future status as a regional great power. Not only did Sweden play a major role on the European scene for the rest of the Thirty Years War; her government also saw a real chance of now carrying its old strategy to its logical conclusion: that of obtaining complete control over the Baltic by mutilating or even incorporating her old enemy in a new Great-Sweden, by now the undisputed strongest military power in Northern Europe.

The next two wars between Denmark and Sweden – in 1643–45 and 1657–60 – consequently took the form of determined Swedish attempts at a total eradication of Denmark while, from a Danish viewpoint, they amounted to desperate struggles for mere survival. In point of fact, Denmark escaped her fate only after the merciful intervention of foreign powers, in particular the United Provinces, which – being the great commercial nation of the seventeenth century – were taking over Lübeck's old role as arbiter in the Baltic, in line with the mercantilist ideas of the time. According to those ideas, a single great power controlling the entire Baltic region was not compatible with the commercial interests of the Dutch, who preferred a divided and open Baltic Sea to a closed one. On this account, Denmark was allowed to survive, albeit in a reduced shape: with the exception of the island of Bornholm, all Danish provinces east of the Sound were ceded to Sweden at the Peace of Copenhagen in 1660. In this process, Denmark lost nearly a third of her original territory, and the Danish state was thus reduced to the shape which it kept until her separation from Norway in 1814, in the aftermath of the Napoleonic wars and the loss of the Duchies in 1864 after the short war with Germany.

The last two Dano-Swedish wars – those of 1675–79 and 1709–20 (the short skirmish in 1700 is disregarded in this context) – were in a sense the Baltic counterparts to Louis XIV's European wars. Both were, from a Danish viewpoint, motivated by a wish to exploit favourable international conditions for reconquering the lost provinces in the Scandinavian peninsula, while Sweden was forced into the wars by her French ally. Neither of those undertakings met with any success, nor did the waning great power of Sweden succeed in conquering further Danish territory. In the larger picture, those wars were indeed only minor Baltic sideshows to the great European showdowns of the late seventeenth century, thus indicating that both Nordic countries had by then become integral members of the greater European alliance-systems, while the real causes of these wars were to be found in conflicts outside Scandinavia. They were, in short, only expressions of the fact that the Scandinavian kingdoms after the Thirty Years War had finally joined the new international system in Europe after 1648, the Westphalian system.

Sweden's time as a regional great power was definitely over by the signing of the peace treaties after the Great Northern War in 1720–21. Sweden and Denmark were so weakened by their many wars and so hemmed in by the new European balance-of-power system that any thought of further territorial changes in Scandinavia on their own instigation became unrealistic. Accepting this fact, and realising that a much greater common threat in the shape of the emerging great power of Russia was looming on the horizon, both sides at last came to terms with the status quo and eventually adopted a policy in tune with the new realities. Sweden's wars with Russia in 1741–43, during the War of the Austrian Succession, and again in 1788–90, during Russia's ongoing war with the Turks, were certainly, like her war with Prussia in 1757–62 as the ally of France, dictated by her wish to reduce the Russian threat and protect Finland, but they can best be seen as local manifestations of the European cabinet wars, the concomitant to the emergence of the classical great power system of the *ancien régime* in Europe. The same is true for Denmark's mobilisation against Russia in 1762 and her short war with Sweden in 1788. The latter was motivated by the need to protect Norway against a Swedish attack, but was in reality initiated by Russian pressure. The Baltic wars of the eighteenth century were symptoms of the fact that Russia had by then emerged as the crucial political and military factor in the region.

Only after the breakdown of the international system during the French Revolution and the Napoleonic wars did decisive changes in the political geography of the Nordic area again take place. At the Peace in Fredrikshamn in 1809, after the Russo-Swedish war of 1808–09, Sweden had to surrender Finland to Russia, while Denmark, at the Peace in Kiel in 1814, had to cede Norway to Sweden. The resulting political geography remained stable, until the unification of Germany in 1871 and the weakening of Russia after the Russo-Japanese war (1904–05) once again changed the patterns and laid the foundations of the modern situation in the Baltic.[4]

THE MILITARY REVOLUTION AND BALTIC WARFARE

Ever since Michael Roberts gave his famous inaugural lecture on 'The Military Revolution 1560–1660' in 1955, a rich debate has taken place on the nature and consequences of the early modern military transformations.[5] There now seems to be general scholarly agreement that Roberts's analysis was too one-sided and geographically too narrow in its scope, in that he took his point of departure only from technological changes – mainly the introduction of small firearms – and concentrated exclusively on north-west Europe. Roberts has also been criticised for analysing the military transformations in a rather too narrow time-perspective, tending thereby to over-emphasise the early modern changes at the cost of both earlier and later reformations of the military systems.[6]

Recent Scandinavian research has, moreover, seriously questioned the central role, heavily stressed by Roberts, of the Swedish king, Gustav II Adolf, in early modern military transformations. Obviously influenced by the Swedish General Staff's great work *Sveriges Krig 1611–1632*, Roberts portrayed Gustav Adolf as the great reformer of military organisation and the pioneer in tactics and strategy. According to Roberts, such crucial elements as a battle-seeking campaigns, increased mobility and shock-effect in attack were indeed reintroduced in European warfare by his reforms. Following his interpretation, it was Gustav Adolf before anyone else who succeeded in bringing the military operations out of the deadlock imposed on them by a previously inexpedient combination of pikes and firearms.

In contrast to this view, recent Swedish research in particular has raised doubts as to whether Gustav Adolf really was the determined strategist of annihilation and the revolutionary tactician portrayed by Roberts.[7] According to current Swedish views, the hero-king was, rather, a traditional strategist of attrition, even if a very clever one, who, loyally seconded by his hard-headed chancellor Axel Oxenstierna, was extremely successful in creating solid financial foundations for his ambitious military campaigns in Germany and elsewhere. This gift of methodical provisioning – more than novel tactical inventions – was, according to current views, the real secret behind his military successes.

This recent depreciation of Gustav Adolf as a tactical and strategical reformer has its counterpart in a corresponding higher appreciation of the nature of military reforms in Sweden's neighbouring countries in the same period. Notably, Gustav Adolf's most important rival, the Danish king Christian IV, whose military reputation has always been overshadowed by the fame of his great Swedish colleague, is presently experiencing something of a renaissance, accompanied by a more positive appraisal than hitherto of seventeenth-century Danish military organisation.[8]

However, there is no doubt that Michael Roberts's views have greatly influenced our general understanding of the military transformation process in early modern times. His many books on Swedish history, imbued with his admiration of Gustav Adolf, have likewise decisively influenced and shaped general perceptions in the English-speaking world of early modern warfare in the Baltic: it is almost universally perceived as synonymous with the military history of Sweden, while the other Baltic countries are largely ignored. It is, therefore, my intention in this chapter to draw a more shaded picture than the traditional one by also taking Denmark, Sweden's most important rival in the Baltic, into account with more emphasis than usual.

Although it is thus possible to note some disagreement about details in the so-called military revolution, it is fairly safe to assume a general consensus about two major consequences for European warfare of the early modern military transformations. They caused, in the first place, a heavy growth in the format of war: the armies grew larger, the campaigns and battles became more extensive and soldiers were recruited from a broader social basis than earlier. Second, the nobility had to give up their traditional monopoly on the business of warfare. It was, instead, taken over by the new renaissance state-powers who eventually took full responsibility for the recruitment, supplying and management of the war machinery. The use of military force became a state monopoly exercised by means of permanent state armies.

THE MILITARY FORMAT AND THE
STRUCTURE OF WARFARE

Such were the general trends in early modern Europe, and, apart from certain local variations, the development in the Baltic followed the general European trend. Sweden thus built, from the reign of Erik XIV (1560–68), a substantial permanent army, mainly based upon national conscription and financed from direct taxation and crown-land revenue.[9] Denmark followed suit from the beginning of the seventeenth century and, at the same time, greatly expanded her navy. It was her most important arm in the struggle for regional supremacy in view of her geographical position astride the entrances to the Baltic Sea. In full keeping with continental trends, this rearmament also took the form of an extensive construction of fortresses, serving mainly as points of support for the navy's operations. Here, as elsewhere, one can thus observe a quite heavy expansion of the permanent military infrastructure taking place under the auspices of the state powers along lines not dissimilar from those followed in Europe at large.[10]

Against this background, it is not surprising that the military operations in the Baltic area tended to follow the European mainstream both as far as the size of the field-armies and the nature of the operations are concerned. The greatest land-battle in the Northern Seven Years War, that of Axtorna in Halland on 20 October 1565, thus involved about 10 000 combatants on each side. This decisive battle ended with a Danish victory, and the total losses could most likely be counted in hundreds.[11] In the notorious battle at Lutter am Barenberg in the Harz on 17 August 1626, between the Danish king Christian IV and the Catholic general Tilly, the number of combatants on each side was about 20 000. It ended with a disastrous defeat for Christian IV, and the losses amounted to thousands.[12] The bloodiest battle ever in the history of northern warfare was the battle at Lund in Scania on 4 December 1676, which ended with a total Swedish victory. Around 20 000 men were involved all in all, and no fewer than 8000 were killed – a death-rate, incidentally, comparable to the one at Nördlingen in 1634, where 20 000 out of 58 000 combatants are said to have lost their lives.[13]

It appears from these figures that the northern wars in general were fought by smaller armies than was common on the contemporary great European battlefields – a fact that is not unnatural in view of the smaller size of the Nordic theatre of war and the more limited resources behind the armies. However, the smaller scale of northern land warfare may also be explained by the fact that naval war was a more important component of warfare in this region than in many other places: supremacy at sea, the *dominium maris Baltici*, remained, after all, the most important key to military domination in the region. This fact was heavily underlined by the most famous naval battle in the entire history of Baltic warfare, the battle in Køge Bay on 1 July 1677 between the Danish and Swedish fleets. This decisive showdown ended with a crushing Swedish defeat, which paralysed the Swedish navy for the rest of the war and thus prevented Sweden from exploiting the victory at Lund a few months earlier by invading the Danish islands – a step which, if taken, might have decided the war definitively in favour of Sweden.[14] As it happened, the assertion of Danish naval domination in the Western Baltic ensured that the Scanian War, like so many of the previous wars between Denmark and Sweden, ended in a draw.

The crucial role of naval power for success or failure in Baltic warfare is perhaps even most clearly demonstrated by Sweden's near-successful attempt at conquering Denmark during the wars 1657–60 and incorporating her in a new Great-Sweden. With a 10 000-man army, the Swedish warrior-king, Charles X Gustav, had succeeded in occupying Jutland from the south in the autumn of 1657 in one sweeping attack, but, from then on, his lightning war operations had come to a halt because he was prevented by the powerful Danish navy from advancing eastwards across the straits and islands towards the Danish capital, Copenhagen.

Around New Year 1657–58, however, nature came to the assistance of the Swedes. A continuous hard frost made the inner Danish waters freeze, thus paralysing the Danish navy but, on the other hand, making it possible for Charles X Gustav to venture one of the most daring operations ever in the history of warfare: he marched an expeditionary force of 8000 men, infantry and cavalry, across the ice-clad straits from Jutland over Funen, Langeland and Lolland to Zealand in the course of only two weeks. One can only guess what the Swedish soldiers must have felt while marching in darkness for mile after mile over the boggy ice, up to their knees in meltwater. However, the result justified this resolute action: Denmark was forced to sign a humiliating peace, and only intervention by the European great powers prevented her total extinction as a sovereign state.[15]

This dramatic event illustrates better than anything else how difficult it was for Denmark to survive without a strong operational navy. Also for Sweden, naval power was crucial both as an instrument in the permanent rivalry with Denmark and as a link between the Swedish mainland and her overseas possessions stretching from Finland to Pomerania. Those needs account for the fact that the arms race in the Baltic predominantly took the shape of a competition in naval capability, as illustrated in Figure 7.1.[16]

The very similar evolution of the sizes of Danish and Swedish navies until 1720 is a telling expression of the direct and close rivalry of the two leading Baltic powers in that period. Obviously, the naval building programmes of the two powers took the form of a close competition, with the goal of having disposal of a navy that could at least match the opponent's. The growing gap between the two curves after 1720 can, on the other hand, best be interpreted as signifying that the two countries after the Great Northern War were no longer military rivals, but lived in relative peaceful coexistence. The receding trend of Swedish naval power in the eighteenth century is explained by her loss of regional great power-status, while Denmark – remaining the gateway nation of the Baltic – still endeavoured to preserve a navy able also to match the emerging new naval power in the region, Russia. Lastly, the dramatic decline in Danish naval capability between 1800 and 1810 was the deplorable result of Great Britain's confiscation of her navy after the British attacks on Copenhagen in 1801 and 1807. On this account, Denmark lost her most important asset for influence in the Baltic, and in reality she ceased, from that point, to be a Baltic power of consequence.

The picture is markedly different, however, if we turn to the size of the armies in various Baltic countries. These are shown in Table 7.1.[17]

The figures reflect the increasing emphasis on army size, which was one main effect of the early modern military revolution. Contrary to the naval expansion, however, it is hardly possible here to discover any distinct correspondence between the growth-rates in the individual states: on the contrary, the figures are an illustration of the widely divergent conditions and local interests of the states around the Baltic.

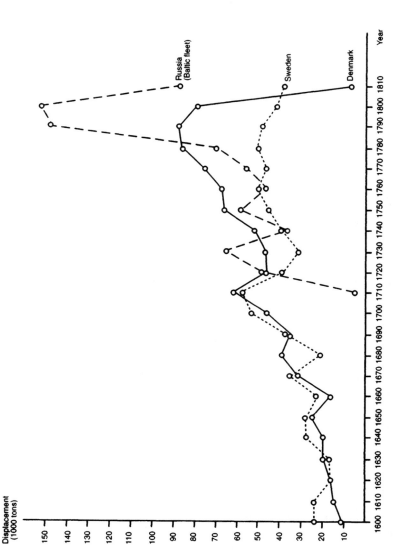

Figure 7.1 *Size of the Danish, Swedish and Russian navies (displacement) 1600–1810*

Table 7.1 *Approximate size of armies in various Baltic states*

Year	Denmark	Sweden	Prussia	Poland	Russia
c.1600	5000	15000	–	–	–
c.1650	25000	70000	800	10000	–
c.1700	70000	100000	41000	35000	170000
c.1750	50000	50000	135000	17000	200000
c.1800	74000	47000	200000	–	300000

As far as Denmark is concerned, her military readiness was at first determined by the antagonism with Sweden, later on by the necessary mobilisation during the French Revolution and the military alert caused by the Napoleonic wars. The steep increase in the size of Sweden's armies in the seventeenth century was a consequence of her temporary great power-status, while the Prussian figures reflect the systematic build-up of the Prussian military state. The modest Polish army was an adequate expression of this country's weak international position, while the heavy increase of the Russian army-size was a true representation of her widespread interests and a telling expression of Russia's road towards a European great power-status in the eighteenth century.

Measured against the figures for the overall population and compared with other European powers, however, the figures are also a striking demonstration that the armies of Denmark, Sweden and Prussia were unusually large. Taken together, these three states formed probably the most heavily militarised region in Europe at the beginning of the eighteenth century – a fact reflected in the remark by Sir Robert Molesworth, the British envoy to Denmark, in his description of Denmark in the 1690s: 'Denmark resembles . . . a Monster that is all Head and no Body, all Soldiers and no Subjects.'[18] This extremely high level of militarisation was, as far as Sweden and Denmark were concerned, a direct effect of their prolonged rivalry for supremacy in the Baltic, while for Prussia, it was an inevitable consequence of her incessant struggle for survival with hostile neighbours on all sides.

WAR AND THE TRANSFORMATION OF SOCIETY

The almost permanent state of war in the Baltic region from the mid-sixteenth to the early eighteenth centuries imposed a permanently heavy burden upon the shoulders of the relatively poor and backward peasant societies of the region. The constant warfare was, however, also the most important single dynamic factor in the profound process of modernisation, which, over the same time-span, transformed the area from a cluster of distant medieval church provinces on the fringe of the permafrost – as it was once described by an obviously frostbitten French diplomat – into modern European state formations equipped with well-functioning power-structures. If we look at the eighteenth century, they were all well-integrated parts of the general European balance-of-power system – the Westphalian system – that emerged from the international anarchy of the Thirty Years War. In other words: one effect of the permanent regional warfare was the opening of the Baltic towards Europe – a process of Europeanisation.

Another significant effect was, as mentioned above, a thorough modernisation of the machineries of state and the structures of society, most marked in Denmark, Sweden and Prussia. On the economic level, financing by direct taxation gradually took over from the traditional method of domain-financing, while the administrative machinery was centralised and turned into a regular bureaucracy. The political system gradually tended towards absolutism – in Prussia de facto from the mid-seventeenth century, in Denmark from the constitutional revolution in 1660, and in Sweden from 1680. These general effects of the growing military format are discussed by Ronald Asch in Chapter 2 of the present volume. The same processes, with similar effects, were also in play in the Baltic region.

Another question, not unconnected with the general process of modernisation, should be considered: how was it that the isolated and poor Sweden emerged victorious from the long drawn-out struggle over the Baltic and, even for a few decades, rightfully claimed a great, regional power-status? Why not the better situated and better-off Denmark?

The short answer to this question is, paradoxically enough, that the Swedish king at the outset of the sixteenth century was markedly poorer than his Danish colleague. For this reason, the Swedish king was under heavy pressure from almost permanent warfare from 1560 onwards and had to press on with a determined effort of optimising financial policy and modernising the machinery of government. Those efforts – in particular under chancellor Oxenstierna's resolute leadership – eventually created one of the most efficient war economies in the region – until the mid-seventeenth century, far more efficient and powerful than, for instance, its Danish counterpart.

In order to understand the background to this asymmetrical development, it is necessary to point out a few significant differences between the political systems and socioeconomic structures of the two leading Scandinavian powers. In a political sense, the Swedish king was considerably stronger than his Danish colleague. Since Gustav Vasa's days the Swedish crown had been hereditary, while the Danish king was, until 1660, elected and limited in his executive power by a restrictive coronation charter. This fact alone endowed the Swedish king with much greater power. Moreover, the different conditions were further enhanced by the fact that the Swedish power-elite, the nobility, was a far weaker corporation and fewer in number than that of Denmark. Around 1560 the Swedish nobility thus only owned 22 per cent of the land, while the Danish nobility controlled no less than 44 per cent of arable land in Denmark. This fact, combined with the more democratic Swedish *riksdags*-constitution, explains why the weak Swedish nobility did not constitute a serious threat to the crown. On the contrary, the noble estate in general submitted to the crown and acted as its partner – in stark contrast to Denmark, where, up to 1660, an extremely powerful nobility exercised an overwhelming political influence not dissimilar from contemporary conditions in Poland, by far the most aristocratic republic of Europe.[19]

The Swedish crown, however politically powerful, was, in economic terms, poor in comparison to the Danish king. Thus, around 1560, crown lands totalled only about 30 per cent of Sweden's arable land, while the Danish king controlled around 50 per cent of the fertile Danish farmland. In Sweden revenues from crown lands were thus considerably lower than those in

Denmark, to which should be added the substantial incomes from the Sound Toll and from the Swedish war indemnities after the Northern Seven Years War and the Kalmar War.

When, from the mid-sixteenth century, Sweden became engaged in almost permanent warfare, the relatively poor Swedish government had at a very early stage to resort to direct taxation in order to complement the modest ordinary revenue. In other words, the Swedish war economy became, very early on, an economy based upon taxes and handled by an efficient government machinery built up for the purpose. Therefore, under the constant pressure of permanent warfare, the medieval domain-state Sweden was already from the early seventeenth century transformed into a modern tax-state with a strong, centralised and smoothly working government run by a politically powerful king. The foundations were by then already in place for the later Swedish great power, capable of harvesting the full profit from the weakness of her more backward neighbours. Only as these neighbours, by the end of the seventeenth century, gradually regained some of their former strength through modernisation – while the fortune of war at the same time failed the Swedish forces – did the great Swedish power collapse like a house of cards when challenged by the other Baltic states. Sweden's sudden and total collapse by 1720 was at the same time a telling exposure of the weak foundations of her virtual great power-status: the Swedish great power rested in reality only upon the temporarily favourable combination of a weak, but efficiently managed Swedish economy, the weakness of her neighbours and the fleeting friendship of powerful allies among the real great powers in Europe.

In Denmark things evolved differently. After the conclusion of the Northern Seven Years War in 1570 the country experienced more than forty years of unbroken peace and her state finances were in a healthy shape. Contrary to Sweden, therefore, there was no need for an instant reformation of the traditional, old-fashioned system of domain-financing which could perfectly meet the government's needs and, at the same time, exactly reflected the delicate balance of power between king and nobility. An urgent need for administrative reforms only arose after Christian IV's disastrous and expensive involvement in the Thirty Years War in 1625–29. This ill-fated adventure emptied the government's coffers and, at the same time, exposed the urgent need for heavy investment in a modernisation of the army and the navy. Only then did Denmark's transformation into a modern, centralised tax-state begin. This process was not completed until about 1700 – and had, along the way, changed the old aristocratic kingdom into a highly centralised, absolutist state with a modern, efficient power-structure ready to meet the challenges of war.

It was precisely in this decisive transitional phase when, by the mid-seventeenth century, the country was weakened by the fierce internal struggle between new and old power-structures, that the balance of power between Denmark and Sweden tipped definitely in favour of Sweden. The fully modernised Sweden, with her high level of military readiness, was by then in a good position to exploit the temporary Danish weakness. In a couple of decisive wars she succeeded in taking the lead in the Baltic at the expense of Denmark and, at the same time, acquiring important territorial gains, which meant a permanent weakening of Denmark's position both in the Baltic and internationally.

This outcome of the prolonged rivalry between the two Scandinavian powers can thus, in large part, be explained by this asymmetrical process of modernisation in the two countries. Both countries had modernisation forced upon them by the pressure of war, but it struck, as demonstrated, earliest and strongest in Sweden, and thus gave this country a decisive advantage, when the rivalry with the better-off, but old-fashioned Denmark entered the crucial phase in the mid-seventeenth century. When the Swedish great power definitely collapsed in 1720–21 a new balance was re-established between a reduced Sweden and a now fully modernised Denmark – but by then in the shadow of Russia, the rising new great power in the Baltic.

MERCANTILISM AND THE BALTIC WARS

With the peace treaty at Nystad in 1721 between Sweden and Russia, the last great war in the Baltic so far finally came to an end. This treaty was, at the same time, the beginning of almost a century of relative peace in the region – a situation contrasting strongly with the endless conflicts and the almost permanent state of war during the preceding 150 years.

Regarded in a longer perspective, this belligerent phase forms a long and painful period of transition in the history of the Baltic region, during which it underwent a transformation from one status to another. At the outset, in the sixteenth century, the region was an isolated, mainly self-sufficient area, dominated by the local commercial great power – the Hanseatic League. However, during the long period of conflict and open war that followed, the region – because it was eventually dragged into the focus of great power-interests – was transformed into becoming an integral part of the greater European system, usually described as the Westphalian system. The militant mercantilism of the seventeenth century – the precondition of which was the notion of the modern state – was an important driving-force in this great process of transformation. Those two phenomena are, therefore, as shown, closely interconnected in Baltic history, as they are in the history of Europe as well.[20]

The most famous of all Danish kings, Christian IV, who happened to be the one who came to preside over great parts of this transformation, once gave his understanding of what mercantilism was all about in an official statement. It is an economic system, he said, 'that should be to the honour of Us – and, with the help of God, do no harm to the merchants'. With hindsight, it may be pointed out that the militant mercantilism, which helped to shape the early modern Baltic history and was a dynamic force behind most of the wars described in this chapter, did not serve the honour of Christian IV. And the merchants who profited most from it were certainly neither the king's own subjects nor those of his Swedish colleague, but first and foremost the participants in the great commercial companies in the United Provinces and England who, in the end, were the ones who designated the local winners and losers in the regional contest and, by their choice, determined the modern political geography of the Baltic.

This proved to be part of the price that the peoples in the Baltic region had to pay for being changed from distant church provinces into proper European nation-states. Another price was the ordeal of almost permanent warfare for a century and a half. And – who knows – it may have been worth the price. The ordinary people in the Baltic region were never asked, and were never given a choice.

8. Gaelic Warfare 1453–1815

J. MICHAEL HILL

I

Scottish and Irish warfare from the mid-fifteenth to the early eighteenth centuries has largely been neglected by European military historians. One reason for such neglect is that both Scotland and Ireland are sparsely populated and lie on the fringes of Europe, far out of the main current of historical development. Another is because the Gaels practised a non-traditional, alternative style of warfare that contrasted markedly with the traditional, uniform model represented by the 'Great Powers' of the early modern era: Spain, France, England, the Netherlands and Sweden, among others. The Scots and Irish combined mobility with devastating offensive shock power, thus falling outside Michael Roberts's 'military revolution' paradigm.[1]

The arrival of the *gallóglaigh*, a professional Scottish military class, in Ireland in the thirteenth century heralded a martial counterweight to the Anglo-Norman *gendarmes*. Thenceforth, Gaelic warfare relied on attack tactics designed to destroy the opposition in one terrible blow. By the late sixteenth century, however, Shane O'Neill and his nephew Hugh O'Neill, second earl of Tyrone, combined traditional Scottish *gallóglaigh* heavy-infantry tactics with a novel type of warfare based mainly on the use of gunpowder weapons in guerrilla-style operations. This combination of blade and gunpowder weaponry, superior mobility, surprise and an effective use of rugged terrain fused the best elements of traditional and new warfare by 1600.[2]

In his wars against the English in the 1590s, Hugh O'Neill enjoyed a good deal of success by combining formational flexibility, firepower and heavy-infantry shock tactics against English armies unaccustomed to such irregular warfare. But when he threw off this manner of fighting at Kinsale in 1601, in

201

favour of the unfamiliar intricacies of the Spanish *tercio* formation, O'Neill suffered defeat at the hands of a competent English army under the command of Charles Blount, Lord Mountjoy. It was not until the mid-seventeenth century that the Gaelic Scots and Irish began to develop a style of war that allowed them to win frequently against professional armies. The Gaels had been reluctant to adopt the military technologies and theories so often used in England and on the Continent among the larger dynastic states; however, by employing the musket, the Scots and Irish were able to unleash the fearsome 'Highland (or, properly speaking, Irish) charge'.[3]

The Irish charge, which originated in the last third of the sixteenth century, allowed the Gaels to solve Michael Roberts's dilemma of combining 'hitting power [and] mobility'. Unlike conventional armies, the Gaels' use of firearms did not sacrifice offensive striking power and mobility for static defensive firepower. Although the Irish charge depended for its success primarily on the one-handed broadsword and target (a round, leather-covered shield), it effectively used the musket (without the cumbersome fork-rest that limited the attack capabilities of both Maurice of Nassau's and Gustav Adolf's armies) as an offensive weapon.[4]

The Irish charge employed both the new linear and the old columnar attack formations, thus giving it a tactical flexibility absent in most other European armies of the day. At the start of battle, the Gaels would array themselves on a piece of high ground from which they advanced against the enemy. Then, within some forty yards of the opposing line, they fired a wild musket volley in order to cause confusion from flying shot and powder smoke. Next they threw aside their firearms, formed up into wedges or columns twelve to fifteen men wide, drew broadswords and continued toward the adversary. Usually, the enemy could fire only one potentially deadly volley before close-quarter combat became the order of the day. Armies lacking sufficient firepower, hand-to-hand combat skills and defence in depth frequently were overwhelmed by the Irish charge. This blending of old tactics and new technology led to a decisive and distinctive type of offensive warfare unique in Western Europe for over a century. The Irish charge, evolving as it did from 1642 to 1746, became the centrepiece of Gaelic tactical doctrine during what was called their 'Golden Age' of warfare.[5]

During this era, Scottish and Irish armies won eight major battles by using offensive tactics on harsh terrain, with the broadsword rather than the musket as the principal weapon. Unlike most other European armies, Gaelic forces were not hampered by the trappings of modern warfare. They were not restricted to defensive operations, the conduct of sieges or massive frontal assaults due to immobility or inflexibility. Rather, they were flexible enough to attack from the front or the flank, the latter option depending initially upon superior mobility instead of sheer striking power. The Scots and Irish often used mobility and shock power in deadly combination, as demonstrated at Auldearn and Kilsyth (1645), Killiecrankie (1689) and Prestonpans (1745). At other times, they sought (with varying degrees of success) simply to overwhelm the enemy: Tippermuir and Aberdeen (1644), Inverlochy (1645), Sheriffmuir (1715) and Falkirk and Culloden (1746).[6]

After 1689, Celtic offensive tactics were first blunted and then broken by tactical and technological improvements worked out on European battlefields. The introduction of the socket bayonet, the more efficient flintlock musket, and mobile field artillery firing grapeshot and canister, permitted the defence to develop better close-quarter tactics and to generate more firepower. Moreover, as the British during the Jacobite uprisings of 1715 and 1745–46 fielded armies comprising co-ordinated infantry, cavalry and artillery arms, the Gaels could no longer expect to triumph by their customary methods of fighting. Indeed, the duke of Cumberland's destruction of Prince Charles Edward Stuart's Highland army on the open ground of Culloden Moor was the death-knell to an alternative style of warfare that had dominated British battlefields for a century. From 1746 to 1815, certain elements of the Gaelic way of war would be introduced on the battlefields of Europe and abroad in the armies of the great colonial powers.[7]

II

The Swiss pikemen's defeat of the Burgundian heavy cavalry in the 1470s marked the end of an era in European warfare. Since the Welsh wars of independence in the mid-thirteenth century, the footsoldier had shown his ability (when properly

armed, well led, and operating on favourable terrain) to defeat
levies of feudal horsemen. The effectiveness of infantry against
heavy cavalry was further manifested by the intrepid Swiss when
they dealt severe blows to the Austrian chivalry at Morgarten
and Laupen (1315) and Sempach (1386); and by the English
longbowmen at Crécy in 1346. Thus, the diminished role of
feudal cavalry and the increased importance of infantry marked
a revolutionary turn in the mainstream of European warfare by
making possible a dramatic increase in the size of armies. The
approaching 'gunpowder revolution' would give the wheel yet
another turn.[8]

But in the Gaelic world of the late Middle Ages no such revolution was necessary, for the Scots and Irish had always employed
infantry as the backbone of their military forces. The most important Gaelic infantry of this era were the *gallóglaigh* – West Highland and Hebridean mercenaries who settled in Ireland from the
mid-thirteenth through to the sixteenth centuries. One contemporary observer described the *gallóglaigh* as

> picked and select men of great and mighty bodies and cruel
> without compassion. Their order of fight is much like the
> Suizes [Swiss], for the greatest force of the battle consisteth
> upon them choosing rather to do than to yield, so that when it
> cometh to handy blows they are either quickly slain or win the
> field. They are armed with a shirt of mail, a skull [helmet] and
> a skayne [knife]. The weapon which they most use is a battleaxe
> or halbert five foot long, the blade whereof is somewhat like a
> shoemaker's knife, but broader and longer without pike, the
> stroke whereof is deadly where it lighteth. And being in this
> sort armed reckoning also to him a man for his arms bearer
> and a boy to carry his provision, he is named a sparre as his
> weapon or axe is so termed, 80 of which sparres make a battle
> of galloglas.[9]

The term *gallóglaigh* (anglicised as 'gallowglass' or 'galloglas')
literally means 'foreign' (*gall*) 'warrior' (*óglaigh*). *Gallóglaigh*
first appeared in the Irish annals in 1290, but they had been
employed by Irish chiefs since mid-century. A fierce admixture
of Gaelic and Norse blood descended from the line of the
great twelfth-century warrior-chief, Somerled MacGillebride, the

gallóglaigh who, under the leadership of Angus Oge of the Isles, had introduced into Ireland a style of warfare that revolutionised the island's military system. Whereas before, the native Irish chiefs had depended on a general levy, not unlike the Anglo-Saxon *fyrd*, to raise troops, the coming of the *gallóglaigh* gave them a permanent force of professional soldiers.[10]

Because Ireland in the late Middle Ages had no permanent military establishment, the Irish fought few formal, pitched battles on open terrain. Instead, they preferred various forms of guerrilla warfare, using the nimble and lightly accoutered *catharn* (kerne). When Edward Bruce invaded Ireland in the early fourteenth century, he found that the native chiefs favoured running skirmishes with missile weapons (mainly bows and spears) instead of set-piece battles that called for the use of close-quarter blade weapons. Such fighting techniques brought fewer casualties; thus this was a type of warfare conducive to the chiefs' main objective of acquiring tenants rather than wantonly destroying life and property.[11]

But guerrilla warfare was of little use against the Normans, who in Ireland practised war by encastellation. The old Irish proverb, 'better a castle of bones [i.e. a large, well-organised field army] than a castle of stones', had little relevance for a force of light infantry that was capable of nothing more than the ambush and the skirmish.[12] But this was not so with the *gallóglaigh*, whose objective it was to engage the enemy in the open and destroy him with the use of blade weapons at close quarters. Indeed, the arrival of the *gallóglaigh* in Ireland precipitated what might be termed a Gaelic 'military revolution' in the thirteenth and fourteenth centuries.

Commonly, the *gallóglaigh* units in Ireland received their compensation in the form of land grants and *buannadha*, a payment system similar to coyne and livery wherein troops were billeted upon the population of a lordship (*tuath*). Other bands – freelance mercenaries – roamed the countryside, hiring themselves out to the highest bidder. This system undoubtedly increased the level of chaos in Ireland, but the services of the redoubtable *gallóglaigh* were indispensable in driving out the Normans.[13]

The battlefield tactics of the *gallóglaigh* can perhaps be best illustrated by examining the battle of Knockdoe (meaning 'the hill of the axes') in 1504. Arraying on open ground, the *gallóglaigh* under Ulick Burke deployed on either wing to profit from their superior mobility, and in the centre so that they could either deliver or absorb a shock assault. Even at this relatively late date, the tactics of the Scots mercenaries had changed little from those of the past two centuries. Each warrior, or, to be precise, each *sparre*, combined the use of both missile and close-quarter blade weaponry. Since bows were absent from the ranks of the *gallóglaigh*, the opening missile volley consisted of light spears and javelins, designed to disorder the enemy rather than cause severe casualties. In place of an initial volley of heavy missiles, the Scots troops delivered a powerful shock attack. Lacking reserves, the Scots obviously risked all on carrying the enemy position with the first assault. This plan demanded that each warrior be resolute in pressing home the charge, because disaster would likely befall the army should they be repulsed by the defenders. As late as 1543, the Irish Lord Deputy, Sir Anthony St Leger, informed Henry VIII that the *gallóglaigh* swore an oath before battle not to abandon the field; therefore, they remained 'the one part of an Irish army that could be entrusted to stand its ground to the end'.[14]

III

G. A. Hayes-McCoy did not compare the *gallóglaigh* tradition with contemporaneous European military institutions. Before 1500, only among the Italian *condottieri* and the roving 'Great Companies' and the Swiss were there similar military organisations. However, the respective societies that fostered the *gallóglaigh* and the *condottieri* could not have been more dissimilar. The Celtic world, on the one hand, was arguably Europe's most pastoral, non-commercial region; northern Italy, on the other, was its most urbane and commercially advanced. Yet both areas gave rise to small, elite professional infantry forces, some of which were as competent as any in Europe until the close of the fifteenth century.[15]

Celtic and most pre-1500 European infantry forces differed primarily in weaponry, tactics and the role of the individual soldier on the battlefield. The Scots and Irish had no chivalric tradition, as such (though they did have the inspiring Red

Branch and Fenian cycle tales); thus cavalry played only a minor role in their military system. Most of Scotland's and Ireland's harsh and rugged terrain was unsuited for cavalry tactics, and this, along with the lack of adequate mounts, most certainly deterred the Gaels from becoming expert horsemen. Instead, they preferred to fight on foot, amid bog, mountain and glen. Scottish and Irish 'irregulars' were proficient with the bow, but, with occasional exceptions, they relegated it to a secondary status behind blade weapons. In Gaelic society, the individual footsoldier became a self-contained fighting unit. Armed with sword or axe, he acted under the inducements of personal honour and fiery impetuosity rather than of collective discipline. On the Continent and in English armies, conversely, an increased tactical use of the pike resulted in an emphasis on the disciplined body of the whole rather than on the individual warrior. Standard European warfare, in which men 'would act as cogs in a machine', was becoming a science. In the Gaelic world, it remained a proud art.[16]

In order to better understand post-1500 Celtic military developments, perhaps we should look briefly at the type of warfare that played itself out among the Great Powers of Europe. When Charles VIII of France invaded Italy in the last decade of the fifteenth century, his armies brought about some salient changes in the way European wars were fought. Between the battles of Fornovo (1495) and Pavia (1525), combat became uncharacteristically costly and decisive. Larger armies began to appear on the field of battle, and they tended to suffer more casualties because of the dominance of infantry utilising gunpowder weapons. But these factors alone did not ensure the increased level of carnage during this quarter-century. Rather, combat had become so destructive because tactics had yet to adapt to new technologies. The shock of the pikemen's charge, which had dominated attack tactics for well over a generation, no longer won the day on a battlefield studded with field fortifications and swept by fire from personal firearms and artillery. These defensively-orientated tactical innovations, first employed by the great Spanish general, Gonzalo de Córdoba, allowed his troops to win at Cerignola (1503). Moreover, the same method of fighting resulted in a French victory at Marignano (1515) and a Spanish triumph again at Bicocca (1522). All three of these engagements witnessed the victors employing superior firepower from behind strong field fortifications to break the backs of attacking infantry and cavalry forces. The decline of the pike as an effective offensive weapon and the concurrent rise in the defensive use of gunpowder weapons initiated an era in which mainstream European warfare would be dominated by defensive tactics.[17]

If we exempt such battles as Muhlberg (1547), Zutphen (1586) and White Mountain (1620), and the First and Second Polish–Swedish wars (1600–11 and 1617–29, respectively), the decisive battle all but disappeared in Western and Central Europe from Pavia (1525) to Breitenfeld (1631). A number of general military developments account for this change: the defensive superiority of combining firearms and elaborate field entrenchments; the innovative military architecture of the *trace italienne* – a novel style of low, thick walls that neutralised siege artillery; and the spread of military entrepreneurship from northern Italy beyond the Alps. Joined with the increased financial costs of war because of the sixteenth-century price revolution, these factors caused kings and commanders across Europe to seek means other than battle to attain their political and military objectives. Battle, some observers now believed, was the resort of the incompetent captain.[18]

Tactical employment of the two standard infantry weapons – pikes and personal firearms – caused the century between Pavia and Breitenfeld to be marked, with some important exceptions, by the indecisive battle. The Spanish *tercio*, common to battlefields in the first half of the sixteenth century, 'so far from producing a fruitful collaboration between [shot and pikes] . . . , succeeded only in inhibiting the characteristic qualities of each'. The complex tactical nature of the *tercio* and other formations discouraged infantry from engaging in close-quarter combat. Conversely, it encouraged ineffective long-range musket duels. Few battles were either won or lost with such tactics. The initial stage of the battle of Ceresole (1544) demonstrated the indecisiveness of long-range fire fights. There, the French and Imperial armies spent much of the day engaged in an exchange of ineffectual fire; hence, nothing of import was decided.[19]

Personal firearms – the arquebus, caliver and matchlock musket – because of their short range, slow rate of fire, inaccuracy and cumbersome nature, proved inadequate for offensive tactics in the hands of most European soldiers. The musket, most powerful of the three weapons, was able to penetrate the heaviest armour, but could not be fired without a fork-rest; this precluded its use except for defensive purposes. In the sixteenth century, firearms assumed the role of disorganising the enemy ranks in preparation for a pike assault. J. R. Hale, undoubtedly aware of the musket's limited and passive role, contends that firearms 'raised problems of tactics, equipment, and supply..., but they had little effect on the fortunes of campaigns....'. Hale is correct, but only from an offensive standpoint. The problems of logistics and immobility rendered firearms virtually useless as weapons of attack. Thus, as musketeers displaced pikemen in European armies, the roles of the weapons underwent salient changes. Firepower became the main responsibility of both infantry and cavalry, the latter being 'transformed ... from an instrument of shock into one of mobile firepower', while the pikemen now were employed to form a barrier behind which the musketeers could safely reload. Barring small numbers of mounted arquebusiers and pistoleers, Spanish sword and buckler troops, and German *landsknecht* pikemen, conventional European armies enjoyed little mobility or striking power during this century.[20]

The artillery also was virtually useless for offensive war in the sixteenth century. Charles VIII of France employed the first mobile field guns during his 1494 invasion of Italy. Fornovo (1495), a French victory over the Italian alliance, was the first battle in which artillery played a significant role, but Ravenna (1512) was the first engagement actually decided by artillery. At Ravenna, some fifty French pieces bombarded the Spanish fortified lines, forcing them into a desperate attack in which they were destroyed by superior French firepower. French field guns also annihilated the attacking Swiss pikemen on the second day at Marignano (1515). The century's end saw the advent of lighter, more mobile artillery pieces. Maurice of Nassau improved the Dutch artillery arm by standardising types (24-, 12- and 6-pounders) and by using limbers to increase mobility.[21] But once his guns were put into position on the battlefield, he found it difficult to move them in support of an infantry advance. In pre-1600 field operations, artillery was useful only for softening up an enemy position prior to attack or for defending a position against assault.

IV

The defensive use of personal firearms and artillery by most European powers after 1500 contrasted sharply with the continued offensive use of blade weapons by the Gaels. Firearms and pikes, so important in continental military developments, did not come into common use among the Highland Scots and Irish until the late sixteenth and early seventeenth centuries. Even then, both musket and pike were of secondary import compared to the broadsword and target (a small, round, leather-covered shield). Since being introduced on to European battlefields, firearms had been condemned by some as the weapons of cowards; however, they were eventually accepted even by the most honourable of soldiers. In the Gaelic world, firearms were never given equal weight with the fearsome claymore or the broadsword, weapons that, if dexterously wielded, earned eloquent praise from the *aés dana* (the learned classes that transmitted the histories and genealogies from generation to generation). The armies of the Tudor and early Stuart dynasties lagged behind their continental counterparts, but even the best trained and armed troops from England, Lowland Scotland and the Irish Pale were virtually powerless to stand against the Gaels' cold steel at close quarters. In fact, until the advent of a reliable bayonet in the late seventeenth century, successful offensive and defensive tactics throughout Europe were predicated on the attacking infantryman's competence with the sword or other hand-held blade weapons and the defender's ability to counter him with a combination of shot and pike.[22]

The changing roles of gunpowder weaponry and the pike and the new science of military fortification wrought a re-examination of European tactics between Pavia and Breitenfeld. During this century, however, the Highland Scots, and particularly the redshanks, continued to use the heavy infantry tactics of the *gallóglaigh*. At the same time, the Irish were developing a new style of warfare predicated on superior mobility, stealth and the employment of firearms in guerrilla-type ambushes. The blending of shock power and finesse, together with the individual prowess of their warriors, allowed Gaelic military leaders an offensive capability unmatched on the European continent from about 1550 to 1640. Perhaps the only exceptions were certain elements in the Spanish and Swedish armies, the latter under the great military reformer Gustav Adolf.

Shane O'Neill demonstrated the effective nature of this new style of Gaelic warfare by forcing the English out of Ulster in the early 1560s and then by defeating his old allies, the MacDonnells of Antrim, at Glentaisie (Glenshesk) in 1565. The Scottish redshank army under brothers James and Sorley Boy (Somhairle Buidhe) MacDonnell fought at Glentaisie in the traditional *gallóglaigh* fashion, drawn up in formal alignment and using the Lochaber axe and the two-handed claymore. O'Neill's troops – both heavy infantry and light skirmishers (kerne) – combined blade weapons and gunpowder weapons with mobility, the element of surprise and a judicious use of the surrounding terrain, thus pulling together the best offensive tactics of the traditional and the new Gaelic warfare. While there were many similarities between the weaponry and tactics of the two armies at Glentaisie, there were enough marked differences to support the claim that Shane O'Neill had begun to revolutionise the Irish military system. But when he abandoned his new formula, he was roundly defeated by the Tyrconnell O'Donnells at Farsetmore in 1567. Hugh O'Neill, Shane's nephew and the second earl of Tyrone, built on his kinsman's success in the 1590s. At Clontibret, the Yellow Ford and the Moyry Pass, the younger O'Neill more than held his own against the best commanders England could put in the field by blending stealth, speed, formational flexibility, firepower and, above all, shock tactics. O'Neill suffered defeat only when he fought the English at Kinsale in 1601 on open ground and under conventional circumstances. His futile attempt to employ the complicated *tercio* formation threw his troops into confusion and permitted Charles Blount, Lord Mountjoy's men to assume the tactical offensive against the disordered Irish. As a result, O'Neill's army was routed by a combination of Mountjoy's infantry and cavalry. The Irish loss at Kinsale undermined their entire campaign to rid Ireland of Elizabethan dominance in the last decade of the sixteenth century.[23]

From the advent of the *gallóglaigh* until the middle of the seventeenth century, the Gaels had sought the most useful combination of tactics and weaponry to suit their particular military organisation. In three and a half centuries their methods of war had evolved quite differently from those of the continental powers. The Highland Scots and Irish, as a rule, eschewed most of the ideas and technologies upon which Roberts's 'military revolution' had been founded. Unlike most of their continental counterparts, Gaelic armies did not grow in size and complexity as a result of Europe's general economic prosperity. Nor did they reorder their military strategies based on such factors as the defensive innovations of Maurice of Nassau. However, there were some fundamental changes in Gaelic tactics that resulted from their adoption of new gunpowder technologies. When the Gaels ultimately did embrace gunpowder weaponry as an important element of their tactics, it was in a fashion uniquely their own. The Scots and Irish,better than any other forces in Europe, solved what Roberts defines as the tactical problem 'of how to combine missile weapons with close-action; how to unite hitting-power, mobility and defensive strength'. Their use of personal firearms did not undermine offensive shock power and mobility, and it mattered little to the Gaels whether they had to sacrifice modern defensive- and siege-orientated military practices to conduct offensive warfare. By effectively blending old tactics and new technology, the Scots and Irish created a type of war distinct from any other practised in Western Europe.[24]

Maurice of Nassau's and Gustav Adolf's military reforms in the last years of the sixteenth century and the first third of the seventeenth had little effect on the development of warfare in the Gaelic world. While Maurice's introduction of a smaller, more manageable infantry unit – the 550-man battalion – paralleled the standard tactical organisation of the old clan regiments, this was one of the few similarities between modern military units and those of the Gaels. Both drew up their forces in wide, shallow formations, but the Maurician battle-line, according to Roberts, 'was essentially passive . . . [and] not apt for the offensive. . . . Of an offensive tactic he had little idea; of a campaign culminating in annihilating victory, none at all.' Because Gustav Adolf is his champion, Roberts posits that Maurice failed to solve the pressing military problems of his day, and thus left the great Swede 'to restore, both to horse and foot, the capacity for the battle-winning tactical offensive'.[25]

Gustav increased the percentage of blade (pikes) to missile (muskets) weapons among his infantry 'squadrons' (units of comparable size to Maurice's battalions) and introduced the 'salvo' for greater missile shock power. He also increased the effectiveness of his footsoldiers by arming them with shorter, lighter matchlock muskets, but did not introduce the more advanced wheel-lock or snaphance musket. He also continued to use the cumbersome fork-rest. Gustav initiated the employment of mobile field artillery – two- and three-pounder 'leather guns', and restored the striking power of the cavalry arm (which, by the early 1630s, made up nearly one-third of his forces). The advance of Swedish musketeers, pikemen and mobile field guns firing pre-loaded cartridges of 'hail shot' (canister) gave Gustav a 'fire-shock' which he tried to exploit with his pikemen (standing at a 2:3 ratio to muskets, as compared to the standard seventeenth-century ratio of 1:2 pikes to muskets) who were trained to charge the enemy after a salvo rather than to stand passively and defend the musketeers. But personal firearms, including those borne by cavalry, and artillery made up his main capability. The concerted salvo of Gustav's musketeers alone, for example, threw out such a heavy weight of fire at Breitenfeld that they broke the attack of the Imperial cavalry. When the squadron artillery was included, the Swedes possessed greater firepower than any previous European army. Gustav's reforms did not result in an increase in his infantry's speed, mobility and close-combat shock power; rather, they led to increased firepower, hardly a revolution in offensive tactics. His heavily-laden footsoldiers found it impossible to keep pace with the cavalry moving ahead at a trot. It was necessary, therefore, for the horse to advance at a snail's pace, thus greatly reducing mobility and hitting power. Nor could the leather guns, not to mention heavier pieces, keep up with the infantry, except over smooth terrain for limited distances. Roberts, then, is forced to concede that under Gustav Adolf 'the dilemma – speed or firepower – remained unresolved'.[26]

If we credit Maurice of Nassau and Gustav Adolf with restoring organisational flexibility, offensive tactics and the decisive battle to European warfare, we thereby ignore contemporaneous developments in Gaelic warfare, however outside the main-stream such developments might have been. As Gustav lay dying at Lützen (1632), the Scots and Irish were undertaking a series of tactical innovations that would usher in their military 'Golden Age' (1644–1746). Scottish historian David Stevenson, in his *Alasdair MacColla and the Highland Problem in the Seventeenth Century* (1980), posits that the 'Highland charge' was first employed in Ireland at the battle of the Laney (1642) by the intrepid military adventurer, Alasdair MacColla. A decade later, Stuart Reid challenged this assertion by dismissing the Highland charge as insignificant when compared to conventional seventeenth-century tactics and by calling the Highlanders 'a half-armed, undisciplined mob'.[27]

Though both Stevenson and Reid make some provocative arguments, further explanation of this tactical innovation is needed if we are properly to understand the origins and development of warfare in the Celtic fringe. MacColla indeed introduced a dynamic new tactical configuration from Ireland into Scotland in the 1640s and won at least five major victories – Tippermuir (1644), Aberdeen (1644), Inverlochy (1645), Auldearn (1645) and Kilsyth (1645) – for the Royalist cause. His tactical development should not, however, be called the 'Highland' but the 'Irish' charge. This matter of nomenclature leads quite naturally into the second issue: Reid's claim that the Highlanders themselves were not proper instruments to carry out the charge. Up to a point, he is correct; it was MacColla's Irish veterans (mainly men from Clan Donald's Irish branch, the Antrim MacDonnells) who usually executed the tactics in question in 1644–45. However, Reid is mistaken in his implication that the Highland clans thereafter did not successfully adopt the charge from Killiecrankie (1689) to Culloden (1746).[28]

Upon thorough study, it is clear that an evolving Irish charge (in several variations) had become the centrepiece of Gaelic tactical warfare by the 1640s. Thus the charge antedates the battle of the Laney in 1642. In fact, certain important tactical elements of the 'Highland charge' had already been developed in Gaelic Ulster and the Hebrides from *c*.1560 to 1600. Moreover, the charge's tactical principles and its execution underwent some important changes during the 1640s. It may be argued that the Irish charge had its immediate origins in the latter half of the sixteenth century after the introduction of firearms into the

Gaelic periphery of the British Isles. As we have seen, firearms were first employed in Irish warfare at the battle of Knockdoe in 1504, and a Galway ordinance of 1517 prohibited the sale of guns, ammunition and powder to the native Irish, a sure indication that already there was a thriving market for firearms in the island. The use of personal firearms became commonplace in Irish military units after 1550, and from there spread to Scottish 'redshanks' in the 1560s.[29]

Though firearms were indispensable to the Irish charge, the single-handed broadsword and target were its primary instruments of destruction. Unlike their Scottish cousins, the Irish had seldom used the great two-handed swords of the Middle Ages, and by the 1560s Scottish redshanks had begun to abandon the traditional claymore in favour of the single-handed broadsword and target. This effective combination of missile and blade weaponry as early as the 1560s was shown in Shane O'Neill's victory over the MacDonnells of Antrim at Glentaisie (1565).

If there was a revolution in Gaelic warfare in the seventeenth century, it hinged on the use of personal firearms as *offensive* weapons. Other European military establishments would not begin to consider firearms as offensive weapons until the advent of a reliable socket bayonet near the end of the century. Even then, the musket–bayonet combination had more use as a blade rather than a missile weapon. Until the eighteenth century, hand-held firearms continued to be primarily defensive missile weaponry, employed *en masse* by well-drilled soldiers drawn up in linear formations and devoid of any sort of expertise in close-quarter combat. This tactical shortcoming was evinced, for example, by the government armies (though they were not so well drilled) at MacColla's and Montrose's triumphs at Tippermuir, Aberdeen and Inverlochy. The Irish charge further distinguished itself from continental tactics by stressing both the new linear and the old columnar attack formations, a flexibility that eluded most European tacticians until the eighteenth century.[30]

V

From 1644 to 1746, the Gaelic Scots and Irish won eight major battles by using variations of the Irish charge, thereby disproving Roberts's assertion that after Gustav Adolf's death the 'careful

combination of firepower and shock became rarer'. The Gaels
practised their novel tactics with terrific effect on adversaries un-
used to such fury. Arrayed in line formation, usually on a stand of
high ground, the Celtic warriors advanced quickly with broadsword, target and musket. When between sixty and twenty yards
distant from their foes, the Gaels fired a wild musket volley designed to confuse the defenders with lead and smoke. They then
cast away their firearms, formed wedges or rough columns twelve
to fifteen men wide, and drew broadswords for hand-to-hand
combat. The musket volley, when followed rapidly by the impact
of the charge at several selected *Schwerpunkten* along the
enemy line, most often routed numerically-superior government
armies that lacked defence in depth, skill with blade weapons and
sufficient time to reload their muskets. The tactics of the Irish
charge frequently resulted in the normally elusive 'decisive battle'
so desired (but so often unattained) by generations of European
commanders, especially when the enemy attempted to fight
without benefit of field fortifications or well-served artillery.[31]

Gaelic warfare in the period 1644–1746 emphasised the frontal
shock attack across rugged terrain, with the broadsword – and not
the musket – as the primary weapon. The combined use of blade
and missile weapons in executing this sort of offensive tactics
distinguished the Gaels from most other European armies as late
as the mid-eighteenth century. Moreover, while other armies
were weighed down by sheer size and complicated logistical requirements, the Highland Scots and Irish kept great freedom of
manoeuvre, speed and range. The Gaels were not limited to siege
warfare or frontal assaults because of a lack of mobility. Rather,
they possessed the tactical flexibility that permitted them to
choose their method of attack – frontal or flank. Frontal attacks
depended upon shock power; flank attacks initially upon superior mobility. Often, however, the Scots and Irish combined the
two capabilities, using mobility to enhance their shock power by
forcing an adversary to turn 'front to flank', thereby disrupting
his formation and creating confusion in his ranks. Highland
armies indeed could be an efficient melding of regular line troops
and light 'rangers'. This type of tactical flexibility was used successfully at Auldearn (1645), Kilsyth (1645), Killiecrankie (1689)
and Prestonpans (1745). In the remaining six major engagements
during the 1644–1746 period – Tippermuir (1644), Aberdeen

(1644), Inverlochy (1645), Sheriffmuir (1715), Falkirk (1746) and Culloden (1746) – the Gaels chose, for better or worse, the hard-charging frontal assault.[32]

A number of eighteenth-century French commanders – the Chevalier de Folard, the Comte de Guibert and Marshal de Saxe – realised that most *ancien régime* armies lacked the Gaels' mobility that forced an opponent to give battle under unfavourable circumstances and their offensive shock power that finished him off. Folard was disappointed with the results of linear warfare and attempted to 'devise tactical changes . . . to add flexibility and shock to the line's firepower'. He advocated massive assault columns with half the troops armed with pikes.[33] Guibert advocated use of both line and column assault tactics, but understood that the column had restricted shock power because it comprised individual soldiers and thus was not a solid, cohesive mass.[34] Indeed, the massive columns envisioned by Folard and Guibert were never widely used in the eighteenth century. They were seen as being deficient in firepower (which should not be the *ultima ratio* for a column assault anyway), vulnerable to crossfire and difficult to maintain in proper order once an attack was begun. And in most cases, the formation and maintenance of attacking columns were matters of sheer chance rather than of sagacious leadership, as exemplified by the English at Fontenoy (1745).[35]

Marshal Saxe's opinions were more in line with Gaelic tactical doctrine and practice. He attempted to enhance mobility, flexibility and shock power by organising mixed 'legions' of four or five regular and light regiments. As opposed to Folard's attack with massed columns, Saxe's assault was initiated by light skirmishers, who drew the opponent's fire, forcing them to re-load in the face of a brutal bayonet charge by heavy infantry. The Marshal downplayed the effects of musketry against an attacking force, except at very close range. Which army wins the day, he asked, 'the one that gives its fire in advancing, or the other that reserves it? Men of any experience . . . give it in favour of the latter. . . .' He wrote of having

> seen whole volleys fire without even killing four men, . . . and if any single discharge was ever so violent as to disable an enemy from advancing afterward, to take ample revenge by pouring

in his fire, and at the same instant rushing in with fixed bayonets, it is by this method only that numbers are to be destroyed and victories obtained.[36]

Saxe's tactics closely resembled the Irish charge. However, his dismissal of the horrid effects of musketry and grape shot and canister levelled at an attacker within a range of thirty to fifty yards was rather foolhardy (as it was with the Jacobite commanders at Culloden). Despite Saxe's advocacy of the bayonet charge in the teeth of enemy fire, evidence suggests that close-quarter combat with swords and musket-butts was unusual in eighteenth-century European warfare. A contemporary British observer noted that 'There is not probably an instance of modern troops being engaged in close combat; our tactics, produced by the introduction of firearms, are opposed to such a mode of action. . . .' A French authority believed that 'firearms are the most destructive category of weapon, and now [1749] more than ever. If you need convincing, just go to the hospital and you will see how few men have been wounded by cold steel as opposed to firearms.'[37]

VI

A crisis beset Gaelic warfare in the late seventeenth century, brought on by tactical and technological innovations on the battlefields of Europe. The invention of the socket bayonet gave infantry troops a close-quarter, defensive blade weapon and thus eliminated the need for massed pike deployments. Moreover, the advent of the flintlock musket, lighter and more reliable than its predecessors, permitted infantry virtually to double its rate of fire. This change allowed a decrease in the number of firing ranks from five to three; thus more men could fire at once than before. Because of light field artillery, commonly firing grapeshot and canister, the basic European infantry battalion enjoyed much greater defensive capabilities by the onset of the Nine Years War (1688–97). The increased effect of missile weapons enhanced the infantry's role as a provider of static firepower. Hand-to-hand combat between footsoldiers remained a rare occurrence on European battlefields, even during the large-scale campaigns of the War of the Spanish Succession (1701–14). David Chandler noted that during that war, despite the emerging importance of infantry, 'most of the great engagements . . . were won, in the last analysis, by the cavalry, closely supported by the foot'.[38]

Because the Scots and Irish nearly always assumed the tactical offensive on foot, and because a vastly improved British army had learnt, especially after 1688, to co-ordinate infantry, cavalry, and artillery forces, the Irish charge no longer destroyed opposing armies the way it had done since the 1640s. The battle of Killiecrankie (1689), though a stunning Gaelic tactical success, cost the Highland regiments a 30 per cent casualty rate (600 of 1900 men engaged). When this figure is compared with their lowest casualty rate during the campaigns of MacColla and Montrose a half-century earlier (e.g. at Inverlochy the Royalist clans lost only 200 of 1500 men engaged), clan losses at Killiecrankie demonstrated that general improvements in defensive-orientated warfare could blunt – and eventually break – the most ferocious offensive tactics.[39]

Most European infantry commanders continued to stress static firepower over the attack between 1688 and 1750; however, a succession of Gaelic captains, along with Charles XII of Sweden, continued to prefer the assault. But all proponents of offensive warfare now faced opposition much worse than that faced by John Graham, Viscount Dundee, at Killecrankie. There was little headway to be made by attacking an adversary armed with improved muskets, bayonets and artillery and who practised rigorous methods of fire-control. Though Charles XII succeeded against a much larger Russian army at Narva (1700) with tactics similar to the Irish charge, he was defeated by static Russian firepower and strong field fortifications at Poltava (1709). Fortunately for the Gaels, their British opponents from 1689 to 1746 never once sought to mimic the Russians by erecting field fortifications to absorb the shock of the Irish charge. Thus it remained for the British to devise another means of dealing with Gaelic offensive tactics.[40]

Formal combat in eighteenth-century Europe was relatively indecisive largely because of the complexities and ritualistic nature of warfare. Barring such conclusive contests as Steenkerke (1692), Blenheim (1704) and Almanza (1707), as well as the battles of the Gaels and Swedes, war tended to be a slow, cautious and indecisive affair even under the most favourable conditions. This is evidenced by an examination of the career of John Churchill, duke of Marlborough. Marlborough, unlike most of his contemporaries, disapproved of siege warfare and elaborate manoeuvre and sought to fight decisive battles whenever possible. Moreover, he often used mobile tactics on the flanks or wings of his opponent to achieve, or at least to set up, his victories. The *coup de grâce* usually came with a massed frontal cavalry attack because infantry assaults were difficult to execute (since the attackers normally lacked hand-to-hand combat skills) and because fire control was all but impossible to maintain. A British military authority wrote of this problem in 1727:

> In advancing towards the enemy, it is with great difficulty that the officers can prevent the men (but more particularly when they are fired at) from taking their arms, without orders, off from their shoulders, and firing at too great a distance. How much more difficult must it be to prevent their firing, when they have their arms in their hands already cocked, and their fingers on the triggers? I won't say it is impossible though I look upon it to be almost so.

In the early eighteenth century, Marlborough favoured the use of superior mobility and infantry shock power, but often found it difficult, or impossible, to loose the shackles of defensively-orientated warfare.[41]

Marlborough, like his continental counterparts, had at his disposal the resources of the modern nation-state. According to historian Geoffrey Parker, the 'foundation of the Bank of England [in 1694], Parliament's guarantee of all government loans, and the organization of a sophisticated money market in London made it possible for a British army of unprecedented size – 90000 men – to fight overseas for years [during the War of the Spanish Succession]'.[42] But such seeming benefits also had their shortcomings, and the frequent result was a logistical nightmare; those abundant resources made war a rather ponderous undertaking. A typical eighteenth-century infantryman carried well over sixty pounds of equipment (including weapons), which meant that he could carry virtually no rations. Such a burden limited an average day's march to no more than fifteen miles over hospitable terrain in good weather. This limitation, in turn, created the need for larger and larger numbers of transport vehicles which further slowed movement, and tons of forage for the draught animals further exacerbated the problem. If armies, replete with large contingents of cavalry and artillery, became too large to be supported by pack trains, logistics dictated that they either live off the land or establish supply depots and magazines. The former alternative certainly was impracticable for large forces, except for brief periods in productive regions such as the Netherlands, Picardy or northern Italy. The latter alternative surely made more sense, but sharply reduced an army's range of operations. War, then, with all its trappings of modernity, was conducted 'with . . . deadening slowness and lack of decisiveness'. Only a Marlborough or a Frederick the Great 'proved occasionally capable of transcending these . . . limitations, and thus returned something of pace, colour, and decisiveness to the conduct of warfare'.[43]

When the continental powers' ability to conduct war was impaired by the sheer size and complexity of their military forces after 1700, the Scots and Irish continued to fight much the same as always. There were some similarities between the Gaelic and various other military systems, but it must be admitted that even greater differences separated them. The Gaels did not have the modern nation-state from which to draw organisational, economic or technological benefit. These fundamental shortcomings precluded the establishment of any sort of long-term strategies by Gaelic chiefs and commanders. Therefore, the Highland Scots and Irish concerned themselves more with the short-term tactical aspects of war. This allowed them to win most of the battles and still lose the wars. When the Gaels did secure access to modern implements of war, such as firearms and artillery, they either relegated them to places of secondary import (as with firearms in the Irish charge) or neglected them altogether. But by eschewing then engines and theories of modern warfare, they were able to field highly mobile, though small armies usually commanded by men who led by example rather than from a secure post in the rear. The Gaels, then, were little concerned with logistics because they had need of but limited quantities of shot and powder, fodder or other necessities and niceties so common among conventional armies. The resulting increase in mobility allowed them to range far and wide in nearly any season and to traverse the rugged, boggy terrain of their homelands. Because of their mobility and ability to surprise the enemy, the Gaels' battles usually were short, but decisive. At Prestonpans (1745), for instance, the Highlanders needed only some fifteen minutes to destroy Sir John Cope's army. And because of the short duration of their battles, the Gaels, at least before 1689, suffered relatively light casualties. But perhaps most importantly, they enjoyed the option of choosing the sort of battle they fought: flank attack or frontal assault.[44]

The British solution to the Irish charge arose from improvements in eighteenth-century warfare that previously had restricted the scope of offensive tactics and strategy on the Continent. In the end, it took a force of well-trained, steady British regulars, armed with the socket bayonet and 'Brown Bess' musket, supported by mobile field artillery and cavalry, to break the shock power of the intrepid Gaelic offensive. The Gaels, however, contributed to their own defeat in no small manner. Despite superb mobility, rather primitive weaponry and small armies, they chose variations of the frontal assault time and again against an opponent who already was quantitatively superior and rapidly was becoming qualitatively competitive. Even under the most astute commanders, few eighteenth-century armies won victories with the frontal assault and close-quarter tactics.

Under such circumstances, it is remarkable that between 1689 and 1746 the Scots and Irish normally won on the tactical level. But the headlong frontal attack was finally and completely smashed on the open killing-ground of Culloden Moor by a combination of the duke of Cumberland's infantry, cavalry and artillery fighting under conventional dictates with methodical defensive tactics. Unlike at Falkirk some months earlier in 1746, the Highlanders at Culloden did not possess suitable ground over which to execute their traditional attack tactics. But even at Falkirk, where they 'held almost every conceivable tactical advantage, . . . [the Gaels] did not destroy the enemy as their forebears had done in earlier campaigns'. By mid-century the British army could no longer be overwhelmed by the Irish charge. At Culloden, Lord George Murray, Prince Charles Edward Stuart's most able commander, realised that if the Gaels were forced to fight on the open moor they would be quickly slaughtered.

Murray, a widely-travelled professional soldier, knew that modern weaponry (the Brown Bess, socket or sleeve bayonet, and grape- and canister-firing field artillery) gave defensive tactics almost every advantage over offensive tactics on a formal, conventional battlefield. Because the prince ignored Murray's pleas to move the Highland army from the open moor, the Jacobites were left to do the only thing they knew: attack, sword in hand. The subsequent carnage testified to the superiority of hot lead and British discipline over cold steel and Gaelic impetuosity, at least for the time being.[45]

Those who write of a 'military revolution' in early modern Europe (*c.*1400–1750) generally omit developments in Gaelic warfare. This is unfortunate, but understandable, especially when one considers that most contemporary observers showed little interest in the Scottish Highlands and Ireland. The Gaelic system, because it did not fit the mould set by major continental powers, offers a unique perspective for the study of the conduct of war in the early modern era. The uniqueness of Gaelic tactical warfare until its demise at Culloden – and its temporary resurrection as part of post-1750 British tactics in the Seven Years War, the War for American Independence and the wars of the French Revolution and Napoleon – lay in its stubborn insistence on offensive combat. The Frenchman Guibert might just as well have been referring to the Highlanders and the dreadfulness of their attack when he penned the following a generation after Culloden: 'The closer you approach the enemy the more fearsome you become, and a coward, who will fire at a brave man at one hundred paces, will not dare to so much as aim at him at close range.'[46] When attacking not cowards but steady regulars, the Scots and Irish faced seemingly insurmountable defensive odds brought on by technological and organisational innovations that fundamentally altered the nature of European conflict until the age of Napoleon. And it took no less a man than the Corsican to revitalise and reintroduce a style of tactical offensive war based on mobility, flexibility and shock power that the Gaels, in their simple but effective manner, had never forsaken.

9. Revolutionary and Napoleonic Warfare

JEREMY BLACK

PRE-REVOLUTIONARY BACKGROUND

As Peter Wilson indicates in his chapter, it would be mistaken to see the armies of Revolutionary France as impacting on a static military system. Such an approach is attractive to some commentators, for it permits a ready counterpointing of Revolutionary novelty and *ancien régime* conservatism, a contrast that can be held to account for the military success of the Revolutionary forces; but the reality was far more complex. It is necessary to understand the dynamic character of *ancien régime* military theory and practice, in order to appreciate better the degree to which the warfare of the Revolutionary and Napoleonic periods represented a continuation of earlier trends. To note the already strong currents of change in European armies, alongside an emphasis on the impact of the French Revolution, both in the scale of forces and in the political and social context of warfare, helps explain the numerous successes of Revolutionary France's opponents.

The sources of this current of change were varied. In part, it was an aspect of the continual process of testing and adaptation that had long characterised European warfare. However, in this case, three particular points are worthy of note, first, widespread demographic and economic expansion in Europe from the 1740s, second, the emphasis on the value of reform and the application of reason to problems that characterised the Enlightenment thought of the age, and, third, the impact of the protracted warfare of 1740–62. The first produced the resources for military expansion: large numbers of young men and the metallurgical industries capable of providing munitions for the sustained conflict of 1787–1815. The situation thus prefigured the demographic and economic background to the First World War.

The emphasis on the value of reform encouraged a questioning of established precepts and practices and an interest in new ideas. This can be seen in criticism of linear tactics, as in Campbell Dalrymple's *A Military Essay* (1761), Jacques Antoine Hippolyte de Guibert's *Essai Général de Tactique* (Paris, 1772) and two works by an Austrian veteran, Jakob von Cognazo, *Freymüthiger Beytrag zur Geschichte des österreichischen Militärdienstes* (Frankfurt/Leipzig, 1780) and *Geständisse eines oesterreichischen Veterans politisch-militärischer Hinsicht* (Breslau, 1788–91). Aside from reform explicitly as change, there was also considerable backing for reform understood as improvement, especially in administrative practices. This helped ensure that governments were better able to exploit their domestic resources and thus to wage war.

The warfare of 1740–62 was a period of testing, not least in the desperate battle of survival facing, first, Austria and, then, Prussia. It led to a determination to replace what had been found inadequate, and a drive to ensure that armies (and societies) were in a better state for future conflicts. Thus in 1763 the Portuguese army was reorganised along Prussian lines, so as to be better able to confront a future Spanish invasion, by Count Wilhelm von Schaumburg-Lippe-Bückeburg. The outbreak of new wars was seen as likely. Rulers were not planning for the French Revolutionary War, nor for large-scale conflict in Western Europe. Italy, the Rhineland and the Low Countries had been largely peaceful since 1748, and there had been no major war in any of these regions. The extension of the French frontier by the acquisition of Lorraine in 1766 had been peaceful, the working-out of a dynastic gain, and, although the acquisition of Corsica in 1768 had led to resistance on the island, there had been no wider reverberations: France had purchased Corsica from Genoa.

Instead, war was feared in Central and Eastern Europe. It was assumed that there would be another conflict between Austria and Russia, to follow the War of the Bavarian Succession in 1778–79. The fate of the Ottoman Empire also appeared to threaten peace, although the Russian occupation of the Crimea in 1783 was achieved without the wider struggle that was feared. However, in 1787 a period of major warfare did begin. A Turkish attack on Russia broadened out to include conflict between Austria and Turkey (1788–90) and Sweden and Russia (1788–

90), as well as a very short struggle between Denmark and Sweden in 1788. Although these conflicts did not expand to encompass the planned-for war between the Prussian alliance system and both Austria and Russia in 1790–91, they did lead to renewed Russian intervention in Poland in 1792, to the Second Partition of that country in 1793, to rebellion in 1794 and to the Third Partition in 1795.

Thus. Europe was scarcely waiting militarily for the French Revolution. This was especially true in France where humiliation by the armies of Prussia and Britain, at Rossbach (1757) and Minden (1759) respectively, had led to much experimentation in theory and practice, and a willingness to challenge and change the operation, organisation, equipment and ethos of the army. In what was to be a particularly influential work, his *Essai Général de Tactique*, Guibert stressed flexibility, movement and enveloping manoeuvres, advocated living off the land in order to increase the speed of operations, criticised reliance on fortifications and urged the value of a patriotic citizen army. His subsequent criticism of Frederick the Great's tactics was given greater impact because it was published in German as well as French: *Bemerkungen über die Kriegsverfassung der preussischen Armee. Neue, verbesserte und vermehrte Auflage* (Cologne, 1780).

Guibert was not the sole source of new ideas. In 1763 Bigot de Morogues criticised the prescritive approach and geometrical teachings of Hoste's *Art des Armées Navales* (1697), and claimed that they had misled French naval officers during the Seven Years War. On land, the concept of a division, a standing unit in peace and war, composed of elements of all arms and, therefore, able to operate independently, developed in France under the Duc de Broglie. Such a unit was designed to be effective, both as a detached force and as part of a co-ordinated army operating in accordance with a strategic plan. The divisional plan evolved from 1759, and in 1787–88 army administration was arranged along divisional lines.

There was also interest, both within France and elsewhere, in different fighting methods, a development of earlier ideas by writers such as Saxe. His *Mes Rêveries*, posthumously published in 1757, had criticised reliance on firepower alone, and instead, advocated a combination of individually aimed fire and shock attacks with bayonets. Saxe was important, because he encouraged fresh thoughts about tactics and strategy. He was not alone. In contrast to the customary emphasis on firepower and linear tactics, two other French writers, Folard and Mesnil-Durand, stressed the shock and weight of forces attacking in columns. Manoeuvres in 1778 designed to test the rival systems failed to settle the controversy.

In practice, linear tactics was a general concept, including a substantial variety of precepts among which line formations were only one. Therefore, formations in columns were not in themselves in opposition to linear tactics as a whole, as long as their deployment was not intended to break up the closely knit network of tactical rules and customs, and mechanistic creeds, that informed the ideas behind linear tactics. In particular, war against the Turks and overseas warfare allowed and even required more frequent deviations from the conventions of linear tactics than warfare in Western and Central Europe, as traditionalists, such as George Washington's adviser Steuben, admitted.

Allowing for this flexibility, the changes of drill enforced by the French *Règlement* of 1791 were still important. In concert with Guibert's ideas, the new French tactical manual and its vigorous implementation by the armies of Revolutionary France organised by Lazare Carnot, made a major impact on tactics.

It was not only tactical thought that was active and developing in pre-Revolutionary France. The army was also given better weaponry, in what was, increasingly, a more important arm of battle, the artillery. Jean de Gribeauval (1715–89), who had served during the Seven Years War with the Austrian army, then the best in Europe, regularised the French artillery from 1769, being appointed Inspector General of Artillery in 1776. He used standardised specifications: 4-, 6-, 8- and 12-pounder cannon and 6-inch howitzers, in 8-gun batteries. Standardisation aided the flow of force on the battlefield: the projection of fire in a rapid, regular, even predictable, fashion. This was further helped by the introduction of prepackaged rounds. The artillery of the French artillery was also increased by stronger, larger wheels, shorter barrels, lighter-weight cannon, more secure mobile gun carriages, and better casting methods. Horses were harnessed in pairs, instead of in tandem. Accuracy was improved by better sights, the issue of gunnery tables and the introduction of inclination markers.

The theory of war advanced to take note of these changes. In his *De l'Usage de l'Artillerie nouvelle dans la guerre de campagne* (Paris, 1778), the Chevalier Jean du Teil argued that the artillery should begin battles and be massed for effect, in short that they should play a more active operational role, dictating the timetable and topography of the battlefield.

However, the absence of French forces from the European battlefield in 1763–91 ensured both that these ideas were not tested under fire and that the potential impact of the developments on French military effectiveness was not realised.

REVOLUTIONARY WARFARE

Thanks to Gribeauval's reforms, Revolutionary France had the best artillery in Europe. In several other respects, the army of Revolutionary France, especially in terms of capability and effectiveness, though not social practice, was a product of pre-Revolutionary changes. Napoleon, who had been taught to use Gribeauval's guns, admired Guibert's work. The regular army was disrupted in 1790–92 through desertion and emigration by disenchanted and fearful officers, but it still played a major role in the successes of 1792 against Austria and Prussia, not least because the regulars were better trained than new levies.

Yet the political context of warfare was very different, especially in providing both a frenetic energy to the conduct of war and far larger armies. In August 1793 the Revolutionary government issued the *levée en masse*; the latest in a series of experiments to raise manpower and improve the status of the troops that had already led to the encouragement of volunteers and the dismissal of foreign mercenary regiments. Now, the entire population could be obliged to serve in the war and all single men between 18 and 25 were to register for military service. The distinction between the professional army and the militia had in effect been ended. Such powers of conscription were not new in Europe, and, particularly due to draft avoidance and desertion, it anyway proved difficult to raise the numbers that had been anticipated.

However, the armies raised were both larger than those deployed by France hitherto that century, and enabled her to operate effectively on several fronts at once, to sustain casualties and to outnumber opponents. In 1793–94 alone, nearly 7000 new cannons and howitzers were cast by the French. A large powder factory was founded at Grenelle, capable of producing 30 000 lb of gunpowder daily.

The greater size of the forces at France's disposal was a factor, but by no means the sole one, in the greater pace of French advances. Mass had to be complemented by system and ideology: the new logistics brought about by the partial abandonment of the magazine system helped the aggressive style of war – both in strategy and in tactics – of Revolutionary armies able to rely on numbers and enthusiasm. Enthusiasm is an intangible factor. It has been argued that the French soldiers were better motivated and, hence, more successful and better able to use the new methods. This is difficult to prove and it has recently been argued that 'The armies of the First Republic were neither as politically motivated nor as militarily innovative and successful as the Jacobins (then and later) claimed was the case.'[1] Revolutionary zeal had greatly declined by 1797. Nevertheless, initially at least, Revolutionary enthusiasm does seem to have been an important element in French capability. It was probably necessary for the greater morale needed for effective shock action, for crossing the killing ground produced by opposing fire. Patriotic determination was also important to counter the effects of the limited training of the early Revolutionary armies.

Enthusiasm was important for more than tactics. The outbreak of war increased the paranoia of French public culture and allowed the Revolutionaries to associate themselves with France. They were also able to demonise their opponents. Waging war by the brutalisation of subjects and the despoliation of foreigners produced resources. The exploitative nature of French rule led to a crucial increase in resources that complemented France's domestic mobilisation, but the exploitation helped to limit the popularity of the Revolution outside France. This encouraged rebellion.

There had been rapid advances earlier in the century, for example in late 1733 by the Russians into Poland and the French into northern Italy. However, the pace of war, or in scientific terms, the volume of force, speeded up in the 1790s. If, by 1748, the French under Saxe had overrun the Austrian Netherlands, that had taken several years campaigning. In 1792, although the initial French attempts to invade the Austrian Netherlands failed, an invasion in November met with overwhelming success, and they fell in a month.

The Austrians regained the Austrian Netherlands after their victory at Neerwinden the following year (18 March 1793); but, by the end of 1794, the French had again conquered it. They had also driven the Spaniards out of Roussillon and made gains in Catalonia. Having triumphed in the Austrian Netherlands, the French went on to overrun the United Provinces: in January 1795 Amsterdam was captured.

The superiority in French numbers was important both in battles, such as Valmy (20 September 1792, essentially an artillery duel), Jemappes (6 November 1792) and Wattignies (15–16 October 1793), and in offensives, such as that against the Spaniards in Roussillon. Tactics were also important. The characteristic battlefield manoeuvre of French Revolutionary forces, and the best way to use the mass of new and inexperienced soldiers, most of whom went into the infantry, was the advance in independent attack columns. This was best for an army that put an emphasis on the attack. Column advances were more flexible than traditional linear formations and rigid drill. Indeed, in 1787, Earl Cornwallis, one of the most experienced British generals, had echoed Guibert in criticising the regulations for field exercises drawn up by Sir William Fawcett, the British Adjutant-General:

> [Its] impossible for battalions dressing to their own centres to march together in line. For it often happens, and indeed almost always in action, that the centres cannot see each other. But if they did the least deviation of any leader of a centre from the direction of the march would either enlarge the intervals or throw the battalions upon one another.

In contrast, at Jemappes the French were able to advance in columns and get back into line at close range, defeating the less numerous Austrians. The French combination of mobile artillery, skirmishers, assault columns and lines was potent, a successful and disconcerting ad hoc combination of tactical elements matched to the technology of the times and the character of the new republican soldier. The integration of close-order and open-order infantry, so that every battalion could deploy its own skirmishers, proved especially effective.

The politics of revolution ensured that systems of command differed from those of the *ancien régime*. There was a more 'democratic' command structure, at least at battalion level. The social gap between non-commissioned officers and their superiors was less than hitherto. At the strategic level, the greater number and dispersal of units meant that command and co-ordination skills became more important, and the French benefited from young energetic and determined commanders. Careers were open to talent, commanders including Jean-Baptiste Jourdan, a former private, Lazare Hoche, a former corporal, and Napoleon Bonaparte, initially a junior artillery officer from the recent acquisition of Corsica. Those who found themselves denounced for failure, or who were suspected of treachery, risked the death penalty. Eight days after the outbreak of war, one French army murdered its unsuccessful commander, Théobald Dillon. Other generals followed. Houchard was even executed for achieving only moderate success at Dunkirk in 1793. Punishment, politicisation and the policy of the Committee of Public Safety ensured that the generals were willing to accept heavy losses among their troops.

Initial confusion was followed by a measure of organisation, as the government struggled to equip, train, feed and control the new armies. This owed much to Lazare Carnot, head of the military section of the Committee of Public Safety. The process of forming the new armies and using them with success was instrumental in the transition from a royal army to the nation in arms. The way was open for the ruthless boldness that Napoleon was to show in Italy in 1796–97.[2]

Yet the French did not push all before them. The Austrians proved tough opponents, especially in Germany in 1796 under Archduke Charles, and the Russians were often to show impressive staying-power and fighting quality, both in the 1790s and subsequently. The disciplined fire of the Austrian lines initially checked the French at Jemappes and Hondschoote (8 September 1793), and helped to defeat them at Neerwinden. Further afield,

Napoleon's victories over the Mamelukes in Egypt in 1798 are a less than complete account of French effectiveness. It is as pertinent to note the failure of French forces to recapture newly-independent Haiti in 1802–03: 40000 French troops, including Napoleon's brother-in-law, Charles Leclerc, died, the vast majority as a result of yellow fever.

The French were driven out of Haiti by Jean-Jacques Dessalines, who proclaimed himself Emperor Jacques I. This lesser-known imperial counterpart of Napoleon indicated that in Haiti, as elsewhere, the successful use of force was crucial to power. That was certainly demonstrated by Napoleon. The conduct of the war had created an atmosphere of expediency in which it became easier for Napoleon to mount his coup.

Napoleon, the new commander of the French Army of Italy, developed in 1796 the characteristics of his generalship: self-confidence, swift decision-making, rapid mobility, the concentration of strength, and, where possible, the exploitation of interior lines. Victory by French columns over outnumbered defenders at Mondovi (27 April 1796) knocked the leading independent Italian ruler, the King of Sardinia, out of the war. At Lodi (10 May), Bassano (8 September), Arcole (15–17 November) and Rivoli (14 January 1797), Napoleon's tactical genius and ability to manoeuvre on the battlefield brought victory over the Austrians, and associated Napoleon with military success. His siting of the artillery was particularly important. The Treaty of Campo Formio (1797) brought peace, with France dominant in Lombardy and Austria ceding the Austrian Netherlands. The First Coalition of powers against Revolutionary/Napoleonic France had been brought low.[3]

However, neither under Revolutionary governments nor under Napoleon was France able to learn restraint. Repeatedly, victory was followed by a peace settlement that was only temporary. In 1798 a Second Coalition was formed. With Poland partitioned out of existence and Russia at peace with Turkey, the Russians were able to intervene effectively in Western Europe. The Austrians under Archduke Charles defeated a smaller French force at Stockach (25 March 1799), while a Russian army under Suvorov advanced into northern Italy, the first time that the Russians had operated there. Suvorov's victories, particularly Trebbia (17–19 June) and Novi (15 August

1799), were brutal battles, in which repeated attacks finally found weaknesses in the French position.

Like Napoleon, Suvorov was a believer in the strategic and tactical offensive and had little time for sieges. He used methods successfully employed against the Turks in the wars of 1768–74 and 1787–92. Suvorov was willing to accept a high rate of casualties and to mount costly frontal attacks on fortified positions, such as the castle of Novi or the northern approaches to the St Gotthard Pass. He relied on bayonet attacks, not defensive firepower. Suvorov's generalship contrasted with that of his more cautious Austrian allies, who were more concerned with regaining northern Italian positions by sieges, and showed that an emphasis on aggression, attack and risk was not restricted to the French. Russian tactics emphasised the use of the bayonet and troops were trained to fight in columns as well as extended order formations, although in practice they did not do the latter that much. Divisions were employed as tactical units from 1806.

NAPOLEONIC GENERALSHIP

The loss of northern Italy helped to undermine France's Directory government and to make easier Napoleon's seizure of power in the 'Brumaire' coup of 9–10 November 1799. As First Consul, and from 1804 Emperor, Napoleon was in a position not only to act as an innovative general, but also to control the French military system and to direct the war effort. He enjoyed greater power over the army than any ruler since Louis XIV. Furthermore, in many respects, Napoleon was more powerful than Louis. His choice of commanders was not constrained by the social conventions and aristocratic alignments that affected Louis, and both armies and individual military units were under more direct governmental control than had been the case with the Bourbon dynasty. Furthermore, Napoleon was directly in command of the leading French force throughout the wars of his reign. Although he had to manage many campaigns from a distance, they were always those of subsidiary forces.

Under Napoleon, French resources were devoted to the military with a consistency that the Revolutionary governments had lacked. The conscription system, which had become less effective in the mid-1790s, was strengthened. Napoleon raised 1.3 million conscripts in 1800–11 and one million in 1812–13 alone.[4] In August 1813 he had a reserve of 18 million musket cartridges.

Napoleon also developed the corps, a unit at a level above that of the division that could include all the arms and also be large enough to operate effectively: both corps and divisions were given effective staff structures. Thus, the corps added to the flexibility of the earlier divisional system the strength necessary both for the punishing battles of the period – where opposing forces would not collapse rapidly as a result of well-planned battlefield moves, and for Napoleon's campaigns of strategically applied force. Corps allowed the French to pack a heavier punch and operated effectively, both as individual units, for example at the battle of Auerstädt (1806) and in much of the Peninsular War, and in concert.

Greater numbers and operational flexibility ensured that skilled staff work was important to Napoleon. It was necessary to deploy rapidly and effectively the massive resources he controlled, in particular to be able to move many large corps by different routes, yet enable them still to support each other. In 1805 Napoleon speedily moved 194 000 men and about 300 cannon from northern France, where they were preparing to invade Britain, eastwards, in order to attack the Austrians in south-west Germany. The logistical basis of the campaign in 1805 was inadequate and the French were forced to live off the countryside, but they were able to move rapidly in order to surround the Austrians in Ulm. More generally, better roads and better map-making facilitated the swifter movement of troops. Napoleon's Chief of Staff, Louis-Alexandre Berthier, was a crucial figure in a French command structure that was better than those of her opponents. Henri Clarke, Minister of War from 1807, was an effective and energetic administrator, responsible for the drafting of troops, the organisation of new units and the management of the armies of occupation. However, Napoleon's centralised direction of campaigns became a problem from 1809 when he limited the autonomy of his commanders in the distant Peninsular War, and it even proved difficult to control effectively the large armies of his later years that were under his direct command. Several of his commanders, including Davout, Masséna, Ney and Soult, were talented, but Napoleonic intervention lessened their capability for effective independent command.

The French organisational and command structures were vital to Napoleon's characteristic rapidity of strategic and tactical movement, and his troops also travelled more lightly than those of Frederick II. Napoleon employed this mobility to strategic effect. He concentrated on a single front, seeking in each war to identify the crucial opposing force and to destroy it rapidly. For temperamental reasons, and because he sought glory, and rapid and decisive results, Napoleon sought battle. Although he fought for much of his reign, his individual wars with Continental opponents were over fairly rapidly. Warfare might be a long-term process for Napoleon, but war became an event. Thus, for example, wars with Austria in 1805 and 1809 ended the same year, while the war with Prussia that began in 1806 ended in 1807. Such rapid results were the product of a concentration of military resources on a single front, a contrast with the situation in the 1790s.

On campaign, Napoleon took a central position in order to divide more numerous opposing forces and then defeat them separately. A strategy of envelopment was used against weaker forces: they were pinned down by an attack mounted by a section of the French army, while most of the army enveloped them, cutting their lines of supply.

Napoleon was a strong believer in the value of artillery, organised into strong batteries, particularly of 12-pounders. At Wagram, he covered the reorganisation of his attack with a battery of 102 guns. Napoleon also massed his cavalry for use at the vital moment, as with Murat's charge through the Russian centre at Eylau (1807). He initially successfully employed *l'ordre mixte* of the 1790s for the infantry: a mixture of lines and columns with many sharpshooters to precede the attack. The use of these formations were enhanced by effective tactical plans and detailed staff planning. However, French tactics degenerated later on, and it can be argued that Napoleon devoted insufficient attention to tactical details. He was limited by the continual need to adapt tactics to his large numbers of inexperienced troops.[5]

On the whole, Napoleon has been applauded as a great operational genius, especially as a manoeuvrer and strategist. On the whole, he was an able planner and knew when and how to strike, although he usually left tactics to the discretion of his field officers. His campaigns and battles are, for example, still important in the West Point course on military history. Recently, however, there has been more criticism of his generalship, although it has been questioned by many scholars. Owen Connelly presented Napoleon as an improviser who did not care if he initially blundered, since he had confidence that he could devise a strategic or tactical plan in the field, based on the enemy's movements and/or errors, and win. *Improviste* is what he called himself at St Helena. Impressed by Napoleon's ability to improvise, Connelly claimed that:

> Napoleon began almost every campaign with a strategic blunder. . . . He began many battles with a tactical error . . . he did careful planning, paying particular attention to movement and maximizing his numbers. But that done, he simply charged towards his enemy's presumed location . . . his awesome energy; his ability to scramble, to make his men follow him, to hit again and again; and his inability to accept defeat . . . he always charged ahead and rewrote his plans as he went, although in mid-career he acquired superior numbers which covered his blunders and ensured his victories.

Napoleon manipulated the historical record to disguise his failings and seize credit from others. He had official accounts of the Battle of Marengo (14 June 1800) rewritten in order to conceal his mistakes and to present the battle as going according to plan.[6] Furthermore, it has been argued that, having changed European warfare himself, Napoleon failed to understand and respond to further developments:

> Napoleon's mistakes prior to 1809 did not have catastrophic consequences because his opponents made more mistakes and their armies were less effective in war. But Napoleon's usual mistakes were magnified as his opposition improved. Convinced that his personality and genius could overcome all obstacles, Napoleon was blinded to the changing realities of warfare.[7]

The last point is a valuable reminder that, as with Gustav Adolf, Marlborough and Frederick the Great, as well as less famous commanders, it is necessary to avoid a static account of their generalship and, instead, to consider them in terms of a dynamic situation, specifically shifting relative capability and effectiveness. This was as much a case of 'political' as of more narrowly 'military' factors, but, even in terms of the latter, the variety of opponents and the pace of change were such that it was necessary to be continuously flexible and adaptable.

Napoleon's generalship should not be simplified into a trajectory of success to failure, however attractive that might be in terms of the parallel idea of a ruler brought down by hubris. Indeed, in both 1813 and 1814 he displayed impressive generalship against superior odds. Throughout, Napoleon was dominated by the desire to engage and win. By launching campaigns and forcing battles whose likely shape was unclear, Napoleon placed great reliance on the subsequent effectiveness of his armies. This rewarded the fighting quality of individual units, the initiative and skill of subordinates, and the ability to retain reserves until the crucial moment. Napoleon confronted grave problems, not least the number and fighting quality of his opponents and the difficulty of establishing their positions, let alone intentions, the primitive communications of the period, and the need to raise the operational effectiveness of his conscripts. He deserves credit for developing an effective military machine, even as he undermined it by the strains of near-continuous warfare, and eventually overwhelmed it in 1813–14 by failing to avoid or end a multi-front struggle. Able to adapt rapidly to changing circumstances and fresh intelligence, Napoleon had a remarkable ability to impose his will upon war. He won close to fifty major battles in his career, including the largest, most convoluted engagements hitherto seen in the gunpowder age. Most martial reputations rest only on a victory or two. Indubitably, Napoleon, like so many other great commanders, committed errors of judgement, but they were relatively few. His successes owed something to weight of numbers, but Napoleon should be given credit for the skill with which he achieved (usually local) superiority, generally by manoeuvre over vast distances. Leadership and morale were also important. Napoleon, for all his faults,

was a superlative military leader who commanded the respect
and affection of troops and officers.

NAPOLEON'S CAMPAIGNS, 1800–1807

Napoleon's opening campaign as First Consul was an invasion of
northern Italy, boldly begun with a crossing of the Great St
Bernard Pass so that he arrived in the Austrian rear. At Marengo,
however, he found the Austrians a formidable rival, and his
enforced retreat for much of the battle was only reversed because
of the arrival of reinforcements and the successful counter-attack
they mounted. A quarter of the French force became casualties. A
further French victory, at Hohenlinden (3 December 1800), by
an army that was flexible in defence commanded by Jean
Moreau, led the Austrians to conclude peace at Lunéville.

Napoleon next attacked the Austrians in 1805, in the War of
the Third Coalition. The Austrians were preparing for an attack
from the west through the Black Forest, but they were outmanoeuvred by the rapid advance of the French from the middle
Rhine to the Danube in their rear. From the outset, Napoleon
hoped and planned to get behind the Austrians. The overly
cautious Austrian response left an army bottled up in Ulm. It
surrendered on 20 October, and Napoleon then overran southern Germany and Austria. Success in Germany was helped by the
situation in northern Italy, where a French force of only 50 000
under Masséna contained the 90 000-strong Austrian army
under Archduke Charles.

Napoleon's advance brought him closer to the advancing Russians, deliberately so as he wanted to inflict a heavy defeat on
them, and on 2 December 1805 Tsar Alexander I and a 85 000-
strong Austro-Russian army attacked the 75 000-strong French at
Austerlitz. A strong assault on Napoleon's right was held and, in
a surprise attack, the French turned the weak flank of this
Russian attack in order to win. The French were better able than
their Russian counterparts to use numerical superiority at the
point of contact they had sought.[8] Aside from Napoleon's superior generalship, the French command system proved better able
to integrate the different arms effectively. Austria left the war.
The following year poorly commanded and outmanoeuvred

Prussian forces were defeated at Jena and Auerstädt (14 October), although French fighting quality played a major role at Auerstädt. At Jena, massed artillery and substantial numbers of skirmishers inflicted heavy losses on the Prussian lines. Victory over the Russians at Friedland (14 June 1807) brought peace with Prussia and Russia.

The conflicts of this period indicated the superiority of the French corps and divisional structure over the less coherent and well-coordinated opposing forces. French staff work, at army and corps level, was superior to that of both Austria and Russia, and this helped to vitiate the numbers France's opponents put into the field. The quality of French staff work enabled Napoleon to translate his wide-ranging strategic vision into practice, to force what might have been a segmented war into essentially a struggle in one major theatre of operations where he could use the *Grande Armée* effectively. The French had benefited from the years of peace on the Continent from 1801 in order to train their infantry, increase their artillery and cavalry, and produce better balanced corps. The earlier years of war had provided experienced troops and an officer corps sifted by merit.

NAPOLEONIC CAMPAIGNS, 1808–1812

Napoleon encountered many serious problems before his unsuccessful invasion of Russia in 1812. At Eylau (8 February 1807), the Russians proved a tough foe, inflicting heavy casualties with their artillery and fighting off successive attacks before withdrawing during the night. The following year, Napoleon's attempt to seize Spain led to a popular uprising. A surrounded French corps surrendered at Bailén (21 July 1808) and an advancing French army was stopped by the firepower of a British force under Sir Arthur Wellesley, later Duke of Wellington, at Vimeiro (21 August 1808). Napoleon, however, intervened, defeating poorly trained and commanded, and outnumbered Spanish forces, and entering Madrid on 4 December.

The following year, war resumed with Austria, and Napoleon found her a tougher opponent than in 1805, although the Austrians were handicapped by poorly conceived war aims, inadequate and divided central leadership and a foolish strategy.

At Aspern-Essling (21–22 May 1809), his bold attack on a superior Austrian force was repelled and he had to abandon the
battlefield in the face of a serious Austrian advance and better
Austrian generalship.

At Wagram on 5–6 July, however, Napoleon proved the better
general and the French corps commanders were superior to
their Austrian counterparts. Napoleon's counter-attack drove the
Austrians from the field, but it was no Austerlitz: the Austrians
were not routed. Thanks in part to the heavy artillery power of
both sides, there were no tactical breakthroughs. The Austrian
corps structure was effective, and the French victory was essentially due to leadership and to their overall superiority in troops
and material in what was a battle of attrition. Unlike in 1805, the
Austrians had no Russian support, while Frederick William III of
Prussia refused promised support.

In 1812 Napoleon's hegemonic policies and unwillingness to
accept other points of view led him to war with Russia. As with his
earlier attacks on Austria, Prussia and Spain, and his planned
invasion of Britain in 1805, he resolved to strike at the centre of
his opponent's power, thus gaining the initiative and transferring
much of the logistical burden of the war to his enemy. Napoleon
invaded on 24–25 June with half a million men, most of whom
were allied, principally German, Polish and Italian troops. The
Russians, however, fell back, denying Napoleon a decisive battle.
Russian scorched earth and guerrilla activity hit supplies, and the
French lost men through hunger, disease and fatigue. Finally, at
Borodino on 7 September, the Russians sought to stop the advance on Moscow. In a battle of attrition that involved 233 000
men and 1227 cannon, the Russians resisted successive attacks
and were driven back without breaking. Russian casualties were
heavier, but Napoleon lost a quarter of his army. He repeatedly
pressed Clarke to forward troops from all available sources
within the empire. Napoleon followed up Borodino by entering
an undefended Moscow, but the city was set ablaze, probably by
the Russians. Alexander refused to negotiate, and, in the face of
a deteriorating supply situation and encroaching Russian forces,
Napoleon retreated. The retreat turned into a nightmare as
heavy snowfalls, supply breakdowns and Russian attacks, especially as the French crossed the Berezina River on 26–27 November, combined to cause heavy casualties.[9]

This disaster was far more serious than the checks at Eylau and Aspern-Essling; or the British victories in the Peninsular War in Portugal and Spain at Talavera (27–28 July 1809) and Salamanca (22 July 1812), for the French were winning the Peninsular War until 1812. Napoleon was fatally weakened, not least because there would never thereafter be anywhere near such an opportunity to defeat the Russians. The failure on 23 October 1812 of the attempted coup in Paris by ex-General Claude-François Malet was scant consolation.

NAPOLEONIC CAMPAIGNS 1813–1815

The idea of Napoleonic invincibility was shattered by defeat in Russia, although the defeat was in large part attributed to General Winter. In early 1813 Napoleon's diplomatic position collapsed as the French retreated before the Russian advance. In March 1813 Prussia declared war on France. Napoleon rebuilt his army to a force of over 400000 plus his artillery, but the new recruits were more like the fresh troops of 1792 than the veterans of his earlier campaigns, and, unlike in 1792, France's opponents were not outnumbered. In addition, Napoleon was unable to create a new cavalry to match the troops lost in Russia. His victories over the Prussians and Russians at Lützen (2 May) and Bautzen (20–21 May) were achieved over outnumbered forces, and neither was decisive; they might have well have brought victory had Napoleon pressed on, but he could not, in part for lack of cavalry. Bautzen led both sides to agree to an armistice.

Napoleon rejected peace terms that summer, Austria and Sweden joined his opponents and the French became heavily outnumbered. In the autumn of 1813 Napoleon confronted his opponents again. Austrian, Prussian, Russian and Swedish forces exceeded 600000, while Napoleon's total field army was only 370000. The allies adopted the Trachenburg Plan: battle with Napoleon was to be avoided while independent forces under his subordinates were to be attacked. The plan reflected the Allies' respect for Napoleon's generalship. The Prussians defeated detached French forces at Grossbeeren (23 August), on the Katzbach river (26 August) and at Dennewitz (6 September); and the Austrians won at Kulm (30 August). Napoleon's failure to train his marshals to operate as independent commanders, and their lack of supporting staffs, cost the French dear. The marshals could not concentrate their armies at the decisive point in order to achieve victory, and they were unable to operate in order to fulfil strategic objectives. The scale of war was too great for Napoleon to control everything, and he also suffered due to the raw nature of many of his troops.

Only at Dresden, when Frederick Willian III insisted on fighting on 27 August, was Napoleon victorious, thanks to strong attacks by his flanks. Nevertheless, this was not the triumph of envelopment that the French required were they to win. By failing to concentrate his forces during the campaign, Napoleon had allowed their attenuation, and this had preserved neither the territory under French control nor the strategic advantage.

Instead, it was Napoleon who was outmanoeuvred, his line of retreat threatened by the converging Allied forces. At the Battle of the Nations at Leipzig (16–19 October) Napoleon was heavily outnumbered: by 195 000 to 365 000 by the time both sides were fully engaged. Unable to defeat his opponents, whom he, nevertheless, held off, Napoleon decided to retreat, but the premature destruction of the Elster bridge trapped four corps, leading to French losses of 68 000 in the battle.

Artillery played an important role in the battles of 1813, as more generally in Napoleonic warfare. Thus, before attacking the Saxons, then backing Napoleon, at Grossbeeren, Bernadotte bombarded his opponents with 62 cannon he had massed together.

After Leipzig, Napoleon's position in Germany collapsed as former allies deserted and the French fell back. Too many troops, however, were left in fortresses in Germany and Spain, a sign of Napoleon's refusal to face facts. In France, Napoleon was affected by falling tax revenues, widespread draft avoidance, a serious shortage of arms and equipment and a marked decline in the morale and efficiency of officials. The economy was in a parlous state, hit by British blockade and by the loss of continental markets.

In the early months of 1814, Napoleon took the initiative and, with some success, attacked the Austro-Prussian forces that invaded eastern France, manoeuvring with skill in order to destroy the most exposed units. Numbers, however, told. In place of the

80 000 opposing troops he had anticipated, there were about 200 000, and his own army was 70 000 strong, not the 120 000 men he had anticipated.[10] Both Napoleon and his subordinates were defeated. Finally, the Austrians and Prussians marched on Paris, ignoring Napoleon's position on their flank. After its defenders were driven back in the suburbs, Paris surrendered. A provisional French government deposed Napoleon and, with his marshals unwilling to fight on, Napoleon abdicated on 6 April 1814. Four days later the British army under the Duke of Wellington, that had earlier driven back the French in Spain, crushing them at Vitoria (21 June 1813), defeated Marshal Soult at Toulouse.

Napoleon was exiled to Elba, but he returned to France in March 1815 and seized power from the weak Louis XVIII. Rather than wait for the opponents to invade in overwhelming force, Napoleon attacked their nearest concentration, invading the Low Countries on 15 June. Three days later a 68 000-strong Anglo-Dutch–German army under Wellington on a ridge at Mont-Saint-Jean was attacked by Napoleon's 72 000-strong force. In the battle of Waterloo, defensive firepower beat off successive French frontal attacks. Flank attacks or yet more frontal assaults might have succeeded, but the arrival of the Prussian forces on the French right spelled the end.

A NOVEL FORM OF WAR?

If the context of judgement is late nineteenth-century warfare then it is possible to stress continuity rather than change, to argue that there was a use of yet greater resources of people, *matériel* and funds to pursue familiar military courses. Much that Napoleonic warfare is noted for had been anticipated in earlier conflicts: large armies, a strategy of movement, a preference for battles over sieges, a greater emphasis on artillery, light infantry. In this context, Napoleon was more of a consolidator than an innovator.

However, if the political and social context is to be seen as crucial, then the period was more of a departure than would appear if attention was concentrated on weaponry and naval conflict. Large conscript armies, organised into corps, were a new development in Western Europe. Possibly the greatest tactical difference was that of scale and the resulting organisational, operational and logistical problems. The military effectiveness, in the widest sense, of European states, increased, as formidable resources were devoted to warfare, and the practice of the mobilisation of a large proportion of national manpower and warfare both became more insistent. This greater effectiveness posed a serious problem for popular uprisings, such as those in and south of Rome in 1798. Such uprisings were not new, but they were more important in the period, in part because the French destroyed or took over existing power structures, and because they accelerated processes of reform that the population already found inimical.

CONCLUSIONS

The nature of war at the close of the period was different to that at the outset in part due to an increase in scale. Again, this is a matter of perspective. Whilst coming close to Gettysburg in 1863, Waterloo was closer to the battle of Pavia of 1525 than is was to the battle of Kursk of 1943. Furthermore, a notion of change in military arrangements and methods was already well established from the fifteenth century, so that the interest in novelty that was an important characteristic of thought in Enlightenment, Revolutionary and Napoleonic periods did not impact in military affairs on a static, rigid or conservative society.

However, although change was already well established from the fifteenth century, the warfare of the period did not yet witness the co-ordination of large-scale operations that was to characterise land and sea warfare in the Napoleonic period. The potential effectiveness of the military system was demonstrated by Napoleon's ability to force Austria, Prussia and Russia to terms in 1805–07, and by the simultaneous large-scale French operations against Austria and Spain in 1808–09. The role of land and sea power was demonstrated in 1798–1815 by the British. They suppressed rebellion in Ireland, made extensive gains in India, fought a war with the USA and resisted France and her allies, eventually playing a major role in Napoleon's overthrow.[11]

In Britain, France, and more generally in Europe, war reflected the ability of governments to tap economic activity and demographic potential. By 1813 the Prussians had 100 000 regulars and a 120 000-strong milita, the *Landwehr*. War increasingly became a matter of the intersection of capitalism and government, but an intersection that was mediated by political processes and social practices that reflected the dynamic cooperation of rulers and political elites. The Napoleonic enterprise was defeated not by an unreconstructed *ancien régime*, but by states that had absorbed many of France's developments. Across much of Europe, the modernisation of political structures and administrative practices was influenced by French occupation or models, or by the need to devise new political and administrative strategies to counter the French. The changes introduced in the Prussian army and society after defeat by Napoleon in 1806 are an important example, although there was also considerable continuity with the Enlightenment reforms of the pre-Revolutionary period.

It is, however, important not to exaggerate the effectiveness of military administration in this period. Despite manufacturing large quantities of munitions, including 110 000 muskets in 1812, Russia was short of arms and ammunition and musket calibres were not standardised. Yet, in part, this was due to the pressures created by the mass recruitment of the period. The year 1812 was an exceptional one for Russia, but in it 420 000 regulars were recruited, as was a 200 000-strong militia.

War involves far more than resources and governmental structures, but both were important to the other factors that tend to absorb more attention. They were also important in Napoleon's failure. It was far from inevitable, but he was gravely weakened both by the ability of Britain to use the resources of worldwide trade in order to finance opposition to France, and by the precarious nature of the new imperial system and the limited support it enjoyed across much of the continent that he could otherwise dominate militarily. Napoleon's failure to bring lasting peace was in part a testimony to his unwillingness to compromise, but was also the product of a widespread reluctance to accept his perspective that reflected the strength of political identities across much of Europe. This might be presented as cyclical by asking how far Charles V and Hitler faced similar situations, but, in each case, the answer must refer to a specific moment in military and political history.

Napoleon benefited from the operational and organisational advantages that the French enjoyed over their opponents from the outbreak of war in 1792, and from the commitment of the Revolutionary political system to war. These relative advantages were, however, eroded in the 1800s, such that in 1807–09 the French encountered formidable opposition from Russian, Spanish, British and Austrian forces. As so frequently in European military history, a capability gap within Europe had been closed and, in combination with political factors, the consequence was the end of a drive for hegemonic power.

Notes and References

INTRODUCTION *Jeremy Black*

I would like to thank Tom Arnold, Brian Davies, Charles Esdaile and Richard Harding for their comments on an earlier draft of this Introduction.

1. The extensive literature on this subject can be approached through J. Black, *A Military Revolution?* (Basingstoke, 1991), D. Parrott, 'The Military Revolution in Early Modern Europe', *History Today* (1992), C. Rogers (ed.), *The Military Revolution Debate* (Boulder, CO, 1995), D. Eltis, *The Military Revolution in Sixteenth-Century Europe* (London, 1995) and G. Parker, *The Military Revolution. Military Innovation and the Rise of the West, 1500–1800* (2nd edn, Cambridge, 1996).

2. P. H. Wilson, 'Violence and the Rejection of Authority in Eighteenth-Century Germany: The case of the Swabian Mutinies in 1757', *German History*, 12 (1994), pp. 1–26.

3. H. Watanabe-O'Kelly, 'Tournaments and their Relevance for Warfare in the Early Modern Period', *European History Quarterly*, 20 (1990), pp. 451–63.

4. J. Black, *Why Wars Happen* (London, 1998), pp. 47–138.

5. M. C. Finley, 'The Most Monstrous of Wars: Suppression of Calabrian Brigandage', *Consortium on Revolutionary Europe Proceedings* (1989), pp. 251–61.

6. T. M. Barker, *Army, Aristocracy, Monarchy: Essays on War, Society and Government in Austria, 1618–1780* (Boulder, CO, 1982). The Italian aristocracy came to be less prominent: G. Hanlon, *The Twilight of a Military Tradition. Italian Aristocrats and European Conflicts, 1560–1800* (London, 1998).

7. W. Bracewell, *The Uskoks of Senj: Piracy, Banditry and Holy War in the Sixteenth Century Adriatic* (Ithaca, NY, 1992).

8. J. Glete, *Navies and Nations. Warships, Navies and State Building in Europe and America, 1500–1860* (Stockholm, 1993); J. R. Bruijn, *The Dutch Navy of the Seventeenth and Eighteenth Centuries* (Columbia, SC, 1993); R. Harding, *Seapower and Naval Warfare 1650–1850* (London, 1999).

9. N. A. M. Rodger, *The Safeguard of the Sea. A Naval History of Britain. I. 660–1649* (London, 1997), pp. 430–4.

10. J. A. Lynn, 'The Evolution of Army Style in the Modern West, 800–2000', *International History Review*, 18 (1996), pp. 507–45.

11. P. Longworth, *The Cossacks* (London, 1969); J. E. Thomson, *Mercenaries, Pirates, and Sovereigns: State-Building and Extraterritorial Violence in Early Modern Europe* (Princeton, NJ, 1994).

12. M. Howard, *War in European History* (Oxford, 1976).

13. See, for example, M. Fissel (ed.), *War and Government in Britain, 1598–1650* (Manchester, 1991); R. I. Frost, 'The Polish-Lithuanian Commonwealth and the "Military Revolution"', in M. B. Biskupski and J. S. Pula (eds.), *Poland and Europe: Historical Dimensions* (Boulder, CO, 1993).

14. Following, for example, the approach of S. Ross, *From Flintlock to Rifle. Infantry Tactics, 1740–1866* (2nd edn, London, 1996).

15. See, for example, B. P. Hughes, *Firepower. Weapons' Effectiveness on the Battlefield 1630–1850* (London, 1974) and *Open Fire: Artillery Tactics from Marlborough to Wellington* (London, 1983).

16. A readily accessible example is provided by C. J. Duffy, *Siege Warfare. The Fortress in the Early Modern World 1494–1660* (London, 1979) and *The Fortress in the Age of Vauban and Frederick the Great, 1660–1789* (London, 1985).

17. J. Black, *Culloden and the '45* (Stroud, 1990).

18. G. Parker, *The Army of Flanders and the Spanish Road 1567–1659* (Cambridge, 1972).

19. O. Subtelny, 'Russia and the Ukraine: The Difference that Peter I Made', *Russian Review*, 39 (1980), p. 10.

20. P. H. Wilson, *German Armies. War and German Politics 1648–1806* (London, 1998).

21. D. Showalter, 'Tactics and Recruitment in Eighteenth-Century Prussia', *Studies in History and Politics* (1983–84); J. L. H. Keep, *Soldiers of the Tsar: Army and Society in Russia, 1462–1872* (Oxford, 1985).

22. For command and control problems with the French army, D. Parrott, 'Richelieu, the *Grands*, and the French Army', in J. Bergin and L. Brockliss (eds.), *Richelieu and his Age* (Oxford, 1992), pp. 135–73.

23. M. A. J. Palmer, 'The "Military Revolution" Afloat: The Era of the Anglo-Dutch Wars and the Transition to Modern Warfare at Sea', *War in History*, 4 (1997), pp. 148, 168, 174.

24. J. A. Lynn, 'Food, Funds and Fortresses: Resource Mobilization and Positional Warfare in the Campaigns of Louis XIV', in Lynn (ed.), *Feeding Mars. Logistics in Western Warfare from the Middle Ages to the Present* (Boulder, CO, 1993), pp. 137–60.

25. P. H. Wilson, 'War in German Thought from the Peace of Westphalia to Napoleon', *European History Quarterly*, 28 (1998), pp. 19–20.

26. Parker, *Military Revolution*, esp. p. 24. But see criticisms by S. Adams, 'Tactics or Politics? "The Military Revolution" and the Habsburg Hegemony, 1525–1648', in J. A. Lynn (ed.), *Tools of War. Instruments, Ideas, and Institutions of Warfare, 1445–1871* (Champaign, IL, 1990), pp. 28–52, and Lynn, 'The *Trace Italienne* and Growth of Armies: The French Case', *Journal of Military History*, 55 (1991), pp. 297–330.

27. Parker, *Military Revolution*, pp. 120–5.

28. R. Frost, *War in History*, 4 (1997), pp. 485–6. For an emphasis on the period 1642–60 in England, M. J. Braddick, 'An English Military Revolution?', *Historical Journal*, 36 (1993), pp. 965–75.

29. D. Parrott, *War in History*, 4 (1997), p. 479.

30. B. Nosworthy, *The Anatomy of Victory. Battle Tactics 1689–1763* (New York, 1990).

31. C. Storrs, 'The Army of Lombardy and the Resilience of Spanish Power in Italy in the Reign of Carlos II', *War in History*, 4 (1997), p. 376.

32. B. Steele, 'Muskets and Pendulums: Benjamin Robins, Leonhard Euler and the Ballistics Revolution', *Technology and Culture*, 34 (1994), pp. 348–82.

33. Hanlon, *Italian Aristocrats*, p. 346.

34. J. Pritchard, 'From Shipwright to Naval Constructor', *Technology and Culture* (1987), pp. 7, 9, 19–20.

1. WAR IN SIXTEENTH-CENTURY EUROPE: REVOLUTION AND RENAISSANCE
Thomas F. Arnold

1. Michael Roberts, 'The Military Revolution, 1560–1660' (1956), most recently reprinted in Clifford J. Rogers (ed.), *The Military Revolution Debate* (Boulder, CO, 1995), pp. 13–35.

2. Ibid., p. 29.

3. Ibid.

4. Geoffrey Parker, 'The "Military Revolution, 1560–1660" – A Myth' (1976), reprinted in Rogers, *Military Revolution*, pp. 37–54 and Geoffrey Parker, *The Military Revolution: Military Innovation and the Rise of the West, 1500–1800* (Cambridge, 1988 and 1996).

5. Geoffrey Parker, in Rogers, *Military Revolution*, p. 38.

6. Günther E. Rothenberg, 'Maurice of Nassau, Gustavus Adolphus, Raimondo Montecuccoli, and the "Military Revolution" of the Seventeenth Century', in Peter Paret (ed.), *Makers of Modern Strategy from Machiavelli to the Nuclear Age* (Princeton, NJ, 1986), p. 32.

7. Jeremy Black, *A Military Revolution? Military Change and European Society, 1550–1800* (Atlantic Highlands, NJ, 1991), p. 94.

8. Ibid., p. 93. Black's emphasis on a post-1660 chronology is sustained in his article 'A Military Revolution? A 1660–1792 Perspective', in Rogers, *Military Revolution*, pp. 95–116.

9. Clifford J. Rogers, 'The Military Revolutions of the Hundred Years War' (1993), now reprinted in Rogers, *Military Revolution*, pp. 55–94.

10. Ibid., pp. 58, 64, 75.

11. Bert S. Hall, *Weapons and Warfare in Renaissance Europe* (Baltimore, MD, 1996), p. 210.

12. Giovan Mattheo Cicogna, *Il primo libro del trattato militare* (Venice, 1567), pp. 66–67v.

13. François La Noue, *The Politicke and Militarie Discourses* (London, 1587), pp. 203–10.

14. Charles Oman, *The Art of War in the Middle Ages* [1924] (New York, 1958), vol. 2, p. 356.

15. Alessandro Benedetti, *Diario de bello carolino*, ed. Dorothy M. Schullian (New York, 1967), p. 148.

16. Sanuto, quoted in J. R. Hale, *War and Society in Renaissance Europe, 1450–1620* (Baltimore, MD, 1985), p. 70.

17. Frédérique Verrier, *Les armes de Minerve, L'Humanisme militaire dans l'Italie du XVIe siècle* (Paris, 1997).

18. Francesco Patrizi, *Parallelli Militari*, book two (Rome, 1595), title page.

2. WARFARE IN THE AGE OF THE THIRTY YEARS WAR 1598–1648 *Ronald G. Asch*

1. For the war against the Turks see J. P. Niederkorn, *Die europäischen Mächte und der 'Lange Türkenkrieg' Kaiser Rudolfs II. (1593–1606)* (Vienna, 1993).

2. On the situation in Europe before 1618 see G. Parker et al., *The Thirty Years War* (2nd edn, London, 1997), pp. 35–9.

3. H. Schmidt, 'Pfalz-Neuburgs Sprung zum Niederrhein. Wolfgang Wilhelm von Pfalz-Neuburg und der Jülisch-Klevische Erbfolgestreit', in H. Glaser (ed.), *Wittelsbach und Bayern*, vol. ii, 1: *Um Glauben und Reich. Beiträge zur bayerischen Geschichte und Kunst 1573–1657* (Munich, 1980), pp. 77–89; for French policy cf. M. Greengrass, *France in the Age of Henry IV* (2nd edn, London, 1995), pp. 241–50, and J. M. Hayden, 'Continuity in the France of Henry IV and Louis XIII, French Foreign Policy 1598–1615', *Journal of Modern History*, 45 (1973), pp. 1–23.

4. S. P. Oakley, *War and Peace in the Baltic 1560–1790* (London, 1992), pp. 42–66; P. D. Lockhart, *Denmark in the Thirty Years War 1618–1648* (Selinsgrove and London, 1996), pp. 71–3.

5. J. Burkhardt, *Der Dreißigjährige Krieg* (Frankfurt/M., 1992), pp. 10–30, 63–128. Cf. Burkhardt, 'Der Dreißigjährige Krieg als frühmoderner Staatsbildungskrieg', *Geschichte in Wissenschaft und Unterricht*, 45 (1994), pp. 487–99.

6. For the notion of the composite monarchy see H. G. Koenigsberger, 'Dominium Regale or Dominium Politicum et Regale? Monarchies and Parliaments in Early Modern Europe', in Koenigsberger, *Politicians and Virtuosi* (London, 1986), pp. 1–26; J. H. Elliott, 'A Europe of Composite Monarchies', *Past and Present*, 137 (1992), pp. 48–71. See further M. Greengrass (ed.), *Conquest and Coalescence. The Shaping of the State in Early Modern Europe* (London, 1991).

7. R. G. Asch, *The Thirty Years War. The Holy Roman Empire and Europe 1618–1648* (Basingstoke, 1997), pp. 47–59.

8. C. Russell, *The Fall of the British Monarchies* (Oxford, 1991).

9. On the crisis in the Holy Roman Empire before 1618 see Asch, *War*, pp. 9–34, and M. Heckel, 'Die Krise der Religionsverfassung des Reiches und die Anfänge des Dreißigjährigen Krieges', in Heckel, *Gesammelte Schriften. Staat, Kirche, Recht, Geschichte*, ed. K. Schlaich, 2 vols. (Tübingen, 1989), vol. ii, pp. 970–98.

10. For the *ius foederis* and *ius superioritatis* conceded to the individual Estates of the Empire in 1648 see H. Schilling, *Höfe und Allianzen.*

Deutschland 1648–1763 (Berlin, 1989), pp. 131–3, and H. Duchhardt, *Deutsche Verfassungsgeschichte 1495–1806* (Stuttgart, 1991), pp. 163–4, 180.

11. For opposition within France see J. M. Constant, *Les Conjurateurs, le premier libéralisme politique sous Richelieu* (Paris, 1987), and O. Ranum, *The Fronde: A French Revolution 1648–1652* (New York, 1993).

12. D. Albrecht, *Die auswärtige Politik Maximilians von Bayern 1618–1635* (Göttingen, 1962); cf. for Spanish problems with Bavaria E. Straub, *Pax et Imperium. Spaniens Kampf um seine Friedensordnung in Europa zwischen 1617 und 1635* (Paderborn, 1980).

13. A. Gotthard, '"Politice seint wir bäpstisch". Kursachsen und der deutsche Protestantismus im frühen 17. Jahrhundert', *Zeitschrift für historische Forschung*, 20 (1993), pp. 275–320.

14. S. Lundkvist, 'Die schwedischen Kriegs- und Friedensziele 1632–1648', in K. Repgen (ed.), *Krieg und Politik 1618–1648. Europäische Probleme und Perspektiven* (Munich, 1988), pp. 219–41, at p. 223; M. Roberts, *The Swedish Imperial Experience* (Cambridge, 1979), pp. 28–36, and K. Zernack, 'Schweden als europäische Großmacht in der frühen Neuzeit', *Historische Zeitschrift*, 232 (1981), pp. 327–57, at pp. 333–43.

15. J. I. Israel, *The Dutch Republic and the Hispanic World 1606–1661* (Oxford, 1982), pp. 25–74.

16. For the war over Mantua see D. Parrott, 'The Mantuan Succession, 1627–31: A Sovereignty Dispute in Early Modern Europe', *English Historical Review*, 112 (1997), pp. 20–65; R. A Stradling, 'Olivares and the Origins of the Franco-Spanish War, 1627–1635', *English Historical Review*, 101 (1986), pp. 68–94, reprinted in Stradling, *Spain's Struggle for Europe* (London 1994), pp. 95–120, esp. pp. 101–6.

17. D. Parrott, 'The Causes of the Franco-Spanish War of 1635–59', in J. Black (ed.), *The Origins of War in Early Modern Europe* (Edinburgh, 1987), pp. 72–111, and H. Ernst, *Madrid und Wien 1632–37. Politik und Finanzen in den Beziehungen zwischen Philipp IV. und Ferdinand II.* (Münster, 1991), pp. 65–7, 81–5; cf. Stradling, 'Olivares and the Origins', and J. I. Israel, 'Olivares, the Cardinal-Infante and Spain's Strategy in the Low Countries (1635–1643): the Road to Rocroi', in R. L. Kagan and G. Parker (eds.), *Spain, Europe and the Atlantic World. Essays in Honour of John H. Elliott* (Cambridge, 1995), pp. 267–95. As opposed to Stradling, Israel emphasises that Olivares continued to give priority to the fight against the Dutch Republic after 1635, not to the battle against France.

18. For the debate on the military revolution see M. Roberts, 'The Military Revolution', in Roberts, *Essays in Swedish History* (London, 1967), pp. 195–225, reprinted in C. J. Rogers (ed.), *The Military Revolution Debate: Readings on the Military Transformation of Early Modern Europe* (Boulder, CO, 1995), pp. 13–35, and the other essays in the collection edited by Rogers. See further G. Parker, *The Military Revolution* (Cambridge, 1988; 2nd edn 1997), pp. 6–44, and J. Black, *European Warfare 1660–1815* (London, 1994), pp. 3–33, with further references.

19. M. Roberts, *Gustavus Adolphus: A History of Sweden 1611–1632*, 2 vols. (London, 1953–58), vol. ii, pp. 245–64, esp. pp. 255–6.

20. D. A. Parrott, 'Strategy and Tactics in the Thirty Years' War: The Military Revolution', in Rogers, *Revolution Debate*, pp. 227–53, at pp. 230–5: Parrott offers a trenchant criticism of the idea of a military revolution. Cf. M. Junkelmann, *Gustav Adolf. Schwedens Aufstieg zur Großmacht* (Regensburg, 1993), pp. 226–31.

21. Roberts, *Gustavus Adolphus: A History*, vol. ii, pp. 255–6; also G. E. Rothenberg, 'Maurice of Nassau, Gustavus Adolphus, Raimondo Montecuccoli and the "Military Revolution" of the Seventeenth Century', in P. Paret (ed.), *Makers of Modern Strategy from Machiavelli to the Nuclear Age* (Oxford, 1986), pp. 32–63, at pp. 45–9.

22. A. Åberg, 'The Swedish Army from Lützen to Narva', in M. Roberts (ed.), *Sweden's Age of Greatness* (London, 1973), pp. 265–87, at p. 283; Junkelmann, *Gustav Adolf*, pp. 238–9. See also M. Roberts, *Gustavus Adolphus* (London, 1992), p. 106, where Roberts has revised his earlier assessment to some extent.

23. M. Junkelmann, 'Feldherr Maximilians: Johann Tserclaes Graf von Tilly', in Glaser, *Um Glauben und Reich*, pp. 377–99, at pp. 385–6.

24. K. Krüger, 'Dänische und schwedische Kriegsfinanzierung im Dreißigjährigen Krieg bis 1635', in K. Repgen (ed.), *Krieg und Politik 1618–1648. Europäische Probleme und Perspektiven* (Munich, 1988), pp. 275–98. Cf. J. Lindegren, 'The "Swedish Military State" 1560–1720', *Scandinavian Journal of History*, 10 (1985), pp. 305–36.

25. During the years 1625 to 1630 altogether about 50 000 men were conscripted in Sweden, according to a rota system which ensured that every village provided a certain number of men – by no means all adult men had to serve. A further 25 000 were sent to Germany in 1630–31 (Krüger, 'Kriegsfinanzierung', pp. 283–5; Roberts, *Gustavus Adolphus: A History*, vol. ii, p. 207 ff; F. Tallett, *War and Society in Early Modern Europe 1495–1715* (London, 1992), p. 83, Junkelmann, *Gustav Adolf*, pp. 157–68).

26. But cf. the sceptical remarks by J. A. Lynn, 'The *Trace Italienne* and the Growth of Armies: The French Case', in Rogers, *Revolution Debate*, pp. 169–200.

27. Parker, *Revolution*, pp. 6 ff, esp. p. 24, Cf. Parker, 'In Defense of the Military Revolution', in Rogers, *Revolution Debate*, pp. 337–66, at pp. 346–52. This essay has now been reprinted as an appendix to the second edition of Parker, *Revolution*.

28. On warfare in the Low Countries see Israel, *The Dutch Republic and the Hispanic World*.

29. It has also been argued that the prominent role comparatively minor powers played in the Thirty Years War at least until the mid-1630s, for example Bavaria, Denmark or, in some sense, Sweden, accounted for the fact that commanders generally sought a quick decision in open battle. These states just could not afford a prolonged war of attrition along the lines of the Spanish strategy in the Low Countries. See S. Adams, 'Tactics or Politics? "The Military Revolution" and the

Habsburg Hegemony, 1525–1648', in Rogers, *Revolution Debate*, pp. 253–72, at pp. 265–6.

30. Tallett, *War and Society*, pp. 61–6. It is unlikely that it was primarily the Swedish control of numerous fortresses in northern Germany which saved Sweden from total defeat after Nördlingen (Parker, 'In Defense', p. 349). Rather, the unbroken morale of the native Swedish troops and the fact that the Emperor gave priority to the fight against France saved Sweden.

31. P. Sörensson, 'Das Kriegswesen während der letzten Periode des Dreißigjährigen Krieges', in H. U. Rudolf (ed.), *Der Dreißigjährige Krieg* (Darmstadt, 1977), pp. 431–57, esp. pp. 452–3.

32. For the size of armies, see Tallett, *War and Society*, p. 5–6; for a reassessment of Rocroi see R. A. Stradling, 'Catastrophe and Recovery: The Defeat of Spain 1639–43', in Stradling, *Spain's Struggle*, pp. 197–212, at pp. 208–10.

33. The imperial general Gallas, for example, when fighting the Swedes in northern Germany in 1644, had 11 500 horse and 10 000 footsoldiers under his command. Of the cavalry about two-thirds survived the campaign; of the foot only about 50 per cent (H. Salm, *Armeefinanzierung im Dreißigjährigen Krieg. Der Niederrheinisch-Westfälische Reichskreis 1635–1650* (Münster, 1990), p. 43).

34. A. Corvisier, ch. xiv: 'La Paix nécessaire mais incertaine 1598–1635' and ch. xv: 'Renouveau militaire et misères de la guerre, 1635–1659', in P. Contamine (ed.), *Histoire Militaire de La France*, I: *Des origines à 1715* (Paris, 1992), pp. 331–52, 353–82, at pp. 341–2, 347, 361–5. Cf. Corvisier, *La France de Louis XIV* (Paris, 1979), pp. 61, 124, where Corvisier – much more cautiously – puts the average size of the royal armies at between 80 000 and 120 000 men during 1635–59 (p. 124). See also J. A. Lynn, 'Recalculating French Army Growth During the *Grand Siècle*', in Rogers, *Revolution Debate*, pp. 117–48, at pp. 124–30, as well as Lynn, *Giant of the Grand Siècle. The French Army 1610–1715* (Cambridge, 1997), pp. 41–55, and B. Kroener, 'Die Entwicklung der Truppenstärken in den französischen Armeen zwischen 1635 und 1661', in K. Repgen (ed.), *Forschungen und Quellen zur Geschichte des Dreißigjährigen Krieges* (Münster, 1981), pp. 163–220.

35. France lost half a million soldiers between 1635 and 1659 (Corvisier, *La France*, p. 124), not counting deserters. Mass desertions were very widespread in the French army, and the fact that many officers never joined their regiments or were absent for long periods of time certainly did not help to contain this problem (Corvisier, 'Renouveau militaire', pp. 363–6).

36. Parker, *Revolution*, p. 45, and I. A. A. Thompson, '"Money, Money, and yet more Money!" Finance, the Fiscal-State and the Military Revolution: Spain 1500–1600', in Rogers, *Revolution Debate*, pp. 273–98, at pp. 283–4.

37. Parker, *War*, p. 90.

38. M. C. 't Hart, *The Making of a Bourgeois State: War, Politics and Finance during the Dutch Revolt* (Manchester, 1993), pp. 43–5.

39. Junkelmann, *Gustav Adolf*, pp. 303, 405.

40. Salm, *Armeefinanzierung*, p. 42, n. 34; Parker, 'In Defense', p. 349, quoting A. Oschmann, *Der Nürnberger Exekutionstag 1649–1650* (Münster, 1991), pp. 506–20.

41. See Parrott, 'Strategy and Tactics', p. 240, who doubts there is any link between warfare and the growth of the state in this period.

42. The fundamental work on this problem remains F. Redlich, *The German Military Enterpriser and his Workforce: A Study in European Economic and Social History*, 2 vols. (Wiesbaden, 1964–65).

43. G. Mann, *Wallenstein* (Frankfurt/M., 1971; English translation London, 1976), and A. Ernstberger, *Hans de Witte, Finanzmann Wallensteins* (Wiesbaden, 1954).

44. Redlich, *Enterpriser*, vol. i, pp. 234–5; cf. Gustav Droysen, *Bernhard von Weimar* (Leipzig, 1885).

45. Salm, *Armeefinanzierung*, pp. 11–26, 45–6, 172–6.

46. C. Kapser, *Die bayerische Kriegsorganisation in der zweiten Hälfte des Dreißigjährigen Krieges 1635–1648/9* (Münster, 1997), pp. 133–65, 163–95, 212–16.

47. Krüger, 'Kriegsfinanzierung', esp. pp. 288–9; Roberts, *Imperial Experience*, p. 53; Asch, *War*, pp. 164–6, with further references.

48. S. A. Nilsson, *De Stora krigens tid. Om Sverige som militärstaat och bondesambället* (Uppsala, 1990), pp. 284–7.

49. 't Hart, *Bourgeois State*, pp. 118–57, 173–84.

50. Parrott, 'Strategy and Tactics', pp. 241–3; Parrott, 'French Military Organization in the 1630s: the Failure of Richelieu's Ministry', *Seventeenth-Century French Studies*, 9 (1987), pp. 151–67; Parrott, 'The Administration of the French Army during the Ministry of Cardinal Richelieu', unpublished Ph. D. thesis (University of Oxford, 1985), and most recently Lynn, *Giant*, pp. 221–38. Lynn speaks of a 'semi-entrepreneurial' system combining 'the worst of two worlds', at least for the officers (p. 223).

51. P. T. Hoffman, 'Early Modern France, 1450–1700', in P. T. Hoffman and K. Norberg (eds.), *Fiscal Crises, Liberty and Representative Government* (Stanford, CA, 1994), pp. 226–52, at p. 238.

52. Hoffman, 'France', p. 239, and W. Mager, *Frankreich vom Ancien Régime zur Moderne 1630–1830* (Stuttgart, 1980), p. 114, giving the equivalent in labour days of the tax burden for each head of a family in France. If the whole adult population, including women and children, were counted, the burden would, of course, be lower. Hoffmann, 'France', p. 238, gives the equivalent of the revenues of the Crown (including indirect taxes and other income) per head of population as 4.18 labour days in the 1620s and 9.11 days in the 1640s.

53. Hoffman, 'France', pp. 232–5; J. Collins, *Fiscal Limits of Absolutism: Direct Taxation in Early Seventeenth-Century France* (Berkeley, CA, 1988), pp. 98–107.

54. R. Bonney, 'Louis XIII, Richelieu and the Royal Finances', in J. Bergin and L. Brockliss (eds.), *Richelieu and his Age* (Oxford, 1992), pp. 99–135, at pp. 108–10; Collins, *Fiscal Limits*, pp. 135–65.

55. Collins, *Fiscal Limits*, pp. 141, 215, 200–13, 219; Hoffman, 'France', p. 244; Bonney, 'Royal Finances', p. 119; cf. Bonney, *Political Change in France under Richelieu and Mazarin 1624–1661* (Oxford, 1978), pp. 214–37.

56. Collins, *Fiscal Limits*, p. 209.

57. I. A. A. Thompson and B. Yun Casalilla (eds.), *The Castilian Crisis of the Seventeenth Century: New Perspectives on the Economic and Social History of Seventeenth-Century Spain* (Cambridge, 1994); J. Gelabert, 'The Fiscal Burden', in R. Bonney (ed.), *Economic Systems and State Finance* (Oxford, 1995), pp. 539–76, at pp. 568–9; cf. J. Gelabert, 'El impacto de la guerra y del fiscalismo en Castilla', in J. H. Elliott and A. García Sanz (eds.), *La España de Conde Duque Olivares* (Valladolid, 1990), pp. 555–73.

58. D. Flynn, 'Fiscal Crisis and the Decline of Spain', *Journal of Economic History*, 42 (1982), pp. 139–47, and E. J. Hamilton, *American Treasure and the Price Revolution in Spain, 1501–1650* (1934, 2nd edn Cambridge, MA, 1965); however, cf. M. Morineau, *Incroyables Gazettes et fabuleux métaux. Les retours des trésors américains d'après les gazettes hollandaises* (Cambridge, 1985), esp. pp. 77–83, 247–50.

59. I. A. A. Thompson, 'Castile: Polity, Fiscality and Fiscal Crisis', in Hoffman and Norberg (eds.), *Fiscal Crises*, pp. 140–80, at pp. 160–5. On the growing income of the crown in Castile in the sixteenth century see Gelabert, 'Fiscal Burden', pp. 565–6.

60. Thompson, 'Castile', pp. 173–4; cf. Thompson, *War and Government in Habsburg Spain 1560–1620* (London, 1976), pp. 33–45.

61. Thompson, 'The Government of Spain in the Reign of Philip IV', in Thompson, *Crown and Cortes: Government, Institutions and Representation in Early-Modern Castile* (Aldershot, 1993) ch. iv, esp. pp. 27 ff, for the role of the nobility in recruiting soldiers.

62. Thompson, 'The Government of Spain in the Reign of Philip IV', in particular p. 79; cf. Thompson, 'War and Institutionalization: the Military-Administrative Bureaucracy of Spain in the Sixteenth and Seventeenth Centuries', in Thompson, *Crown and Cortes*, ch. iii, esp. pp. 36–7.

63. Thompson, ' "Money, Money, and yet more Money!" ', esp. pp. 290–1.

64. This is the argument of David Parrott, 'Strategy and Tactics', p. 241, based on his thesis 'The Administration of the French Army'.

65. B. Yun Casalilla, 'The Castilian Aristocracy in the 17th Century; Crisis, Refeudalisation or Political Offensive', in Thompson and Casalilla (eds.), *Castilian Crisis*, pp. 277–300. Casalilla comes to the conclusion that 'This "refeudalisation" did not mean any decrease in the institutional power of the state, nor *a fortiori* any political independence for the *señor*, nor any fragmentation of the political system as a whole' (p. 284). He also emphasises that the alienation of revenues to noble magnates was at least as important as the sale of jurisdictional rights. See also I. A. A. Thompson, 'The Nobility in Spain', in H. M. Scott (ed.), *The European Nobilities in the Seventeenth and Eighteenth Centuries*, 2 vols. (London, 1995),

vol. i, pp. 174–236, at pp. 210–19: Thompson here prefers to speak of 'reseñorialization' instead of refeudalisation and admits that the increase in noble power coincided with a serious economic crisis affecting many nobles, due to a considerable extent to the fiscal demands of the crown.

66. Asch, *Thirty Years War*, pp. 189–92, and Asch, 'Estates and Princes after 1648: The Consequences of the Thirty Years War', *German History*, 6 (1988), pp. 113–32.

67. M. J. Braddick, *Parliamentary Taxation in 17th Century England* (Woodbridge, 1994), p. 290 and 127–50, as well as pp. 291–8. For the reality of warfare in England cf. Charles Carlton, *Going to the Wars: The Experience of the British Civil Wars, 1638–1651* (London, 1992).

3. WARFARE IN THE OLD REGIME 1648–1789 *Peter Wilson*

1. For example, E. Luard, *War in International Society* (London, 1986) and J. U. Nef, *War and Human Progress* (Cambridge, MA, 1950).

2. For examples of this view from differing historical perspectives see H. Schnitter and T. Schmidt, *Absolutismus und Heer* (Berlin, 1987) and O. Hintze, *The Historical Essays of Otto Hintze* (ed. F. Gilbert, Oxford, 1975), esp. pp. 180–215.

3. Overview provided by S. P. Oakley, *War and Peace in the Baltic, 1560–1790* (London, 1992).

4. G. E. Rothenberg, *The Military Border in Croatia, 1740–1881* (Chicago, 1966); A. Balisch, 'Infantry Battlefield Tactics in the Seventeenth and Eigtheenth Centuries on the European and Turkish Theatres of War. The Austrian Response to Different Conditions', *Studies in History and Politics*, 3 (1983/84), pp. 43–60.

5. T. M. Barker, *Double Eagle and Crescent: Vienna's Second Turkish Siege and its Historical Setting* (Albany, NY, 1967); I. Parvev, *Habsburgs and Ottomans between Vienna and Belgrade (1683–1739)* (Boulder, CO, 1995); K. A. Roider, *Austria's Eastern Question 1700–1790* (Princeton, NJ, 1982).

6. J. Brewer, *The Sinews of Power. War, Money and the English State, 1688–1783* (New York, 1989).

7. C. Tilly, *Coercion, Capital and European States, A.D. 990–1992* (Oxford, 1992), pp. 122–5.

8. D. E. Showalter, *The Wars of Frederick the Great* (London, 1996), p. 6. For the importance of technology in eighteenth-century weapons production see B. R. Kroener (ed.), *Europa im Zeitalter Friedrichs des Grossen* (Munich, 1989), pp. 47–78.

9. C. Jones, 'The Military Revolution and the Professionalization of the French Army under the Ancien Régime', in C. J. Rogers (ed.), *The Military Revolution Debate* (Boulder, CO, 1995), pp. 149–68, at p. 162. For soldiers' marital status see P. H. Wilson, 'German Women and War, 1500–1800', *War in History*, 3 (1996), pp. 127–60.

10. Good case studies are R. Pröve, *Stehendes Heer und städtische Gesellschaft im 18 Jahrhundert. Göttingen und seine Militärbevölkerung 1713–1756* (Munich, 1995) and J. Chagniot, *Paris et l'armée au xviiie siècle* (Paris, 1985).

11. A good introduction to this important topic is provided by C. Storrs and H. M. Scott, 'The Military Revolution and the European Nobility, *c.*1600–1800', *War in History*, 3 (1996), pp. 1–41. For a slightly controversial view that Italian elites lost interest in military affairs, see G. Hanlon, *The Twilight of a Military Tradition. Italian Aristocrats and European Conflicts, 1560–1800* (London, 1998).

12. O. Büsch, *Military System and Social Life in Old Regime Prussia 1713–1807. The Beginnings of the Social Militarization of Prusso-German Society* (1st edn Berlin, 1962; Atlantic Highlands, NJ, 1997).

13. J. Kloosterhuis, *Bauern, Bürger und Soldaten. Quellen zur Sozialisation des Militärsystems in preussischen Westfalen 1713–1803*, 2 vols. (Münster, 1992) and his article and that by H. Harnisch in B. R. Kroener and R. Pröve (eds.), *Krieg und Frieden. Militär und Gesellschaft in der frühen Neuzeit* (Paderborn, 1996).

14. J. A. Lynn, *Giant of the Grand Siècle. The French Army 1610–1715* (Cambridge, 1997); A. F. Upton, 'The *Riksdag* of 1680 and the Establishment of Royal Absolutism in Sweden', *English Historical Review*, 103 (1987), pp. 281–308; J. Lindegren, 'The Swedish "Military State", 1560–1720', *Scandinavian Journal of History*, 10 (1985), pp. 305–36; J. Childs, *The Army, James II and the Glorious Revolution* (Manchester, 1980); F. G. J. Ten Raa et al., *Het staatsche Leger 1568–1795*, 8 vols. in 11 parts (The Hague, 1911–59).

15. J. Lukowski, *Liberty's Folly. The Polish–Lithuanian Commonwealth in the 18th Century, 1697–1795* (London, 1991). For foreign interference in Polish military reforms see also M. G. Müller, 'Staat und Heer in der Adelsrepublik Polen im 18. Jahrhundert', in J. Kunisch (ed.), *Staatsverfassung und Heeresverfassung* (Berlin, 1986), pp. 279–95.

16. P. H. Wilson, *German Armies. War and German Politics 1648–1806* (London, 1998); K. O. V. Aretin, *Das alte Reich 1648–1806*, 3 vols. (Stuttgart, 1993).

17. F. Redlich, *The German Military Enterprizer and his Workforce*, 2 vols. (Wiesbaden, 1964–65); A. Guy, *Oeconomy and Discipline. Officership and Administration in the British Army 1714–63* (Manchester, 1985); A. Bruce, *The Purchase System in the British Army 1660–1871* (London, 1980); G. Holler, *Für Kaiser und Vaterland. Offizier in der alten Armee* (Vienna, 1990).

18. J. Kunisch, *Staatsverfassung und Mächtekonflikt. Zur Genese von Staatskonflikten im Zeitalter des Absolutismus* (Berlin, 1979) and his *Fürst-Gesellschaft-Krieg. Studien zur bellizistischen Disposition des absoluten Fürstenstaates* (Cologne, 1992).

19. This view is espoused by those who assert the primacy of socio-economic factors in historical development; for example P. Anderson, *Lineages of the Absolutist State* (London, 1979).

20. J. R. Jones, *The Anglo-Dutch Wars of the Seventeenth Century* (London, 1996).

21. For further discussion see P. H. Wilson, 'War in German Thought from the Peace of Westphalia to Napoleon', *European History Quarterly*, 28 (1998), pp. 5–50.

22. The pace was the standard measurement of distance in contemporary drill manuals and battle accounts. Its exact length varied between countries, but was generally similar to that used in Austria, which measured 62 cm.

23. Desertion rates, though serious, were far lower than generally believed and were often exceeded by those experienced by the French revolutionary forces. See M. Sikora, *Disziplin und Desertion. Strukturprobleme militärischer Organisation im 18. Jahrhundert* (Berlin, 1996).

24. The national variations are summarised in B. Nosworthy, *The Anatomy of Victory. Battle Tactics 1689–1763* (New York, 1992) and H. Schwarz, *Gefechtsformen der Infanterie in Europa durch 800 Jahren*, 2 vols. (Munich, 1977).

25. D. Chandler (ed.), *Robert Parker and Comte de Mérode-Westerloo* (London, 1968), pp. 87–8. Kriegsarchiv [Austria], *Kriege gegen die Französischen Revolution 1792–1797*, 2 vols. (Vienna, 1905), vol. ii, pp. 391–3.

26. See E. von Warnery, *Remarks on Cavalry* (London, 1798, repr. 1997).

27. C. Duffy, *Fire and Stone. The Science of Siege Warfare 1660–1860* (London, 1975) and his *The Fortress in the Age of Vauban and Frederick the Great 1660–1789* (London, 1985).

4. NAVAL WARFARE 1453–1815 *Robert Harding*

1. J. Morrison (ed.), *The Age of the Galley, Mediterranean Oared Vessels since Pre-Classical Times* (London, 1995), pp. 10–11.

2. J. H. Pryor, *Geography, Technology and War. Studies in the Maritime History of the Mediterranean, 649–1571* (Cambridge, 1988), pp. 135–70.

3. A. C. Hess, 'The Evolution of the Ottoman Seaborne Empire in the Age of Oceanic Discoveries, 1453–1525', *American Historical Review*, lxxv (1970), pp. 1892–1919; 'The Ottoman Conquest of Egypt (1517) and the Beginning of the Sixteenth Century World War', *International Journal of Middle East Studies*, iv (1973), pp. 55–76.

4. J. E. Dotson, 'The Economics and Logistics of Galley Warfare', in Morrison, *The Age of the Galley*, pp. 217–23.

5. See R. Unger, *Cogs, Caravels and Galleons* (London, 1994).

6. J. H. Parry, *The Age of Reconnaissance: Discovery, Exploration and Settlement, 1450–1650* (London, 1963), pp. 19–130; A. J. R. Wood, 'Seamen Ashore and Afloat: The Social Environment of the *Carreira da India*,

1550–1750', *Mariner's Mirror*, lxix (1983), pp. 35–52; G. V. Scammell, 'The Sinews of War: Manning and Provisioning English Fighting Ships, 1550–1650', *Mariner's Mirror*, lxxiii (1987), pp. 351–67; P. E. H. Hair, 'The Experience of the Sixteenth Century English Voyages to Guinea', *Mariner's Mirror*, lxxxiii (1997), pp. 3–13.

7. C. Cipolla, *Guns, Sails and Empires. Technological Innovation and the Early Phases of European Expansion, 1400–1700* (New York, 1965; paperback edn Manhattan, KS, 1996), pp. 21–89.

8. J. Glete, *Navies and Nations, Warships, Navies and State-Building in Europe and America, 1500–1860*, 2 vols. (Stockholm, 1993), vol. 1, pp. 110–13; D. Loades, *The Tudor Navy: An Administrative, Political and Military History* (Aldershot, 1992); J. Thomson, *Mercenaries, Pirates and Sovereigns: State-Building and Extra-Territorial Violence in Early Modern Europe* (Princeton, NJ, 1994). A. Petrotin-Dumon, 'The Pirate and the Emperor: Power and the Law on the Seas, 1450–1850', in J. D. Tracy (ed.), *The Political Economy of Merchant Empires* (Cambridge, 1991), pp. 196–227.

9. Glete, *Navies and Nations*, vol. I, pp. 110–12.

10. R. C. Davis, *Shipbuilders of the Venetian Arsenal: Workers and Workplace in the Pre-Industrial Age* (Baltimore, MD, 1991), pp. 16–17; A. Tenenti, *Piracy and the Decline of Venice, 1580–1615* (London, 1967), pp. 56–80; J. R. Guilmartin, *Gunpowder and Galleys: Changing Technology and Mediterranean Warfare at Sea in the Sixteenth Century* (Cambridge, 1974).

11. R. Murphy, 'The Ottoman Attitude towards the Adoption of Western Technology: The Role of *Efrenci* technicians in Civil and Military Applications', in J.-L. Basque-Grammont and P. Dumont, *Contributions à l'histoire économique et sociale de l'Empire ottoman* (Louvain, 1983), pp. 292–3 and n. 11.

12. G. Parker, *The Military Revolution: Military Innovation and the Rise of the West, 1500–1800* (Cambridge, 1988), pp. 92–9.

13. B. Capp, *Cromwell's Navy: The Fleet and the English Revolution, 1648–1660* (Cambridge, 1989), pp. 15–41, 331–70.

14. J. R. Jones, *The Anglo-Dutch Wars of the Seventeenth Century* (London, 1996), gives a good concise account of all three Anglo-Dutch wars. Naval affairs are covered in more detail by P. Padfield, *Tides of Empire: Decisive Naval Campaigns in the Rise of the West*, 2 vols. (London, 1979 and 1982).

15. C. R. Phillips, *Six Galleons for the King of Spain: Imperial Defence in the Early Seventeenth Century* (Baltimore, 1986), pp. 213–18.

16. See S. R. Gardiner and C. T. Atkinson (eds.), *Letters and Papers Relating to the First Dutch War, 1652–1654* (London, 1899–1930).

17. J. D. Davies, *Gentlemen and Tarpaulins: The Officers and Men of the Restoration Navy* (Oxford, 1991); G. Teitler, *The Genesis of the Professional Officers Corps* (London, 1977); J. Aman, *Les Officiers Bleus dans la Marine Française au XVIIIe Siècle* (Geneva, 1976); A. K. Belik, 'Structure of the Officer Corps of the Russian Navy', in *The War of King Gustavus III and Naval Battles of Ruotsinsalmi* (Kotka, 1993), pp. 49–59.

18. E. H. Jenkins, *A History of the French Navy from its Beginnings to the Present Day* (London, 1973), pp. 38–105; J. Tramond, *Manuel d'Histoire Maritime de la France* (Paris, 2nd edn, 1947), pp. 175–293; C. de la Roncière, *Histoire de la Marine Française*, 6 vols. (Paris, 1906–32), vol. 5; J. W. Konvitz, *Cities and the Sea: Port Planning in Early Modern Europe* (Baltimore, MD, 1978); J. Bruiyn, *The Dutch Navy in the Seventeenth and Eighteenth Centuries* (Columbia, SC, 1993); J. P. Merino Navarro, *La Armada Española en el Siglo XVIII* (Mardrid, 1981); E. J. Phillips, *The Founding of Russia's Navy: Peter the Great and the Azov Fleet, 1688–1714* (Westport, CT, 1995).

19. Tramond, *Manuel*, p. 283; G. Symcox, *The Crisis of French Sea Power, 1688–1697* (The Hague, 1974). For its impact on Britain, see D. W. Jones, *War and Economy in the Age of William III and Marlborough* (Oxford, 1988).

20. D. D. Aldridge, *Sir John Norris and the British Naval Expeditions to the Baltic Sea, 1715–1727*, unpublished Ph.D. thesis (University of London, 1972), pp. 318, 330.

21. Tramond, *Manuel*, pp. 311–13, Padfield, *Tides of Empire*, vol. 2, pp. 145–7.

22. N. Tracy, *Attack on Maritime Trade* (London, 1991), esp. pp. 11–63.

23. J. S. Corbett, *England in the Mediterranean: A Study in the Rise and Influence of British Power within the Straits, 1603–1714*, 2 vols. (London, 1904; repr. Westport, CT, 1987) is still very useful. H. W. Richmond, *The Navy in the War of 1739–1748*, 3 vols. (Cambridge, 1920; repr. Godstone, 1993); J. S. Corbett, *England in the Seven Years War: A Study in Combined Strategy* (London, 1907); P. Bamford, *Prisons and Fighting Ships: The Mediterranean Galleys of France in the Age of Louis XIV* (Minneapolis, MN, 1973), pp. 272–7.

24. Glete, *Navies and Nations*, vol. 1, pp. 233–5.

25. C. Buchet, *La Lutte pour l'Espace Caribe et la Façade Atlantique de l'Amérique Centrale du Sud (1672–1763)*, 2 vols. (Paris, 1991), vol. 1, pp. 164–274.

26. D. Baugh, 'Great Britain's Blue Water Policy, 1689–1815', *International History Review*, x (1988), pp. 35–58; J. Black, *A System of Ambition? British Foreign Policy, 1660–1793* (London, 1991); J. Black, 'British Naval Power and International Commitments: Political and Strategic Problems', in M. Duffy (ed.), *Parameters of British Naval Power, 1650–1850* (Exeter, 1992), pp. 39–59.

27. J. Pritchard, *Louis XV's Navy, 1748–1762: A Study of Organisation and Administration* (Quebec, 1987); Merino Navarro, *La Armada Española*.

28. M. Acerra and J. Meyer, *Marines et Révolution* (Rennes, 1988), pp. 27–43; Merino Navarro, *La Armada Española*, pp. 83–8; S. Gradish, *The Manning of the British Navy During the Seven Years War* (London, 1980).

29. J. R. McNeill, *The Atlantic Empire of France and Spain: Havana and Louisbourg, 1700–1763* (Chapel Hill, NC, 1985); D. G. Crewe, *Yellow Jack*

and the Worm: British Naval Administration in the West Indies, 1739–1748 (Liverpool, 1993), J. D. Harbron, *Trafalgar and the Spanish Navy* (London, 1988); J. Sutton, *Lords of the East: The East India Company and its Ships* (London, 1981); J. Boudriot, *Compagnie des Indies, 1720–1770: Vaisseaux, Hommes, Voyages, Commerce* (Paris, 1993).

30. Richmond, *The Navy in the War of 1739–1748;* P. Woodfine, 'Ideas of Naval Power and the Conflict with Spain, 1737–1742', in J. Black and P. Woodfine (eds.), *The British Navy and the Uses of Naval Power in the Eighteenth Century* (Leicester, 1988), pp. 71–90; J. Black, 'Anglo-Spanish Naval Relations in the Eighteenth Century', *Mariner's Mirror*, lxxvii (1991), pp. 235–8; C. E. Swanson, *Predators and Prizes: American Privateering and Imperial Warfare, 1739–1748* (Columbia, SC, 1991); J. D. Starkey, *British Privateering Enterprise in the Eighteenth Century* (Exeter, 1990), pp. 121–50; C. E. Fayle, 'Economic Pressure in the War of 1739–48', *Journal of the Royal United Services Institution*, lxviii (1923), pp. 434–46.

31. R. Browning, *The War of Austrian Succession* (New York, 1993; paperback edn Stroud, 1995), pp. 307–9, 321–3, 329–44; M. S. Anderson, *The War of Austrian Succession, 1740–1748* (London, 1995), pp. 187–92.

32. Corbett, *England in the Seven Years War;* G. S. Graham, *Empire of the North Atlantic: The Maritime Struggle for North America* (Oxford, 1958); Pritchard, *Louis XV's Navy*; Merino Navarro, *La Armada Española*. R. Middleton, *The Bells of Victory: The Pitt-Newcastle Ministry and the Conduct of the Seven Years War, 1757–1762* (Cambridge, 1985), is a valuable recent study.

33. J. C. Riley, *The Seven Years War and the Old Regime in France. The Economic and Financial Toll* (Princeton, NJ, 1986), pp. 105–7; H. Legoherel, *Les Trésoriers Généraux de la Marine (1517–1788)* (Paris, 1963), p. 221; J. R. Dull, *The French Navy and American Independence: A Study of Arms and Diplomacy, 1774–1787* (Princeton, NJ, 1975).

34. Harbron, *Trafalgar and the Spanish Navy*, pp. 34–42.

35. Glete, *Navies and Nations*, vol. 1, pp. 271–94, 311–13.

36. N. Tracy, *Navies, Deterrence and American Independence. Britain and Seapower in the 1760s and 1770s* (Vancouver, 1988); D. Syrett, *The Royal Navy in American Waters, 1775–1783* (Aldershot, 1989); Dull, *The French Navy and American Independence*.

37. Acerra and Meyer, *Marines et Révolution;* W. S. Cormack, *Revolution and Political Conflict in the French Navy, 1789–1794* (Cambridge, 1995).

38. Glete, *Navies and Nations*, vol. 1, p. 299; R. C. Anderson, *Naval Wars in the Baltic, 1522–1850* (London, 1910; 1969 edn), pp. 241–93.

39. W. C. Chapman, 'Prelude to Chesme', *Mariner's Mirror*, lii (1966), pp. 61–76, at pp. 72–4.

40. Glete, *Navies and Nations*, vol. 2, pp. 375–401.

5. OTTOMAN WARFARE IN EUROPE 1453–1826 *Gábor Ágoston*

1. On the early period of Ottoman history, see Cemal Kafadar, *Between Two Worlds. The Construction of the Ottoman State* (Berkeley, Los Angeles and London: University of California Press, 1995), esp. pp. 19–28, 47–59, 79–90, 118–54.

2. Gyula Káldy-Nagy, 'The First Centuries of the Ottoman Military Organization', *Acta Orientalia Academiae Scientiarum Hungaricae* (henceforth *AOH*), 31 (1977), pp. 147–83.

3. Marshall Hodgson, *The Venture of Islam. Conscience and History in a World Civilization 3. The Gunpowder Empires and Modern Times* (Chicago and London: University of Chicago Press, 1974).

4. Halil İnalcık, 'The Socio-Political Effects of the Diffusion of Firearms in the Middle East', in V. J. Parry and M. E. Yapp (eds.), *War, Technology and Society in the Middle East* (London: Oxford University Press, 1975), p. 204.

5. Vernon J. Parry, 'La Manière de combattre', in Parry and Yapp (eds.), *War, Technology and Society*, p. 224.

6. Halil İnalcık, 'The Ottoman State: Economy and Society, 1300–1600', in İnalcık and Donald Quataert (eds.), *An Economic and Social History of the Ottoman Empire, 1300–1914* (Cambridge: Cambridge University Press, 1994), pp. 88–9.

7. Gábor Ágoston, 'Ottoman Artillery and European Military Technology in the Fifteenth and Seventeenth Centuries', *AOH*, 47 (1994), pp. 15–48.

8. M. J. Rogers and M. R. Ward, *Süleyman the Magnificent* (London, 1988), No. 45b.

9. Caroline Finkel, 'Ottoman Tactics', paper presented at the ISAV Conference, Istanbul, 11 September 1996.

10. Palmira Brummett, *Ottoman Seapower and Levantine Diplomacy in the Age of Discovery* (New York: State University of New York Press, 1994), pp. 89–121. For Gritti's data, see p. 93.

11. John Guilmartin, *Gunpowder and Galleys, Changing Technology and Mediterranean Warfare at Sea in the 16ᵗʰ Century* (Cambridge: Cambridge University Press, 1980).

12. İnalcık, 'The Ottoman State', p. 29.

13. Rhodes Murphey, 'Ma'din', in *Encyclopaedia of Islam* (Leiden, 1954–), pp. 973–85.

14. Gábor Ágoston, 'Gunpowder for the Sultan's Army: New Sources on the Supply of Gunpowder to the Ottoman Army in the Hungarian Campaigns of the Sixteenth and Seventeenth Centuries', *Turcica*, 25 (1993), pp. 75–96.

15. Quoted in Kenneth M. Setton, *The Papacy and the Levant (1204–1571)* 4 vols. (Philadelphia, PA: American Philosophical Society, 1978–85), vol. 4, p. 1075.

16. On this, see Suraiya Faroqhi, 'Crisis and Change, 1590–1699', in İncalcık and Quataert (eds.), *An Economic and Social History*, pp. 411–636.

17. Gábor Ágoston, 'Habsburgs and Ottomans: Defense, Military

Change and Shifts in Power', *Bulletin of The Turkish Studies Association*, forthcoming, 1998.

18. Klára Hegyi, 'The Ottoman Military Force in Hungary', in Géza Dávid and Pál Fodor (eds.), *Hungarian–Ottoman Military and Diplomatic Relations in the Age of Süleyman the Magnificent* (Budapest: ELTE, 1994), pp. 131–48.

19. Ágoston, 'The Cost of Ottoman Defence in Hungary', unpubl.

20. Caroline Finkel, *The Administration of Warfare: the Ottoman Military Campaigns in Hungary, 1593–1606* (Vienna: VWGÖ, 1988), p. 290.

21. Finkel, *Administration*, pp. 121–208.

22. József Kelenik, 'A hadügyi forradalom hatása Magyarországon a tizenötéves háború időszakában', *Hadtörténelmi Közlemények*, 103 (1990), pp. 85–95.

23. Data are from the Ottoman budgets published in various studies of Ö. L. Barkan and summarised in Gábor Ágoston, 'Az európai hadügyi forradalom és az oszmánok', *Történelmi Szemle*, 37 (1995), pp. 478–9.

24. Halil İnalcık, 'Military and Fiscal Transformation in the Ottoman Empire, 1600–1700', *Archivum Ottomanicum*, 6 (1980), pp. 283–337; Finkel, *Administration*, pp. 39–46; William J. Griswold, *The Great Anatolian Rebellion, 1000–1020/1591–1611* (Berlin: Klaus Schwarz, 1983); Karen Barkey, *Bandits and Bureaucrats. The Ottoman Route to State Centralization* (Ithaca, NY and London: Cornell University Press, 1994).

25. Ahmet Tabakoğlu, *Gerileme Dönemine Girerken Osmanlı Maliyesi* (Istanbul: Dergâh, 1985), pp. 14–15.

26. Caroline Finkel, 'The Cost of Ottoman Warfare and Defence', *Byzantinische Forschungen*, 16 (1990) pp. 91–103.

27. Tabakoğlu, *Gerileme*, pp. 183–93.

28. Kurt Wessely, 'Neuordnung der ungarischen Grenzen nach dem großen Türkenkrieg', in *Die k.k. Militärgrenze. Beiträge zu ihrer Geschichte* (Vienna, 1973), pp. 29–93.

29. Here I rely on Virginia Aksan's research and her invaluable studies. Virginia Aksan, *An Ottoman Statesman in War and Peace. Ahmed Resmi Efendi, 1700–1783* (Leiden: E. J. Brill, 1995), pp. 100–69, also 'Eighteenth Century Ottoman-Russian Warfare: New Approaches', paper presented at the 35th ICANAS, Budapest, 6–12 July 1997.

30. Ibid., pp. 139–41.

31. Mehmet Genç, 'XVIII Yüzyılda Osmanlı Ekonomisi ve Savaş', *Yapıt*, 49 (1984), p. 89.

32. Ibid., pp. 54–5.

33. Yavuz Cezar, *Osmanlı Maliyesinde Bunalım ve Değişim Dönemi* (Alan Yayıncılık, 1986), pp. 89–97.

34. Ibrahim Müteferrika, *Milletlerin Düzeninde İlmî Usüller* (Istanbul: Milli Eğitim Basımevi, 1990), pp. 73–112.

35. Quoted by Geoffrey Parker, *The Military Revolution: Military Innovation and the Rise of the West, 1500–1800* (Cambridge: Cambridge University Press, 1996), p. 128.

36. Virginia Aksan, 'Baron de Tott's "Wretched Fanaticks" and Ottoman Military Reform in the Late Eighteenth Century' (manuscript).

6. THE DEVELOPMENT OF RUSSIAN MILITARY POWER 1453–1815
Brian L. Davies

1. A. E. Presniakov, *The Formation of the Great Russian State* (Chicago: Quadrangle, 1970), pp. 199, 266.
2. Gustave Alef, 'The Origins of Muscovite Autocracy: The Age of Ivan III', *Forschungen zur Osteuropäischen Geschichte*, 39 (1986), p. 122.
3. On the political motives and consequences of *mestnichestvo*, see Nancy Shields Kollmann, *Kinship and Politics: The Making of the Muscovite Political System, 1345–1547* (Stanford, CA: Stanford University Press, 1987).
4. Gustave Alef, 'Muscovite Military Reforms in the Second Half of the Fifteenth Century', *Forschungen zur Osteuropäischen Geschichte*, 18 (1973), pp. 77–8, 122; A. V. Chernov, *Vooruzhennye sily russkogo gosudarstva v XV-XVII vv.* (Moscow: Ministerstvo Oborony SSSR, 1954), p. 33; Dianne L. Smith, 'Muscovite Logistics, 1462–1598', *Slavonic and East European Review*, LXXI: 1 (1993), pp. 38–9; J. L. H. Keep, *Soldiers of the Tsar. Army and Society in Russia, 1462–1874* (Oxford: Clarendon Press, 1985), pp. 87–8.
5. Chernov, *Vooruzhennye sily*, pp. 40–1; Marshall Poe, 'The Consequences of the Military Revolution in Muscovy: A Comparative Perspective', *Comparative Studies in Society and History*, XXXVIII: 4 (1996), pp. 614–15.
6. Brian Davies, 'The Town Governors in the Reign of Ivan IV', *Russian History/Histoire Russe* XIV: 1–4 (1987), pp. 80–1; N. E. Nosov, *Ocherki po istorii mestnogo upravleniia russkogo gosudarstva pervoi poloviny XVI veka* (Moscow and Leningrad: Akademiia Nauk SSSR, 1957), pp. 21, 67–75, 79.
7. Sigizmund Gerbershtein, *Zapiski o Moskovii* (Moscow: Moskovskii Gosudarstvennyi Universitet, 1988), pp. 113–14.
8. B. A. Rybakov, 'Voennoe iskusstvo', *Ocherki russkoi kul'tury XIII-XV vekov. Chast' pervaia* (Moscow: Moskovskii Gosudarstvennyi Universitet, 1968), pp. 411–15; Thomas Esper, 'Military Self-Sufficiency and Weapons Technology in Muscovite Russia', *Slavic Review* XXVIII: 2 (1969), pp. 187–9; Djurdjica Petrovic, 'Firearms in the Balkans on the Eve of and After the Ottoman Conquests of the Fourteenth and Fifteenth Centuries', in V. J. Parry and M. E. Yapp (eds.), *War, Technology and Society in the Middle East* (London: Oxford University Press, 1975), pp. 164–5, 187, 190–3. On the diffusion of Italian and Ottoman gunpowder technology through Persia and Central Asia, see Halil İnalcık, 'The Sociopolitical Effects of the Diffusion of Firearms in the Middle East', in Parry and Yapp (eds.), *War, Technology and Society*, pp. 207–8.
9. Gerbershtein, *Zapiski o Moskovii*, p. 114.
10. Alef, 'Muscovite Military Reforms', p. 103; Alef, 'Origins of Muscovite Autocracy', pp. 123–31, J. L. I. Fennell, *Ivan the Great of Moscow* (London: Macmillan, 1963), pp. 171–6.
11. 'Sochineniia Ivana Semenovicha Peresvetova', in L. A. Dmitriev and D. S. Likhachev (eds.), *Pamiatniki literatury drevnei Rusi Konets XV –*

pervaia polovina XVI veka (Moscow: Khudozhestvennaia literatura, 1984), pp. 597, 599, 603, 611, 756; A. A. Zimin, *I. S. Peresvetov i ego sovremenniki* (Moscow: Akademiia Nauk SSSR, 1958), pp. 356–9, 361.

12. A. A. Zimin, 'K istorii voennykh reform 50-kh godov', *Istoricheskie zapiski*, LV (1956), pp. 344–5, 348; Chernov, *Vooruzhennye sily*, pp. 33–6, 53–6, 58; M. M. Denisova, 'Pomestnaia konnitsa i ee vooruzhenie v XVI-XVII vv.', *Trudy Gosudarstvennoi Istoricheskoi Muzei*, XX (1948), p. 32. On the resemblances between *pomest'e*-based cavalry service and the Turkic *soyurgal* and *timar* systems, see Jaroslaw Pelenski, 'State and Society in Muscovite Russia and the Mongol-Turkic System in the Sixteenth Century', *Forschungen zur Osteuropäischen Geschichte*, XXVII (1980), pp. 163–4, and Donald Ostrowski, 'The Military Land Grant Along the Muslim-Christian Frontier', *Russian History/Histoire Russe*, XIX: 1–4 (1992), pp. 327–59.

13. Zimin, 'K istorii voennykh reform', pp. 354–7; A. V. Chernov, 'Obrazovanie streletskogo voiska', *Istoricheskie zapiski*, XXXVIII (1951), pp. 283, 288; Richard Hellie, *Enserfment and Military Change in Muscovy* (Chicago: University of Chicago Press, 1971), p. 161; Esper, 'Military Self-Sufficiency', p. 193; David Nicolle, *The Janissaries* (London: Osprey, 1995), pp. 26, 48.

14. Poe, 'The Consequences of the Military Revolution', p. 615; P. P. Epifanov, 'Voisko i voennaia organizatsiia', *Ocherki russkoi kul'tury XVI veka. Chast' pervaia* (Moscow: Moskovskii Gosudarstvennyi Universitet, 1976), pp. 377–9; Davies, 'The Town Governors', pp. 84–5.

15. Davies, 'The Town Governors', pp. 78, 87–143.

16. Chernov, *Vooruzhennye sily*, pp. 69–73, 82–3; Denis J. B. Shaw, 'Southern Frontiers of Muscovy, 1550–1700', in James Bater and R. A. French (eds.), *Studies in Russian Historical Geography. Volume One* (London and New York: Academic Press, 1983), pp. 122–6.

17. N. I. Nikitin, *Sluzhilye liudi v zapadnoi Sibiri* (Novosibirsk: Nauka, 1988), p. 6.

18. N. I. Nikitin, *Sibirskaia epopeia XVII veka* (Moscow: Nauka, 1987), pp. 52–7.

19. Giles Fletcher, 'Of the Russe Commonwealth', in Lloyd Berry and Robert O. Crummey (eds.), *Rude and Barbarous Kingdom: Russia in the Accounts of Sixteenth-Century English Voyagers* (Madison: University of Wisconsin Press, 1968), pp. 184–6; V. A. Zolotarev (ed.), *Voennaia istoriia otechestva s drevnikh vremen do nashikh dnei. Tom pervyi* (Moscow: Mosgorarkhiv, 1995), pp. 156–7.

20. Michael Roberts, *The Early Vasas: A History of Sweden, 1523–1611* (Cambridge: Cambridge University Press, 1958), pp. 257–8; David Kirby, *Northern Europe in the Early Modern Period: The Baltic World, 1492–1772* (London and New York: Longman, 1990), pp. 47, 136–9, 146, 150.

21. Zolotarev, *Voennaia istoriia*, pp. 153–4; A. N. Kirpichnikov, 'Oborona Pskova v 1615 g', in Iu. G. Alekseev et al. (eds.), *Srednevekovaia i novaia Rossiia. Sbornik nauchnykh statei* (St Petersburg: Sankt-Peterburgskii Universitet, 1996), pp. 424–50.

22. Zolotarev, *Voennaia istoriia*, pp. 150–1.

23. V. I. Buganov, 'Perepiska gorodovogo prikaza s voevodami livonskikh gorodov v 1577–1578 godakh', *Arkheograficheskii ezhegodnik za 1965 g.* (1965), pp. 290–315; Norbert Angermann, *Studien zur Livlandspolitik Ivan Groznyjs* (Marburg and Lahn: J. G. Herder-Institut, 1972).

24. Janet Martin, *Medieval Russia, 980–1584* (Cambridge: Cambridge University Press, 1995), p. 371; G. V. Abramovich, 'Novgorodskoe pomest'e v gody ekonomicheskogo krizisa poslednei treti XVI v.', *Materialy po istorii sel'skogo khoziaistva i krest'ianstva SSSR. Sbornik* VIII (1974), pp. 5–26.

25. Peter B. Brown, 'Early Modern Russian Bureaucracy: The Evolution of the Chancellery System from Ivan III to Peter the Great', unpublished Ph.D. thesis (University of Chicago, 1978), pp. 231–3, 292; E. D. Stashevskii, *Ocherki po istorii tsarstvovaniia Mikhaila Fedorovicha. Chast' pervaia* (Kiev, 1913).

26. Hellie, *Enserfment*, pp. 104–40.

27. V. M. Vazhinskii, *Zemlevladenie i skladyvanie obshchiny odnodvortsev v XVII v.* (Voronezh: Voronezhskii Gosudarstvennyi Pedagogicheskii Institut, 1974).

28. V. M. Vorob'ev, 'Konnost', liudnost', oruzhnost' i sbruinnost' sluzhilykh gorodov pri pervykh Romanovykh', in Iu. G. Alekseev et al. (eds.), *Dom Romanovykh v istorii Rossii* (St Petersburg: Sankt-Peterburgskii Universitet, 1995), pp. 93–108.

29. E. D. Stashevskii, *Smolenskaia voina 1632–1634 gg.* (Kiev, 1919). pp. 2–8, 128, 316.

30. Pistols still had to be imported, however, and garrison troops remained equipped with matchlocks of sixteenth-century design. Esper, 'Military Self-Sufficiency', pp. 198–9, 201–5; E. E. Kolosov, 'Razvitie artilleriiskogo vooruzheniia v Rossii vo vtoroi polovine XVII v.', *Istoricheskie zapiski*, LXXI (1962), pp. 259–61.

31. V. P. Zagorovskii, *Belgorodskaia cherta* (Voronezh: Voronezhskii Universitet, 1969); V. P. Zagorovskii, *Iziumskaia cherta* (Voronezh: Voronezhskii Universitet, 1980); Carol Belkin Stevens, *Soldiers on the Steppe: Army Reform and Social Change in Early Modern Russia* (De Kalb: Northern Illinois University Press, 1995), pp. 111–14.

32. G. N. Bibikov, 'Opyt voennoi reformy 1609–1610 gg', *Istoricheskie zapiski*, XIX (1946), pp. 1–16.

33. Hellie, *Enserfment*, p. 171; William C. Fuller, Jr., *Strategy and Power in Russia, 1600–1914* (New York; Free Press, 1992), p. 31.

34. Chernov, *Vooruzhennye sily*, pp. 114–15, 137–8; Hellie, *Enserfment*, pp. 168–72.

35. Brian Davies, 'Village Into Garrison: The Militarized Peasant Communities of Southern Muscovy', *Russia Review*, LI (1992), pp. 481–501.

36. Keep, *Soldiers of the Tsar*, p. 91. Carol Stevens's *Soldiers on the Steppe* is particularly detailed on the fiscal burden on the southern frontier service population.

37. P. P. Epifanov, 'Uchenie i khitrost' ratnogo stroeniia pekhotnykh liudei', *Uchenye zapiski moskovskogo gosudarstvennogo universiteta. Kafedry*

istorii SSSR, CXXXVII (1954), pp. 77–98; A. Baiov, *Kurs istorii russkago voennago iskusstva* (St Petersburg, 1909), vol. I, pp. 140–5; V. N. Zaruba, *Ukrainskoe kazatskoe voisko v bor'be s turetsko-tatarskoi agressiei* (Kharkov: Osnova, 1993), pp. 72–3.

38. A. N. Mal'tsev, *Rossiia i Belorussiia v seredine XVII veka* (Moscow: Moskovskii Gosudarstvennyi Universitet, 1974), pp. 69–70, 121–6; Yuriy Tys-Krokhmaliuk, 'The Victory at Konotop', *Ukrainian Review*, VI: 3 (1959), pp. 34–45; Baiov, *Kurs*, pp. 152–9; Catherine S. Leach (trans. and ed.), *Memoirs of the Polish Baroque: The Writings of Jan Chryzostom Pasek* (Berkeley: University of California Press, 1976), pp. 73–92, 99, 168, 177; Janusz Sikorski (ed.), *Polskie tradycje wojskowe* (Warsaw: Ministerstwo Obrony Narodowej, 1990), vol. I, p. 300; Robert I. Frost, 'The Polish–Lithuanian Commonwealth and the "Military Revolution"', in M. B. Biskupsi and James S. Pula (eds.), *Poland and Europe: Historical Dimensions. Volume One* (New York: Columbia University Press, 1993), pp. 35, 41–2.

39. Zaruba, *Ukrainskoe kazatskoe voisko*, pp. 46–50, 63–4; Stevens, *Soldiers on the Steppe*, pp. 76–97; Epifanov, 'Uchenie i khitrost'", p. 84.

40. M. D. Rabinovich, 'Formirovanie reguliarnoi russkoi armii nakanune severnoi voiny', in V. I. Shunkov (ed.), *Voprosy voennoi istorii Rossii: XVIII i pervaia polovina XIX vv.* (Moscow: Nauka, 1969), pp. 221–32; Keep, *Soldiers of the Tsar*, pp. 103–4.

41. A. I. Zaozerskii, *Fel'dmarshal B. P. Sheremetev* (Moscow: Nauka, 1989), pp. 53–5, 57, 60, 62, 65; Keep, *Soldiers of the Tsar*, pp. 110–14; L. G. Beskrovnyi, *Russkaia armiia i flot v XVIII veke* (Moscow: Ministerstvo Oborony SSSR, 1958), pp. 111–13.

42. This did not include garrison forces, cossack and Tatar iregulars, and the *sloboda* regiments defending parts of the southern frontier. Keep, *Soldiers of the Tsar*, pp. 105–6; Beskrovnyi, *Russkaia armiia*, p. 26.

43. Fuller, *Strategy and Power*, pp. 44–6, 54–6; P. P. Epifanov and A. A. Komarov, 'Voennoe delo. Armiia i flot', *Ocherki russkoi kul'tury XVIII veka. Chast' vtoraia* (Moscow: Moskovskii Gosudarstvennyi Universitet, 1987), pp. 197–9; Beskrovnyi, *Russkaia armiia*, pp. 130–3, 135, 141, 168–9, 176.

44. O. Leonov, I. Ul'ianov, *Reguliarnaia pekhota, 1698–1801* (Moscow: AST, 1995), pp. 33–4; Beskrovnyi, *Russkaia armiia*, pp. 75–8.

45. John Le Donne, *Absolutism and Ruling Class* (New York, Oxford: Oxford University Press, 1991), pp. 76–8.

46. Peter reassured officers they had the right to use their own good judgement in subsequently altering or abandoning the council's plans on the battlefield. Ibid., pp. 69–73; Fuller, *Strategy and Power*, pp. 71–5; Epifanov and Komarov, 'Voennoe delo', p. 197.

47. Keep, *Soldiers of the Tsar*, p. 107; Fuller, *Strategy and Power*, pp. 48–9; Beskrovnyi, *Russkaia armiia*, p. 118; Arcadius Kahan, *The Plow, the Hammer, and the Knout: An Economic History of Eighteenth-century Russia* (Chicago and London: University of Chicago Press, 1985), pp. 321, 330–2.

48. The Russian army was used in Poland in the War of the Polish Succession (1733–35), the War Against the Confederation of the Bar

(1768) and the Partitions of Poland (1772, 1793 and 1795); against the Swedes in 1741–43 and 1788–90; against Prussia in the Seven Years War (1756–63); against the Turks in 1735–39, 1768–74, 1787–91 and 1806–12; against Persia in 1803–13; and against France in 1798–1800, 1805–07 and 1812–15.

49. Walter Pintner, 'The Burden of Defense in Imperial Russia, 1725–1914', *Russian Review*, XLIII: 3 (1984), p. 232; Christopher Duffy, *Russia's Military Way to the West* (London: Routledge and Kegan Paul, 1985), pp. 69–72; Beskrovnyi, *Russkaia armiia*, pp. 91–3.

50. Walter Pintner, 'Russia's Military Style, Russian Society, and Russian Power in the Eighteenth Century', in A. G. Cross (ed.), *Russia and the West in the Eighteenth Century* (Newtonville, MA: Oriental Research Partners, 1983), pp. 262, 264; Fuller, *Strategy and Power*, pp. 171–4; Keep, *Soldiers of the Tsar*, pp. 222–3.

51. Beskrovnyi, *Russkaia armiia*, pp. 61–2, 148–9, 289, 310–11, 384–92.

52. B. G. Kipnis, 'Razvitie taktiki russkoi armii v russo-turetskoi voine 1768–1774 g.', in T. G. Frumenkov (ed.), *Rossiia v XVIII veke. Voiny i vneshnaia politika, vnutrennaia politika, ekonomika i kul'tury* (St Petersburg: Minerva, 1996), pp. 4–5; Bruce W. Menning, 'Russia and the West: The Problem of Eighteenth-century Military Models', in Cross (ed.), *Russia and the West in the Eighteenth Century*, pp. 282–8; Iu. R. Klokman, *Fel'dmarshal Rumiantsev v period russko-turetskoi voiny 1768–1774 gg.* (Moscow: Akademiia Nauk SSSR, 1951), p. 106.

53. Bruce W. Menning, 'Russian Military Innovation in the Second Half of the Eighteenth Century', *War and Society*, II (1984), p. 37.

54. J. L. H. Keep, 'Feeding the Troops: Russian Army Supply Policies During the Seven Years' War', *Canadian Slavonic Papers*, XXIX: 1 (1987), pp. 24, 43; Zenon Kohut, *Russian Centralism and Ukrainian Autonomy* (Cambridge, MA, Harvard University Press, 1988), pp. 104–24; Bruce W. Menning, 'G. A. Potemkin and A. I. Chernyshev: Two Dimensions of Reform and the Military Frontier in Imperial Russia', *Consortium on Revolutionary Europe. Proceedings*, I (1980), pp. 241–3.

55. Le Donne, *Absolutism*, pp. 83–6, 306; Beskrovnyi, *Russkaia armiia*, p. 341.

56. Kahan, *The Plow*, pp. 333, 336.

57. Ibid., pp. 345–9; V. S. Abalikhin, 'Rol' Ukrainy v obespechenii armii v otechestvennoi voine 1812 g', in Shunkov (ed.), *Voprosy voennoi istorii Rossii*, pp. 187–204.

58. Kahan, *The Plow*, p. 337; Pintner, 'The Burden of Defense', p. 248.

7. WARFARE AND SOCIETY IN THE BALTIC 1500–1800 *Knud J. V. Jespersen*

1. *Axel Oxenstiernas skrifter och brefvexling* (Stockholm, 1888–), vol. II. 1, pp. 395–400; quotation in translation from Michael Roberts,

Gustavus Adolphus. A History of Sweden, 1611–1632 (London, 1958), vol. II, pp. 362–3.

2. Stewart Oakley, 'War in the Baltic, 1550–1790', in Jeremy Black (ed.), *The Origins of War in Early Modern Europe* (Edinburgh, 1987), pp. 52–71. A more extensive treatment is offered in Göran Rystad, Klaus-R. Böhme and Wilhelm Carlgren (eds.), *In Quest of Trade and Security. The Baltic in Power Politics 1500–1900*. Vol. I (1500–1890) (Stockholm, 1994). The general context, unfortunately in a somewhat disorganised shape, is provided by David Kirby, *Northern Europe in the Early Modern Period. The Baltic World 1492–1772* (London, 1990).

3. The following survey of the Baltic conflicts is based mainly upon the works listed in note 2.

4. The classical European great power system is thoroughly described in Derek McKay and H. M. Scott, *The Rise of the Great Powers, 1648–1815* (London, 1983). The Swedish wars are outlined and interpreted by Göran Behre, Lars-Olof Larsson and Eva Österberg, *Sveriges historia 1512–1809. Stormaktsdröm och småstatsrealiteter* (Stockholm, 1985), pp. 261 ff. Cf. also Gunnar Artéus, *Krigsmakt och samhälle i Frihetstidens Sverige* (Stockholm, 1982) and Gunnar Artéus (ed.), *Gustav III:s ryska krig* (Stockholm, 1992). Denmark's situation in the eighteenth century is best described in Ole Feldbæk's volume 4 of *Gyldendals Danmarks historie* (Copenhagen, 1982), covering the period 1730–1814. For the repercussions of those wars upon the military organisation in Denmark, see Knud J. V. Jespersen, 'Claude Louis, Comte de Saint Germain (1707–1778): Professional Soldier, Danish Military Reformer and French War Minister', in Abigail T. Siddall (ed.), *Soldier-Statesmen of the Age of the Enlightenment* (Manhattan, KS, 1984), pp. 305–21.

5. Michael Roberts, *The Military Revolution, 1560–1660* (Belfast, 1956); reprinted in slightly amended shape in Michael Roberts, *Essays in Swedish History* (London, 1967), pp. 195–225.

6. Geoffrey Parker, 'The "Military Revolution, 1560–1660" – a Myth?', in his *Spain and The Netherlands, 1559–1659. Ten Studies* (London, 1979), pp. 86–103; further elaborated in the same author's *The Military Revolution. Military Innovation and the Rise of the West, 1500–1800* (Cambridge, 1988); cf. J. M. Black, *A Military Revolution? Military Change and European Society, 1550–1800* (London, 1991); Brian M. Downing, *The Military Revolution and Political Change. Origins of Democracy and Autocracy in Early Modern Europe* (Princeton, 1992) and Clifford J. Rogers (ed.), *The Military Revolution Debate* (Boulder, CO, 1995). For the repercussions in Denmark, see Knud J. V. Jespersen, 'Social Change and Military Revolution in Early Modern Europe: Some Danish Evidence', *The Historical Journal*, 26 (1983), pp. 1–13.

7. H. Landberg, L. Ekholm, R. Nordlund and Sven A. Nilsson, *Det kontinentala krigets ekonomi. Studier i krigsfinansiering under svensk stormaktstid* (Kristianstad, 1971); Lars Ekholm, *Svensk krigsfinansiering 1630–1631* (Uppsala, 1974) and Klaus-Richard Böhme, 'Building a Baltic Empire', in Göran Rystad et al. (eds.), *In Quest of Trade and Security*, pp. 177–220.

8. Paul Douglas Lockhart, *Denmark in the Thirty Years' War, 1618–1648. King Christian IV and the Decline of the Oldenburg State* (Selinsgrove, 1996); cf. Gunner Lind, *Hæren og magten i Danmark, 1614–1662* (Odense, 1994); Finn Askgaard, *Christian IV – Rigets Væbnede arm* (Copenhagen, 1988) and Jens Carl Kirchmeier-Andersen, 'Christian IV som taktiker', *Vaabenhistoriske Aarbøger*, vols. 33–4 (Copenhagen, 1987–88), pp. 63–157, 5–107.

9. Gunnar Artéus, *Till militärstatens förhistoria. Krig, professionalisering och social förändring under Vasasönernas regering* (Stockholm, 1986); Sven A. Nilsson, *På väg mot militärstaten. Krigsbefälets etablering i den äldre Vasatidens Sverige* (Uppsala, 1989) and, for the navy, Jan Glete, *Navies and Nations: Warships, Navies and State Building in Europe and America, 1500–1860*, 2 vols. (Stockholm, 1993).

10. Cf. Lind, *Hæren og magten i Danmark* and E. Ladewig Petersen, 'Christian IVs skånske og norske fæstningsanlæg 1596–1622' (Danish) *Historisk Tidsskrift*, 95 (1995), pp. 328–41.

11. Frede p. Jensen, *Danmarks konflikt med Sverige 1563–1570* (Copenhagen, 1982), pp. 149ff.

12. Knud J. V. Jespersen, 'Slaget ved Lutter am Barenberg 1626', in *Krigshistorisk Tidsskrift* (Copenhagen, 1973), pp. 80–9.

13. Finn Askgaard and Arne Stade (eds.), *Kampen om Skåne* (Copenhagen, 1983), pp. 194–247; on Nördlingen, see Theodore K. Rabb, *The Struggle for Stability in Early Modern Europe* (New York, 1975), p. 122.

14. Jørgen H. Barfod, *Niels Juel. A Danish Admiral of the 17th Century* (Copenhagen, 1977), pp. 73–88.

15. On the wars of 1657–60 in general and Charles X Gustav's lightning attack on Copenhagen in particular, see Finn Askgaard, *Kampen om Østersøen. Et bidrag til nordisk søkrigshistorie på Carl X Gustafs tid 1654–60* (Copenhagen, 1974).

16. The figures are extracted from Jan Glete's essay, 'Bridge and Bulwark. The Swedish Navy and the Baltic, 1500–1809', in Rystad et al. (eds.), *In Quest of Trade and Security*, pp. 9–60; esp. tables 1 and 2, pp. 27–8.

17. The figures are extracted from Parker, 'Military Revolution', p. 96; André Corvisier, *Armies and Societies in Europe, 1494–1789* (London, 1979), p. 113 and, for Denmark, Knud J. V. Jespersen, *Gyldendals Danmarks historie*, vol. 3, ed. Søren Mørch (Copenhagen, 1989) and Dr P. H. Wilson's Chapter 3 in the present volume.

18. Robert Molesworth, *An Account of Denmark as it was in the Year 1692* (London, 1694; repr. Copenhagen, 1976), p. 224. According to Corvisier, *Armies and Societies in Europe*, p. 113, the ratio of effectives to population was about 1 : 25 in Prussia and in Sweden. My own calculation shows that the same applies to Denmark. In Austria, France and Russia the ratio was only about 1 : 100.

19. For Swedish affairs, see, e.g., Behre et al., *Sveriges historia 1521–1809* and also Michael Roberts's many books on the subject; for a general introduction to the conditions in Denmark, see Jespersen, *Gyldendals*

Danmarks historie; cf. also Jespersen, 'The Rise and Fall of the Danish Nobility, 1600–1800', in H. M. Scott (ed.), *The European Nobilities in the Seventeenth and Eighteenth Centuries*. Vol. II (London, 1995), pp. 41–70.

20. For this important aspect which, owing to lack of space, I have only touched lightly upon in this chapter, see Anja Tjaden, 'The Dutch in the Baltic, 1544–1721' and Stewart Oakley, 'Trade, Peace and the Balance of Power. Britain and the Baltic, 1603–1802', both in Rystad et al. (eds.), *In Quest of Trade and Security*, pp. 61–132 and 221–56 respectively.

8. GAELIC WARFARE, 1453–1815 *J. Michael Hill*

1. Michael Roberts, *The Military Revolution, 1560–1660* (Belfast, 1956), *passim*; Geoffrey Parker, 'The "Military Revolution", 1560–1660 – A Myth?', *Journal of Modern History*, 48 (1976), pp. 195–214.
2. James Michael Hill, *Celtic Warfare, 1595–1763* (Edinburgh, 1986), *passim*; James Michael Hill, 'The Distinctiveness of Gaelic Warfare, 1400–1750', *European History Quarterly*, 22 (1992), pp. 323–45; G. A. Hayes-McCoy, *Scots Mercenary Forces in Ireland, 1565–1603* (Dublin, 1937), *passim*; Andrew McKerral, 'West Highland Mercenaries in Ireland', *Scottish Historical Review*, 30 (1951), pp. 1–14.
3. Hill, *Celtic Warfare*, pp. 22–44; J. Michael Hill, 'The Origins and Development of the "Highland Charge" c.1560 to 1646', *Militärgeschichtliche Mitteilungen*, 53 (1994), pp. 295–307.
4. Hill, 'Distinctiveness of Gaelic Warfare'; Hill, 'Origins and Development of the "Highland Charge"'.
5. Hill, 'Distinctiveness of Gaelic Warfare'.
6. Hill, *Celtic Warfare*, pp. 45–156; Hill, 'Origins and Development of the "Highland Charge"'.
7. Hill, 'Distinctiveness of Gaelic Warfare'; Hill, *Celtic Warfare*, pp. 64–181.
8. Michael Howard, *War in European History* (Oxford, 1976), pp. 3–15; Sir Charles Oman, *The Art of War in the Middle Ages*, rev. and ed. John H. Beeler (Ithaca, NY and London, 1953), pp. 128–9.
9. John Dymmok's description of the Gallowglass, Dublin, National Library of Ireland, MS 669. f. 11 (hereafter cited as NLI).
10. Hayes-McCoy, *Scots Mercenary Forces*, pp. 5–8, 12–17; McKerral, 'West Highland Mercenaries'; Hill, 'Distinctiveness of Gaelic Warfare'.
11. J. F. Lydon, 'The Bruce Invasion of Ireland', *Historical Studies*, 4 (1963), pp. 111–25; Katherine Simms, 'Warfare in the Medieval Gaelic Lordships', *Irish Sword*, 12 (1975–76), pp. 98–108.
12. Eoin MacNeill, *Phases of Irish History* (Dublin, 1937), pp. 324–5.
13. G. A. Hayes-McCoy, *Irish Battles* (London, 1969), pp. 48–53; Hayes-McCoy, *Scots Mercenary Forces*, pp. 23–5, 58, 73.
14. Hayes-McCoy, *Irish Battles*, pp. 48–67; John Dymmok, *A Treatice of Ireland*, ed. Rev. Richard Butler (Dublin, 1842), p. 7; London, Public

Record Office, State Papers, Ireland, St Leger to the king, 6 April 1543, SP 60/11/2 (hereafter cited as SP).

15. Hayes-McCoy, *Scots Mercenary Forces, passim*; Michael Mallett, *Mercenaries and Their Masters: Warfare in Renaissance Italy* (Totowa, NJ, 1974), pp. 25–50; William H. McNeill, *The Pursuit of Power: Technology, Armed Force, and Society since A. D. 1000* (Chicago 1982), p. 77.

16. London, Lambeth Palace Library, Carew MSS, Sir Henry Sidney to Sir Francis Walsingham, 1 March 1583, vol. 601, f. 89; Parker, ' "Military Revolution" ', p. 196.

17. Sir Charles Oman, *A History of the Art of War in the Sixteenth Century* (New York, 1937), pp. 105–207; Howard, *War in European History*, pp. 26–8, 33; Parker, ' "Military Revolution" ', p. 207; J. R. Hale, *War and Society in Renaissance Europe, 1450–1620* (London and New York 1985), pp. 46–74; Gerald de Gaury, *The Grand Captain, Gonzalo de Córdoba* (London 1955), pp. 83–6.

18. Howard, *War in European History*, pp. 26–7, 34, 37; J. R. Hale, 'The Early Development of the Bastion: An Italian Chronology, c.1450–c.1534', in J. R. Hale et al. (eds.), *Europe in the Late Middle Ages* (Evanston, IL, 1965), pp. 466–94; Michael Roberts, 'Gustav Adolf and the Art of War', in Michael Roberts (ed.), *Essays in Swedish History* (Minneapolis, MN, 1967), pp. 56–81.

19. Roberts, 'Gustav Adolf', p. 59; Oman, *Art of War in the Sixteenth Century*, pp. 229–43.

20. H. C. B. Rogers, *Weapons of the British Soldier* (London, 1960), pp. 45–53; George Gush, *Renaissance Armies, 1480–1650* (Cambridge, 1982), pp. 11–12; J. R. Hale, 'Gunpowder and the Renaissance: An Essay in the History of Ideas', in C. H. Carter (ed.), *From the Renaissance to the Counter-Reformation: Essays in the Honor of Garrett Mattingly* (New York, 1965), p. 114; Roberts, 'Gustav Adolf', p. 59; Howard, *War in European History*, p. 34; Theodore Ropp, *War in the Modern World* (New York, 1962), p. 27.

21. Gush, *Renaissance Armies*, p. 109.

22. Hill, *Celtic Warfare, passim*; Hale, 'Gunpowder', pp. 120–1; C. G. Cruickshank, *Elizabeth's Army* (2nd edn Oxford, 1966), p. 1.

23. Cyril Falls, *Elizabeth's Irish Wars* (London 1950; repr. New York, 1970), *passim*; Hayes-McCoy, *Irish Battles, passim*; Rev. George Hill, *An Historical Account of the MacDonnells of Antrim* (Belfast, 1873), pp. 132–40; J. Michael Hill, *Fire and Sword: Sorley Boy MacDonnell and the Rise of Clan Ian Mor, 1538–1590* (London, 1993), pp. 77–122; Shane O'Neill to Lord Justice, 2 May 1565, SP 63/13/34; Sir William Fitzwilliam to Cecil, 16 May 1565, SP 63/13/38; Shane O'Neill to Sir Thomas Cusake, 22 May 1565, SP 63/13/48; Captain Power to Cecil, 27 December 1601, SP 63/210/260; Lord Mountjoy and Council to Lord Chancellor and Council, 1 January 1602, SP 63/210/1, I; Captain Wynfield to Cecil, 25 December 1601, SP 63/209/255; NLI, MS 669, f. 11.

24. Parker, ' "Military Revolution" ', pp. 206–7; Michael Roberts, 'The Military Revolution, 1560–1600', in Roberts (ed.), *Essays in Swedish History*, p. 196; Gush, *Renaissance Armies*, pp. 106–10.

25. Roberts, *Military Revolution*, pp. 33–4; Roberts, 'Gustav Adolf', p. 52.

26. Roberts, 'Gustav Adolf', pp. 60–2, 65–70; Roberts, *Military Revolution*, pp. 33–4; Gush, *Renaissance Armies*, p. 113; Theodore A. Dodge, *Great Captains, Gustavus Adolphus* (Boston and New York, 1895), pp. 42–4.

27. David Stevenson, *Alasdair MacColla and the Highland Problem in the Seventeenth Century* (Edinburgh, 1980), *passim*; Roberts, 'Gustav Adolf', p. 74; Stuart Reid, *The Campaigns of Montrose: A Military History of the Civil War in Scotland, 1639 to 1646* (Edinburgh, 1990), p. 58 and *passim*.

28. Hill, 'Origins and Development of the "Highland Charge"'.

29. Ibid.

30. Stevenson, *Alasdair MacColla, passim*; Hill, 'Origins and Development of the "Highland Charge"'.

31. Roberts, 'Gustav Adolf', p. 75; Hill, *Celtic Warfare*, pp. 45–150; Major-General Hugh Mackay, *Memoirs of the War Carried on in Scotland and Ireland, 1689–1691*, ed. Maitland Club (Edinburgh, 1833), pp. 51–2. A well-trained soldier in the mid-eighteenth century could carry out the complicated tasks of priming, loading and firing his flintlock musket two or three times a minute under optimum battlefield conditions. H. L. Blackmore, *British Military Firearms, 1650–1850* (London, 1961), p. 277; H. Bland, *A Treatise of Military Discipline* (London, 1727), pp. 19–34.

32. Hill, *Celtic Warfare*, pp. 45–150. A description of the brutal effect of the Irish charge at Killiecrankie can be found in Henry Jenner (ed.), *Memoirs of the Lord Viscount Dundee, the Highland Clans, and the Massacre of Glenco, and etc.* (London, 1908), p. 20: 'Many . . . officers and soldiers were cut down through the skull and neck, to the very breasts; others had skulls cut off above the ears. . . . Some had both their bodies and cross belts cut through at one blow; pikes and small swords were cut like willows.' For a recent and thorough study of the Scottish theatre during the War of the Three Kingdoms, see Reid, *Campaigns of Montrose, passim*.

33. Steven Ross, *From Flintlock to Rifle: Infantry Tactics, 1740–1866* (London, 1979), p. 33. For the Chevalier de Folard's ideas concerning columns, see J. Colin, *L'Infantrie au XVIIIe siècle: la tactique* (Paris, 1907), pp. 36–8.

34. J. A. H. Guibert, *Défense du système de guerre moderne ou réfutation complette du système de M. . . . D. . . .* (Neuchâtel, 1779), vol. I, pp. 169–71.

35. Christopher Duffy, *The Military Experience in the Age of Reason* (London and New York, 1987), p. 199.

36. Herman Maurice de Saxe, *Reveries or Memoirs upon the Art of War*, trans. W. Faucett (London, 1757), quoted from Geoffrey Simcox (ed.), *War, Diplomacy, and Imperialism 1618–1763* (New York and London, 1973), pp. 187–8.

37. W. Dalrymple, *Tacticks* (Dublin, 1782), p. 113, trans. from J. F. Puységur, *Art de guerre par principes et par règles*, 2 vols. (Paris 1749), vol. I, pp. 227.

38. Roberts, 'Gustav Adolf', p. 75; B. P. Hughes, *Firepower: Weapons Effectiveness on the Battlefield, 1630–1850* (London, 1974), pp. 10–11; David Chandler, *The Art of Warfare in the Age of Marlborough* (New York,

1976), p. 115; For a close examination of the development of the British Army under William III, see John Childs, *The British Army of William III, 1689–1702* (Manchester, 1987).

39. Hill, *Celtic Warfare*, pp. 54, 64–79; Paul Hopkins, *Glencoe and the End of the Highland War* (Edinburgh, 1986), pp. 157–61; The Marchioness of Tullibardine (ed.), *A Military History of Perthshire*, 2 vols. (Perth, 1908), vol. I, p. 266; John Spalding, *Memorialls of the Trubles in Scotland and in England, A.D. 1624–A.D. 1645*, ed. Spalding Club, 2 vols. (Aberdeen, 1850–51), vol. II, pp. 444–5; George Wishart, *The Memoirs of James, Marquis of Montrose, 1639–1650*, ed. A. B. Murdoch and H. F. M. Simpson (London, 1893), p. 85; Patrick Gordon, *A Short Abridgement of Britane's Distemper, from the yeare of God 1639 to 1649*, ed. Spalding Club (Aberdeen, 1844), pp. 101–2.

40. Chandler, *Art of Warfare*, pp. 127–8; F. G. Bengtsson, *Charles XII* (London, 1960), pp. 85–90.

41. R. Ernest DuPuy and Trevor N. DuPuy, *The Encyclopedia of Military History from 3500 B.C. to the Present* (2nd rev. edn New York, 1986), pp. 608–12; David Chandler, *Marlborough as Military Commander* (New York, 1973), *passim*; C. T. Atkinson, *Marlborough and the Rise of the British Army* (New York and London, 1921), pp. 222–36, 285–97, 339–44, 398–406; Bland, *Treatise of Military Discipline*, p. 80.

42. Parker, '"Military Revolution"', p. 213.

43. Duffy, *Military Experience in the Age of Reason*, p. 168; M. S. Anderson, *War and Society in Europe of the Old Regime 1618–1789* (Leicester and New York, 1988), pp. 36–45; Ropp, *War in the Modern World*, pp. 30–1; Chandler, *Art of Warfare*, pp. 14–15.

44. Hill, *Celtic Warfare*, pp. 2–4, 17, 22–44, 45–63, 64–79, 80–99, 127–56; Katherine Tomasson and Francis Buist, *Battles of the '45* (London, 1962), pp. 67–9.

45. Hughes, *Firepower*, pp. 10–11, 26, 35–6, 81–5; Hill, *Celtic Warfare*, 140–50; Jeremy Black, *Culloden and the '45* (London and New York, 1990), *passim*.

46. Trans. from J. A. H. Guibert, *Essai général de tactique*, 2 vols. (Paris, 1772), vol. I, p. 216.

9. REVOLUTIONARY AND NAPOLEONIC WARFARE *Jeremy Black*

I would like to thank Owen Connelly, Charles Esdaile, Alan Forrest, David Gates, Donald Horward and Harald Kleinschmidt for their comments on an earlier draft of this chapter.

1. S. P. Mackenzie, *Revolutionary Armies in the Modern Era. A Revisionist Approach* (London, 1997), p. 50.

2. S. F. Scott, *Response of the Royal Army to the French Revolution* (Oxford, 1978); P. Wetzler, *War and Subsistence: The Sambre and Meuse Army in 1794* (New York, 1985); J. P. Bertaud, *The Army of the French Revolution* (Cambridge, 1988); J. Lynn, *The Bayonets of the Republic.*

Motivation and Tactics in the Army of Revolutionary France, 1791–94 (2nd edn Boulder, CO, 1996); T. C. W. Blanning, *The French Revolutionary Wars, 1787–1802* (London, 1996).

3. S. Wilkinson, *The Rise of General Bonaparte* (Oxford, 1930); W. G. F. Jackson, *Attack in the West. Napoleon's First Campaign Re-Read Today* (London, 1953).

4. A. Forrest, *Conscripts and Deserters. The Army and French Society during the Revolution and Empire* (Oxford, 1989).

5. D. Chandler, *The Campaigns of Napoleon* (London, 1966); G. Rothenburg, *The Art of Warfare in the Age of Napoleon* (London, 1978); J. R. Elting, *Swords Around a Throne: Napoleon's Grande Armée* (New York, 1988).

6. O. Connelly, *Blundering to Glory: Napoleon's Military Campaigns* (Wilmington, DE, 1987), pp. 1–2; M. Glover, *The Napoleonic Wars: An Illustrated History* (New York, 1978), p. 93.

7. R. M. Epstein, *Napoleon's Last Victory and the Emergence of Modern War* (Lawrence, KS, 1994), p. 182.

8. C. Duffy, *Austerlitz* (London, 1977).

9. M. Raeff (ed.), *The Diary of a Napoleonic Foot Soldier* (London, 1991).

10. Chandler, *Campaigns of Napoleon*, p. 952.

11. See recently, T. Cornell, 'The Military Revolution, Effectiveness, Innovation, and the Duke of Wellington', *The Consortium on Revolutionary Europe 1750–1850. Selected Papers, 1996* (Tallahassee, FL, 1996), pp. 250–9.

Notes on Contributors

Gábor Ágoston is Assistant Professor of Ottoman History at the Department of History, Georgetown University, Washington DC. Until 1998 he taught Ottoman and Hungarian history at the Eötvös Loránd University, Budapest.

Thomas F. Arnold is Assistant Professor of History at Yale University. He received his Ph.D. from Ohio State University in 1993. He is currently completing work on a book about the influence of geometry on European military culture since the Renaissance.

Ronald G. Asch is Professor of Early Modern History at the University of Osnabrück, having taught before for a number of years at the neighbouring university of Münster. His publications include *Der Hof Karls I. von England. Politik, Provinz und Patronage, 1625–1640* (1993) and *The Thirty Years War. The Holy Roman Empire and Europe 1618–1648* (1997). Among the books he has edited or co-edited are *Politics, Patronage and the Nobility, The Court at the Beginning of the Modern Age, c.1450–1650* (1991) and *Der Absolutismus – ein Mythos? Strukturwandel monarchischer Herrschaft ca. 1550–1700* (1996).

Jeremy Black is Professor of History at Exeter University. He is the author of 29 books, including *Culloden and the '45* (1990), *War for America* (1991), *A Military Revolution? Military Change and Governmental Development, 1550–1800* (1991), *European Warfare 1660–1815* (1994), *Why Wars Happen* (1998) and *War and the World 1450–2000* (1998). He has also edited or co-edited 12 books, including *War in the Early-Modern World* (1998).

Brian L. Davies is Associate Professor of History at the University of Texas at San Antonio. A specialist in seventeenth-century Russian social history, he is the author of the forthcoming *State Power and Community in Early Modern Russia* and is working on a monograph on Russia's wars with the Crimean Khanate and Ottoman Empire.

Richard Harding is a Principal Lecturer at the University of Westminster. He has published several articles on the development of Britain's amphibious capability in the eighteenth century. He is author of *Amphibious Warfare in the Eighteenth Century* (1991), *The Evolution of the Sailing Navy* (1995) and *Seapower and Naval Warfare 1650–1830* (1999).

J. Michael Hill is Professor of History at Stillman College, Tuscaloosa, Alabama, and is the author of *Celtic Warfare, 1595–1763* (1986), and *Fire & Sword: Sorley Boy MacDonnell and the Rise of Clan Ian Mor, 1538–1590* (1993). Currently he is working on an expanded version of *Celtic Warfare* that will include the Scottish Wars of Independence, the *gallóglaigh* wars with the Anglo-Normans in Ireland, and the Tudor conflicts in Ireland prior to 1595. He is also completing a study of the Clan Ian Mor in both Scotland and Ireland from 1590 to 1615.

Knud J. V. Jespersen is Professor of Modern European History at Odense University and Royal Historiographer at the Royal Danish Court. His works include volume 3 of the *Gyldendals Danmarks historie: Tiden 1648–1730* (1989), volume 4 of *Det europæiske hus: Stat og nation, 1500–1870* (1992) and several books and articles on European and Danish history and on general military history in the early modern and modern period. He is currently preparing a two-volume work on *SOE and the Danish Resistance, 1940–1945* and a *History of Denmark, 1500–2000*, to be published in English.

Peter H. Wilson is Lecturer in Early Modern European History at the University of Sunderland. He is the author of *War, State and Society in Württemberg, 1677–1793* (1995); *German Armies: War and German Politics 1648–1806* (1998) and various articles on war and society in early modern Europe.

Index

278